The Salt Companion to Mina Loy

Rachel Potter and Suzanne Hobson

S
SALT

CAMBRIDGE

PUBLISHED BY SALT PUBLISHING

Fourth Floor, 2 Tavistock Place, Bloomsbury, London WC1H 9RA United Kingdom

The selection and introduction © Rachel Potter and Suzanne Hobson, 2010
individual contributions © the contributors, 2010

The right of Rachel Potter and Suzanne Hobson to be identified as the
editors of this work have been asserted by them in accordance
with Section 77 of the Copyright, Designs and Patents Act 1988.

Salt Publishing 2010

Printed and bound in the United Kingdom by Lightning Source, UK

Typeset in Swift 10/12

ISBN 978 1 87685 772 1 paperback
1 3 5 7 9 8 6 4 2

Contents

Acknowledgements

The editors would like to extend their deepest gratitude to the Mina Loy Estate for permission to reproduce extracts from Mina Loy's published and unpublished works. This collection could not have taken shape without their support for new scholarship on Loy and generosity in making her writing available for study and citation. Our particular thanks go to Loy's editor and literary executor, Roger L. Conover, who has diligently and patiently responded to numerous enquiries and requests to read submissions. His expertise and guidance has been crucial in bringing this project to a conclusion.

As with all collections of essays, this companion is only as strong as its contributors and we have been extremely fortunate that so many esteemed colleagues have been willing to contribute essays that in our view represent a cross-section of the best British-based scholarship available on Loy at the moment. We are grateful to them, especially for the willingness and generosity with which they have responded to editorial requests and for their patience over what has been the very long process of completing this book.

On behalf of the contributors, the editors would like to thank the staff at the Beinecke Library, Yale University who continue to provide easy access and support to researchers wishing to consult the Mina Loy Papers.

For financial support for the collection, the editors would like to thank the School of Literature and Creative Writing, University of East Anglia (Rachel Potter) and the Department of English, Queen Mary, University of London (Suzanne Hobson). We would also like to thank the *Yearbook of English Studies* for permission to reprint Peter Nicholls's essay. Finally, we would like to thank Kate Holeywell and Lee Smith for their editorial help with this manuscript.

Contributors

Tim Armstrong is Professor of Modern Literature at Royal Holloway, University of London. His publications include *Modernism, Technology and the Body: A Cultural Study* (1998), *Haunted Hardy: Poetry, History, Memory* (2000) and *Modernism: A Cultural History* (2005). He is currently working on a study of the conceptual ramifications of slavery.

David Ayers is Professor of Modernism and Critical Theory at the University of Kent. His publications include *Wyndham Lewis and Western Man* (1992), *English Literature of the 1920s* (1999), *Modernism* (2004) and *Literary Theory: A Reintroduction* (2008). He is currently working on a project concerning the cultural impact of the Russian Revolution in Britain.

Geoff Gilbert is Associate Professor of Comparative Literature at the American University of Paris, where he also directs the MA in Cultural Translation. He writes on literary modernism in *Before Modernism Was* (2005), Scots writing, and sexuality, and is currently working on 'contemporary realism' and its agon with contemporary economics.

Rowan Harris is an independent scholar with a research interest in modernism. Her work focuses on Mina Loy and Dorothy Richardson, and explores the relations between feminine sexuality, the new forms of commodity culture and avant-garde experimentation in the early decades of the twentieth century.

Suzanne Hobson is Lecturer in Twentieth Century Literature at Queen Mary, University of London. She has published articles on modernism and religion in *Literature and Theology* (2008) and *Literature Compass* (2007) and is currently completing a book titled *Modernism, Secularism and Literary Culture: The New Angel.*

Alan Marshall is a writer, teacher and scholar, presently based at King's College London, where he was formerly Head of the

Department of American Studies. He is the author of *American Experimental Poetry and Democratic Thought* (Oxford University Press, 2009) and of numerous articles on modern British and American poetry.

Peter Nicholls is Professor of English at New York University. His publications include *Ezra Pound: Politics, Economics and Writing* (1984), *Modernisms: A Literary Guide* (1995, 2009), *George Oppen and the Fate of Modernism* (2007), and many articles and essays on literature and theory. He co-edited with Laura Marcus *The Cambridge History of Twentieth-Century English Literature* (2004) and is US editor of the journal *Textual Practice*.

Sandeep Parmar received a PhD in English Literature from UCL in 2008. The subject of her dissertation was the unpublished autobiographies of Mina Loy. She has co-edited and introduced a critical edition of Hope Mirrlees' poetry at Newnham College, Cambridge, which is forthcoming from Carcanet Press (Fyfield) in 2011. She has taught literature and creative writing and is currently a Visiting Scholar at New York University where she is completing her forthcoming monograph on Loy entitled *Myth of the Modern Woman* (Editions Rodopi). She is also Reviews Editor for *The Wolf* magazine.

Rachel Potter is a Senior Lecturer in Twentieth Century Literature at the University of East Anglia. Her publications include *Modernism and Democracy: Literary Culture, 1900–1930* (2005), and essays on a range of modernist writers. She is currently working on a book called *Obscene Modernism: Literary Censorship and Experiment, 1900–1940* and an *Introductory Guide to Modernism* for Edinburgh University Press.

Andrew Michael Roberts is Reader in English at the University of Dundee, with research interests in contemporary poetry, modernism, psychoanalytical theory and cognitive processes in literature. His books include: *Conrad and Masculinity* (2000); *Poetry and Contemporary Culture* (co-edited, 2001); *Geoffrey Hill* (2004). He is currently completing a book entitled *Poetry & Ethics*, and a book on *Digital Poetry*.

John Wilkinson is Research Professor in the Department of English at the University of Notre Dame. His book of essays, *The Lyric Touch: Essays on the Poetry of Excess* was published by Salt in 2007. He is now writing chiefly about New York School poets, with essays forthcoming on Barbara Guest, Frank O'Hara and James Schuyler.

Abbreviations

Except in the case of the following abbreviations, full details of works referred to are given in footnotes. Roger L. Conover's edited collection of Loy's poetry, *The Last Lunar Baedeker*, appeared first in 1982 in an edition for the Jargon Society in the USA and then in a later printing for Carcanet in the UK. An updated collection containing a slightly different selection of poems was published as *The Lost Lunar Baedeker* by Farrar, Straus and Giroux in the US in 1996 and then by Carcanet in the UK in 1997. References in the text are to the two Carcanet editions. As advised by Roger L. Conover this companion cites the later collection wherever possible.

BM	Carolyn Burke, *Becoming Modern: The Life of Mina Loy* (Berkeley: University of California Press, 1996)
I	Mina Loy, *Insel,* ed. Elizabeth Arnold (Santa Rosa: Black Sparrow Press, 1991)
LLB I	Roger L. Conover, ed., *The Last Lunar Baedeker* (Manchester: Carcanet, 1985)
LLB II	Roger L. Conover, ed., *The Lost Lunar Baedeker* (Mancheseter: Carcanet, 1997)

Introduction

Rachel Potter and Suzanne Hobson

Mina Loy is a brilliant literary enigma. She ironized her status as a token woman poet among the Italian Futurists, calling herself a 'secret-service buffoon to the Woman's Cause', and was critical of Suffragette feminism; she was friends with surrealist writers but never signed up to their philosophy; she sipped tea at Nathalie Barney's salon but refused to join the group. Her take on life was always idiosyncratic and often slightly perverse. She saw the funny side. She never settled into a received opinion. She was always keen to think the unexpected. These were her greatest strengths as a writer but sometimes also led her to air uncomfortable or odd opinions: from 1909 she was a committed Christian Scientist, she embraced eugenicist ideas, she described herself as a religious and racial 'mongrel' and from the late 1920s she became 'obsessed' with the idea that competitors were out to steal her designs and inventions.[1]

It is difficult to identify her literary precursors: Eliot and Pound saw affinities with the light ironies and grotesque juxtapositions of Jules Laforgue; Nathalie Barney declared that her love songs were 'the best since Sappho'; Marjorie Perloff has suggested prosodic similarities with the skeltonics of John Skelton; Virginia Kouidis connects her writing to Walt Whitman; and a number of readers have seen links with the work of Emily Dickinson. Yet literary antecedents seemed of less interest to Loy than the work of her contemporaries, and she discusses them rarely. Like a number of avant-garde writers in this period, she came at writing by way of visual art and her poems often bear the formal imprint of avant-garde painting, sculpture or collage.

Her first pieces of writing, produced in 1914, were sexual and social satires in a Futurist-feminist vein. In 'Parturition' (1914), 'Virgins Plus Curtains Minus Dots' (1914) and 'Three Moments in Paris' (1914), she satirises the social relationships between the sexes, whilst parodying a pseudo-philosophical avant-garde language: seemingly inappropriate phrases such as 'the extensity / Of intention' or 'dynamic decomposition' can be read either as fragmented philosophies of experience or snippets of avant-garde conversation. Even while she mocked the Italian Futurists, in poems such as 'Three moments in Paris', 'Sketch of a Man on a Platform' (1915) and 'The Effectual Marriage of Gina and Miovanni' (1915) she did so using Futurist tools. This was a time when she was happy to embrace the manifesto and the aphorism; to champion velocity and the leap, the limitless future and gigantic egotism.

She performed her own leap onto a more public cultural platform with the publication of her first four 'Love Songs' in New York in 1915. These poems, the product of a failed love affair with the part-time Futurist Giovanni Papini, remove the narrative or social frame central to earlier poems, and instead create an abstract and fragmented collage of obscene imagery, scientific terminology, discursive satire and psychological insight. They are both similar to Futurist texts and distinctive in their manipulation of psychological and emotional resonances: the lines 'I must live in my lantern / Trimming subliminal flicker' (*LLB II* 53) are too introspective to sit happily in the absurdly inhuman and combative texts of Marinetti. Loy has an ability to juxtapose the painful losses and fractures of love or friendship (or even one-off encounters in later texts) with ironically misplaced scientific or prosaic vocabularies. The resulting tone is both grotesque and intimate: her 'Pig Cupid' rooting away in 'erotic garbage' offers an arrestingly altered perspective on a history of visual and lyrical language. At the same time, she leaves it open whether the internal 'subliminal flicker' is just another bit of romanticized rhetorical garbage or part of a new psychoanalytic language of a self involved in a thoroughly modern love affair. As we read through the full sequence of 'Love Songs', or 'Songs To Joannes' as they became by 1917, we see Loy producing a precarious balancing act in which the lyrical 'I' is both a poetic construction, and a more particularised self collapsing in the face of a specific other.

In 1917, she followed her poems to New York where she hung out with pacifist Dadaists and artists attempting to escape the draft, the most important of whom was Arthur Cravan, the love of her life she met and lost in the space of a year. Her views shifted accordingly. She returned to the social-satirical mode to make more open attacks on the militarist stance of Marinetti and Papini, and, in poems such as 'Lions' Jaws' (1920), pictured their aggression and authoritarianism as both their aesthetic focus, and biggest blind spot.

Her poems of the late 1910s and early 1920s extend this interest in conceptual or artistic authoritarianism to more politicised descriptions of a conflict between modern art and the sinister authority of the State. In some of her most accomplished poems, such as 'Apology of Genius' (1922), 'Perlun' (1921) and 'O Hell' (1919), she combines the light ironies, vivid imagery and alienated rhetorics of earlier texts with a new kind of poetic reflexivity. The 'censor's scythe' as she puts it in 'Apology of Genius' sits poised over the linguistic and prosodic experiments of the international avant-garde, lending a political edge to her images of freedom as well as her own disruptive, obscene, polyglot language.

The early 1920s when she was living in Paris was the period of her greatest productivity: the first collection of her poems, *Lunar Baedecker* [sic] came out in 1923, and her longest and most ambitious poem, 'Anglo-Mongrels and the Rose', was published in instalments in various journals from 1923–1925. This is one of the most remarkable poetic descriptions of the evolution of selfhood in modernist writing, a kind of feminist take on Joyce's, Pound's and Lewis's representations of artistic becoming. Mixing scientific, religious, racist and sociological registers, she traces the evolution of a child from birth to adulthood, focusing in particular on her dual Christian and Jewish parentage. Not only is the poem an attack on what she calls the 'paradox-Imperial' of British nationalism; its polyglot language is implicitly at odds with artistic or political nationalisms.

After 1925, publications of her poems were more intermittent, and we see her working on a number of unpublished novels and prose pieces in which she explores new ways of representing a child's evolving consciousness. With her move to New York in 1936, however, Loy picked up her poetic pen again. She now had a new subject matter: the bums of Manhattan. In poems such as 'On Third Avenue' (1942), 'Mass-Production on 14th Street' (1942) and 'Hot Cross Bum' (1949) she depicted the destitute state of New York itinerants in the context of meditations on more worldly ideas of homelessness.

Despite Loy's presence on the fringes of the key avant-garde groupings of the early twentieth century, her style was always distinctive. She was interested in the discarded particulars of life, a fleck of sperm, a knick-knack, a 'dented dandelion' (*LLB II* 111); or what she saw as the abandoned human beings of the early twentieth century: itinerants, boxers, bums, drunken bohemians, artists, mongrels. While this focus on the discarded fragments of the modern is one that she shares with a number of modernist or avant-garde writers, Loy's poems are unusual in their sheer depth of idiomatic layering, as well as an ability to capture literary style in a condensed image. In her later writing, for instance, she often wrote about other writers or artists (Cunard, Lewis, Joyce, Brancusi) by momentarily squatting in their linguistic and perceptual worlds: her lines 'The press —/ purring / its lullabies to sanity' (*LLB II* 89) seem to be both recognisably within the discursive world of *Ulysses*, and an imagistic summation of some of its formal innovations. Similarly in her novel *Insel*, which focuses on the Surrealist painter Richard Oelze, she mocked the absurdities of Oelze's Surreal liberation of mind from body by means of a robust and deftly handled surrealist lexicon.

Although Loy's ironies make it difficult to pin her down, it is possible and important to try to describe the ideas which run through her work. She ridicules a wide range of contemporary movements and ideas, including Feminism, Futurism, Imperialism, Christianity, Judaism, fascism and psychoanalysis. Yet these attacks never seem simply to cohere to produce a single critical position, something which we might call Loy's politics for instance. Loy will ridicule men's irresponsibility, for example, only then to blame women for inviting this treatment. She has a genius for leading her readers down a particular road only to switch directions at the last moment.

However, if we never know where to find Loy in her texts, many of her targets share common ground. All forms of authority or fixed identity are destabilized by Loy's writing, especially when she detects posturing or egoism. She wanted, in particular, to demystify the calcified ideologies of Victorianisms such as Imperialism, Christianity, Judaism, sentimentalism, femininity, masculinity, Art and philanthropy. This produces moments when Loy's writing becomes more angrily engaged, as for example when she attacks racist Imperialism in 'Anglo-Mongrels and the Rose'. In such moments, she reveals a sophisticated awareness of how different ideologies prop each other up to create damaging forms of psychological and emotional stasis and violence.

Loy often presents the past as a prison from which it is important to break free. Yet she does not follow the Futurists in celebrating modernity as technological progress – the ready-made positions offered by her peers seem no less suspect to Loy than those handed-down from predecessors. She is always attuned to the conflicts and contradictions of modernisation and modernity. In her late poems, for example, she describes the human costs of technological and industrial progress in her depiction of New York bums. At the same time, however, she also destabilizes the progressive discourses of psychiatry, sociology and philanthropy which would seek to explain or describe these individuals. In this she has a fine eye for the contra- dictions at the heart of modern forms of social intervention. Like many of her contemporaries Loy viewed with suspicion discourses which seemingly accommodate individuality while actually promot- ing standardized models of selfhood. In 'Hot Cross Bum' for instance, social workers and psychiatrists are no more able to name and recog- nise the Bum than the clergy whose outdated ideas of 'welfare' they are supposed to have replaced. Loy's own interest in these figures speaks less of a straightforward humanitarianism and more of a collector's interest in those objects and people which do not quite fit. Her collages in the 1940s and 1950s are made out of found and discarded objects and her late poems do the same with words.

By maintaining her aesthetic position within and on the margins of the avant-garde, her texts help us to re-evaluate what we under- stand by Anglo-American modernism. Loy's readers and critics have consistently tried, and failed, to pin her down. She earned the respect of her contemporaries. Eliot, Pound, Stein, Williams, Moore, Bunting, Lewis, all reviewed or valued her work, but there often seems to be an anxiety about where or how she should be positioned. Pound famously mistook her for an American in his review of *Others* 1917, tried hard to connect her writing to that of Marianne Moore, and then went on to see her as too cerebral, which seems to miss the point. Eliot, in arguing that her writing is too abstract, seemed to misread the way that Loy mimics and undermines the idioms of crit- ical and creative language.[2]

While Loy has enjoyed a consistent reputation among poets and writers, she did not feature in mid-century critical accounts of modernism. Jonathan Williams brought out his collection of Loy's poems, *Lunar Baedeker and Time-Tables* in 1958, and this helped to intro- duce Loy to a new generation of writers.[3] It was with the recovery of women writers and the development of more comprehensive exami- nations of an expanded modernist field in the 1980s and 1990s, however, that Loy's work began to be seriously re-positioned. Roger L. Conover paved the way with his timely and important publication of *The Last Lunar Baedeker* in 1982, which spawned a number of critical studies. Early criticism of Loy (particularly from the late 1980s and early 90s) concentrated on establishing the avant-garde and feminist contexts of her poetry, offering analysis of its relationship with Futurism and to a lesser extent with surrealism and Dadaism.[4] It is with the Shreiber and Tuma collection of essays, *Mina Loy: Woman and Poet*, which came out in 1998, as well as Carolyn Burke's biography, and Conover's more streamlined and updated collection of Loy's poems, *The Last Lunar Baedeker* in 1997, however, that Loy was catapulted into the mainstream of modernist criticism.[5]

More recently, the term modernism, which has regulated our sense of Loy's presence in or out of the canon, has itself come under intense scrutiny. This is partly because with the inclusion of writers such as Loy the category of modernism has become itself increasingly slippery. Once described by the *Evening Sun* as an exemplary 'modern' woman, Loy becomes the paradigmatic modernist poet precisely because of her ability to facilitate different critical models.[6] Thus for Cristanne Miller (2005), the manner in which Loy's poetry reworks her urban and metropolitan environment is revealing of a particularly female experience of the city, an experience governed by local laws and customs circumscribing the behaviour and status of women.[7] For Paul Peppis (2002) and Mary E. Galvin (1999), meanwhile, Loy's attack on the sentimentality of love and the sanctity of marriage is consonant with, if not illustrative of, contemporary movements for sex reform.[8] Establishing these alternative modernities has required detailed exploration of Loy's engagement with contemporary realities in her poetry – the 'streetlife' of Italy (Hancock, 2005), the homeless of New York (Potter, 1999 and Cristanne Miller, 2005) and the new technologies of communication and the body (Tyrus Miller, 1999 and Armstrong, 1998).[9]

The proliferation of these different Loys is part of a more general shift in the study of modernism. Tim Armstrong, for instance, in his recent 'cultural history of modernism' surveys a hugely expanded cultural landscape in which the idea of modernism as a number of specific texts or a describable kind of writing truly disintegrates.[10] In Loy's preference for exploring, but never fully identifying with, the writing of her contemporaries, as well as her scepticism about the adoption of cultural or political authority, she is more than ever a poet for our times; a writer who can teach us much about the legislative drives at the heart of critical thinking. Her enigmatic elusiveness, we want to suggest, is one of her key literary achievements.

The essays in this collection continue and strengthen the study of 'Futurist' Loy (Harris), 'feminist' Loy (Harris and Parmar), 'surrealist' Loy (Ayers and Armstrong), 'Christian Science' Loy (Armstrong, Ayers), 'Jewish' Loy (Potter) and 'late' Loy (Hobson, Armstrong) while also acknowledging the difficulties of making Loy fit any particular category. All of the essays pay close attention to Loy as a prosodic and stylistic innovator, finding new vocabularies in which to describe her distinctive voice: thus, for Wilkinson, her poetry 'stumbles', for Marshall, she is an 'ecstatic' writer, for Nicholls, she is a poet of Laforguian 'wit', for Roberts she is a 'jazz' poet, for Potter her language 'wanders', for Ayers she strives towards a 'fugitive kind of truth' and for Gilbert, her poetry produces 'an adolescent experience of language'.

The essays are divided into three sections: first, 'self-constructions', considering the multiple identities that are made and re-made in Loy's poetry and her autobiographical writing; second, 'modern poetics', seeking to understand and to contextualize the innovative characteristics of Loy's poetics; and third, 'art and the divine', which focuses on the turn to matters and 'the matter' of the spirit in her late poetry and prose.

'Self-constructions' contains four essays, all of which explore the cross-currents and influences that comprise the nascent and incomplete self in Loy's 1910s and 1920s work and her later autobiographical prose. Harris's essay revisits the question of Loy's ambivalent relationship with futurism, finding a new manner in which to understand, if not to reconcile, Loy's feminist commitments with futurism's infamous attack on woman. Suggesting an overlap between Otto Weininger's concept of woman as 'mendacious' and futurism's surprising endorsement of the 'fashionable' woman as a driving force of modernity, Harris shows how the Weiningerian-Futurist model of woman served to open up rather than close down possible avenues for the exploration of female identity in Loy's work. Essays by Potter and Roberts offer new interpretations of 'Anglo-Mongrels and the Rose', focusing on what Roberts calls the 'signature elusiveness' of the autobiographical 'I' in this poem. In Potter's essay, the evasive nature of the self is testimony to the 'wandering' and the 'wondering' that together comprise Ova's (and Loy's) legacy from her Jewish father, while in Roberts's piece this elusiveness is understood as a self that is 'always in motion', a self that is modelled on the jazz rhythms and dances that Loy would have witnessed in the cafés and clubs of

Paris in the 1920s. The final essay in this section considers the relationship between the 'autobiographical self' that Loy cultivated in a mass of unpublished writings in the 1930s and 40s and the public self of her poetry. Parmar's work in Loy's archive recovers a 'faltering' and 'inhibiting' concept of self from Loy's autobiographical writings that demands comparison with the 'saint-manqué' of contemporaneous poems such as 'Show Me a Saint Who Suffered' and 'Hilarious Israel'.

The concern to describe the bearing and movement of Loy's poetry is continued in the second section of this companion, 'Modern Poetics'. Peter Nicholls returns to the moment in *Others* in 1918 when Pound identifies Loy's poetry as 'logopoeia', or 'poetry that is akin to nothing but language, which is a dance of the intelligence among words and ideas and modification of ideas and characters.'[11] Nicholls asks whether the flow of ideas and influence between these two poets runs in two directions. Thus he finds echoes of the cadences and abstract vocabulary of Loy's 'Effectual Marriage' in 'Hugh Selwyn Mauberley' and identifies a possible response to and 'reformulation' of Pound's logopoeic formula in Loy's 'Modern Poetry'. The 'dance of the intelligence among words' is here transformed into 'the gait of [the poet's] mentality', suggesting, as Nicholls points out, a banal, down-to-earth and 'pedestrian encounter' with words corresponding to the ordinary subjects of Loy's poetry: the 'garbage' in 'Love Songs', the domestic routine of 'Effectual Marriage' and the offal of 'James Joyce'.

The difficultly of describing the peculiar movement of Loy's poetry has long been a concern for critics. In one of the earliest appreciations of Loy's work published in *The Dial* in 1926, Ivor Winters compares the 'clumsiness' with which the reader is forced to move through Loy's heavy, abstract vocabulary to 'walking through granite'.[12] John Wilkinson invokes another 'walking' metaphor to illustrate the 'gait of Loy's mentality': containing numerous reversals, opposing positions and, at the level of the language itself, awkward lexical and syllabic clusters, Loy's poetry frequently pulls up short, or 'falls over its own feet' before (and thus never succeeding in) taking up a single, definitive position. Alan Marshall finds a very different model for the movement of the mind in Loy's work. In a study of ecstasy drawing on Emily Dickinson, Friedrich Nietzsche and Ralph Waldo Emerson, he develops a language through which to describe the distinctive pulse of Loy's poetry. There is an oscillation in her writing between a self bounded by pain and suffering and a self exploded on to an infinite canvas, 'exceeding its boundaries in every direction'. The challenge presented by Loy's distinctive prosody is taken up again in the final essay in this section. Geoff Gilbert explores one of Loy's late poems, 'Mass-Production on 14th Street' for the insight it provides into the peculiar life of her poetry – a life that draws on the energies of the marketplace and the sexual encounter and is best recognised from a position he identifies as 'adolescent'.

Loy's late poetry and prose has generally received far less attention than the poetry written between 1914 and 1930. Maeera Shreiber explains this neglect with reference to the fact that these texts were 'written in an effort to make manifest the divine'. Critics, she notes, are often wary of this kind of endeavour, suspecting the institutions and the agendas with which it is often associated.[13] The problem with Loy's divine poetry might also, however, be more specific, related in the first instance to the difficulty of squaring Loy's investment in a mystical or spiritual dimension to life with her status as the 'modern woman'. Modernity, when glossed in terms of the triumph of science over superstition, of reason over belief, does not easily accommodate the divine. Yet, as Cristanne Miller has recently pointed out, Loy's effort to manifest a supersensible or Absolute realm is not necessarily incommensurate with her 'modern' commitments. Religion might be a force for conservatism, mystification and oppression, but it might also act as a spur to 'antiparochialism, antimaterialism, and active multiculturalism', all of which appear as key components of modernist poetry in the early twentieth century.[14] The three essays in the final section of this Companion open out this assertion by exploring specific moments at which Loy's 'antimaterialism' incorporates, echoes or reformulates that of her avant-garde contemporaries. David Ayers's essay supplies a context for *Insel*, describing the influence of both Christian Science and Surrealist art on the development of this novel. Tim Armstrong continues this examination of Christian Science and Surrealism in a discussion of the affinities between Loy's late poetry and the visual art of Joseph Cornell. Loy's poetry, he argues, acts as a corrective to the insistent antimaterialism of Christian Science – 'the reduction of matter to mind' – by acknowledging 'the presence of both historical reality and the obdurate actuality of the body in the margins of the text.' In the final essay, Suzanne Hobson examines Loy's challenge to another contemporary school of antimaterialist thought: psychoanalysis which according to Loy was well on its way to exorcising sex and the body from art and culture. Reading Loy's unpublished critique of DH Lawrence alongside her late poetry, Hobson develops the 'angel-bum' as a useful figure through which to understand Loy's curious economy of flesh, spirit and art.

In this book we try to show how Loy's style, so to speak, has substance. We aim through close analysis of her poetry to reveal a poetic idiom that demands comparison to the best of the avant-garde, while through discussion of Loy's interest in fashion, in the fickle whims of popular and high-brow taste, to uncover poetry that is definitive of its time. In essays such as 'Modern Poetry', 'Gertrude Stein' and 'Phenomenon in American Art', Loy demonstrates sensitivity to the modernism of Stein and the fact that Bergson was 'in the air' (*LLB I* 289) just as elsewhere she registers the popularity of contemporary film stars and cultural icons such as the boxers Dempsey and Carpentier. Loy was a writer who recognised the significance of the disparate parts of her culture and it is this ethos, above all, that provides this Companion with its purpose and guiding principle. In the essays that follow we hope to bring to life Loy's embrace of the world in all its forms as well as the seriousness and commitment with which she registered unfolding historical events.

Notes

1 See Roger L. Conover, 'Time Table', *LLB I*, lxxiv.

2 See Ezra Pound, 'Others', *Little Review* 5 no. 11 (4 March 1918), 56–8; and T.S. Eliot [T.S. Apteryx], 'Observations', *Egoist* 5 (1918), 64–71.

3 Jonathan Williams, *Lunar Baedeker and Time-Tables* (Highlands NC: Jonathan Williams, 1958).

4 See for example, Shari Benstock, *Women of the Left Bank: Paris, 1900–1940* (London: Virago Press, 1987); Linda Kinnahan, *Poetics of the Feminine: Authority and Literary Tradition in William Carlos Williams, Mina Loy, Denise Levertov, and Kathleen Fraser* (Cambridge: Cambridge University Press, 1994); Virginia Koudis, *Mina Loy: American Modernist Poet* (Baton Rouge: Louisiana State University Press, 1980); Bonnie Kime Scott, ed., *The Gender of Modernism: A Critical Anthology* (Bloomington: University of Indiana Press, 1990).

5 Maeera Shreiber and Keith Tuma, eds., *Mina Loy: Woman and Poet* (Orono: The National Poetry Foundation, 1998). Future references to this collection abbreviated to Shreiber and Tuma, eds.

6 Anon., 'Mina Loy, Painter, Poet and Playwright, Doesn't Try to Express Her Personality by Wearing Odd Looking Draperies – Her Clothes Suggest the Smartest Shops But Her Poems Would Have Puzzled Granma', *New York Evening Sun* (17 February 1917). See *BM*, 8.

7 Cristanne Miller, *Cultures of Modernism: Gender and Literary Community in New York and Berlin* (Ann Arbor: Michigan, 2005).

[8] Paul Peppis, 'Rewriting Sex: Mina Loy, Marie Stopes and Sexology', *Modernism / Modernity* 9 (2002), 561–70; and Mary E. Galvin, *Queer Poetics: Five Modernist Women Writers* (Westport: Praeger, 1999).

[9] Tim Hancock, 'You couldn't make it up': the love of "bare facts" in Mina Loy's Italian poems', *English: The Journal of the English Association* 54 (2005), 175–94; Rachel Potter, '"At the Margins of the Law": Homelessness in the City in Mina Loy's Late Poems', *Women: A Cultural Review* 10 (1999), 253–65; Tyrus Miller, *Late Modernism* (Berkeley: University of California Press, 1999); and Tim Armstrong, *Modernism, Technology and the Body: A Cultural Study* (Cambridge: Cambridge University Press, 1999).

[10] Tim Armstrong, *Modernism: A Cultural History* (Oxford: Polity, 2005).

[11] Ezra Pound, 'How to Read' (1929), rpt. in T. S. Eliot, ed., *Literary Essays of Ezra Pound* (London: Faber and Faber, 1968), 25.

[12] Ivor Winters, 'Mina Loy', *The Dial* 80 (1926), 496.

[13] Maeera Shreiber, 'Divine Women, Fallen Angels: The Late Devotional Poetry of Mina Loy', in Shreiber and Tuma, eds., 467.

[14] Cristanne Miller, 174.

Mina Loy Chronology

1882	Mina Gertrude Lowy born in London.
1897	She enrols in the St. John's Wood Art School in London
1900	Travels to Munich and enrols for a year in the Society of Female Artists' School.
1901–2	Attends art studio in London taught by Augustus John; meets Stephen Haweis.
1903	Travels to Paris and enrols at the Académie Colarossi. Four months pregnant, she marries Stephen Haweis.
1904	Oda Janet Haweis, her first daughter, born in Paris. Exhibits 6 watercolours at the Salon d'Automne under her new name of Mina Loy.
1905	Oda dies of Meningitis.
1906	She has an affair with Henry Joël Le Savoureux, the doctor who had treated her for neurasthenia after the death of Oda. Elected member of prestigious Salon, d'Automne.
1907	Loy settles with Haweis in Florence; Joella Sinara Haweis born.
1909	John Stephen Giles Musgrove Haweis born. She meets the Christian Scientist, Mrs Morrison, who helps 'cure' Joella of an illness. From now on, she regularly attends the Christian Science church.
1910	Loy meets Mabel Dodge.
1911	She meets Gertrude Stein.

1912	Loy's first one-woman show at the Carfax Gallery in London.
1913	Loy meets Giovanni Papini, Carlo Carrà and Ardengo Soffici, as well as F. T. Marinetti, in Florence. Haweis leaves for Australia and South Seas.
1914	She has affairs with Marinetti and Papini. Her first publications appear: 'Aphorisms on Futurism' in *Camera Work*; 'Café du Néant' in *International: A Review of Two Worlds*; 'Parturition' and 'Italian Pictures' in *The Trend*.
1915	'Love Songs, 1–4' published in *Others*.
1916	She arrives in New York and meets Marcel Duchamp and William Carlos Williams. Loy acts alongside Williams in Alfred Kreymborg's *Lima Beans*.
1917	Mina Loy declared the 'ultimate modern woman' by a journalist for the *New York Evening Sun*. She meets Arthur Cravan. She gets divorced from Stephen Haweis. Her father dies. Loy edits an issue of *Others* and aids Duchamp on editions of *The Blind Man* and *Rongwrong*.
1918	Loy and Cravan arrive in Mexico to avoid the draft. They marry. Cravan disappears in a boat off Salina Cruz. Loy travels on to Buenos Aires alone. Ezra Pound describes Loy's poetry as 'logopoeia' in the *Little Review*.
1919	Returns to London and gives birth to Jemima Fabienne Cravan Lloyd. She travels to Geneva and then on to Florence. 'Psycho-Democracy' published.
1920	Returns to New York; attends the trial of the *Little Review* for publishing *Ulysses*. 'Lions' Jaws' published in the *Little Review*. She meets Djuna Barnes.
1921	Stephen Haweis arrives in Florence and takes Giles to live with him in the Caribbean. Loy returns to Paris via Florence.

1922	'Brancusi's Golden Bird' published in *The Waste Land* issue of *The Dial*. Loy accompanies Djuna Barnes on a visit to Joyce that provides Barnes with the material for an article on Joyce in *Vanity Fair*. Loy moves to Berlin, travelling via Vienna where she meets Freud and draws his portrait. Freud pronounces Loy's work 'analytic'.
1923	Returns to Paris. *Lunar Baedecker* [sic] published by Robert McAlmon's Contact Editions. First three sections of 'Anglo-Mongrels and the Rose' appear in the *Little Review*. Loy's son Giles dies in Bermuda. Peggy Guggenheim and Lawrence Vail organise a lampshade business for Loy in Paris managed by Joella. During this period in Paris Loy begins drafts of several autobiographical prose works focusing on her childhood and early adulthood.
1925	Final sections of 'Anglo-Mongrels and the Rose' published in Robert McAlmon's *Contact Collection of Contemporary Writers*. Peggy Guggenheim Vail organises exhibits of Loy's *Jaded Blossoms* in America.
1926	Lampshade shop opens at 52 rue de Colisée, Paris. Ivor Winters describes Loy as 'the most astounding' of *Others'* poets.
1927	Joella marries Julian Levy; Levy supports Loy when lampshade business begins to fail. Loy reads 'The Widows Jazz' at Natalie Barney's salon.
1929	Loy publishes an essay on Gertrude Stein in the *transatlantic review*. the *Little Review* publishes Loy's responses to its 'Questionnaire'; Loy declares the time spent with Arthur Craven as the happiest years of her life.
1930	Loy sells the lampshade shop; she had for some time been concerned that her ideas were being stolen.
1931	Julian Levy opens a gallery in New York; Loy becomes his advisor, acting as purchasing agent for several European and American artists living in

	Paris. *Pagany* publishes 'The Widows Jazz' and 'Lady Laura in Bohemia'; Loy's poetry is not published again until 1946.
1933	Levy exhibits Loy's paintings in his New York gallery.
c. 1933	Loy meets and becomes friends with the surrealist painter Richard Oelze who provides the inspiration for her novel *Insel*.
1936	Loy returns to New York. Meets Joseph Cornell.
c. 1940–45	Loy reworks the autobiographical material she began in the 1920s.
1944	Kenneth Rexroth publishes 'Les Lauriers Sont Coupés' in *Circle* in which he recognises Loy as a key 'American' modernist.
1946	Loy gains American citizenship.
1946–47	*Accent* publishes four poems: 'Aid of the Madonna', 'Chiffon Velours', 'Ephemerid' and 'Hilarious Israel'.
1949	Loy moves close to the Bowery where she lives in a communal household on Second Street presided over by Irene Klempner. She begins to construct local scenes from objects found on the Bowery streets.
1951	'Hot Cross Bum' published in *New Directions*.
1953	Loy moves to Aspen to be near her daughters.
1958	*Lunar Baedeker and Time Tables*, her second book, published by Jonathan Williams.
1959	Loy's 'Constructions' are exhibited at Bodley Gallery at a show curated by Marcel Duchamp; Loy herself does not attend. Loy receives Copley foundation Award for Outstanding Achievement in Art for her 'experiments in junk'.

1961	Samuel French Morse publishes 'The Rediscovery of Mina Loy and the Avant-Garde' in *Wisconsin Studies in Contemporary Literature*.
1966	Loy is interviewed by Paul Blackburn and Robert Vas Dias; she describes her early life and reads a selection of her poetry. Loy dies in Aspen.
1982	Roger L. Conover publishes *The Last Lunar Baedeker*, which remains the most complete collection of her poetry to date.

With thanks to Roger L. Conover's Time-Table in *LLB I*, Virginia Kouidis's *Mina Loy: American Poet* (Baton Rouge: Louisiana State University Press, 1980) and Carolyn Burke's, *Becoming Modern: The Life of Mina Loy* (Berkeley: University of California Press, 1996).

Futurism, Fashion, and the Feminine: Forms of Repudiation and Affiliation in the Early Writing of Mina Loy

Rowan Harris

1. Antifemininity and manifestos for new womanhood

Living, alone with her children, in Italy on the eve of the First World War and seeking to reinvent herself against the backdrop of a disastrously failed marriage, the London-born artist and poet Mina Loy sent a newly-penned 'Feminist Manifesto' to her close friend Mabel Dodge in New York. Rejecting the reforms of contemporary rights feminism as barely significant and espousing instead a rhetoric of individual self-realisation and creativity, the explosive manifesto was addressed from one aspiring avant-gardist new woman to another – Dodge, whom Loy would describe around this time as 'the only woman yet evolved'.[1] The manifesto called for a transformed feminine psychology. It aggressively harangued women to engage in the '**Absolute Demolition**' of the fictitious values in which they had hitherto invested, in order to emerge as autonomous modern subjects: 'all your pet illusions must be unmasked– the lies of centuries have got to go' (*LLB II* 153). Through this vigorous eschewal of fictitious values it performed a passionate desire to conceive of a truly and radically new woman.

The manifesto's exhortations insisted upon a feminism that would be hard on women. Self-realisation was only to be achieved through extraordinary and strenuous effort; it was to involve 'a devastating psychological upheaval', a '**Wrench**', as well as 'sacrifices' (*LLB II* 154). There is an absolute refusal, here, of a feminism that sees women as being in need of protection, a refusal exemplified in the sharp dismissal of the vice crusades of the Women's Movement. Women, Loy argued, must vigorously repudiate in themselves 'the desire for comfortable protection' which leads the chosen to the parasitic dependency of the 'advantageous bargain' of marriage, a bargain secured at the expense of other women (*LLB II* 156, 155). For the choices available to women under current social conditions were limited, she insisted, to '**Parasitism, & Prostitution – or Negation**'. The manifesto demanded that women cease adapting themselves to values engendered by male desire. It insisted it was imperative that they cease defining themselves negatively relative to men, or adapting 'to a theoretical valuation of their sex as **relative impersonality**', and that they seek instead to realise concrete values in themselves. Perhaps even more radically, in contempt for emotional as well as material dependency, Loy declared that 'Women must destroy in themselves the desire to be loved' (*LLB II* 154–5). This is consistent with an assertion made in her correspondence at this time that 'Love is the parasitism of the weak'.[2] Here, as in the manifesto, love is violently rejected as inextricable from the degradations of femininity.

Eschewing 'fictitious' valuations of women, then, Loy expressed deep antipathy towards a traditional configuration of femininity conceived in terms of dependency, egoic deficiency and 'relative impersonality'. Exemplary amongst such repudiated values, in the manifesto, is 'the fictitious value of woman as identified with her physical purity'. This 'man made bogey' to which women accede is the 'principal instrument of [their] subjection' and an impediment to 'psychic development' (*LLB II* 155). In order to destroy the repressive power of this particular fictitious value, the value of female virtue, a drastic measure is proposed which is deliberately shocking: 'the unconditional surgical destruction of virginity through-out the female population at puberty'. Two further great illusions to be demolished are 'the impurity of sex' and, continuous with this, the division of women into two classes '**the mistress & the mother**', a division which the parasitism of the middle class wife perpetuates (*LLB II* 154–5). The manifesto thus articulates a sex radical position, asserting that the destruction of these illusions will lead to social regeneration. It demands an 'intelligent' and courageous female sexual 'curiosity' (*LLB II* 156). Free (hetero)sexual expression is presented as a primary condition for the evolution of the radical avant-garde new woman.

Lucy Bland has argued convincingly that at the beginning of the century sexology was 'the only current discourse offering a set of ideas with which women could explore the possibility of being sexual *agents* as opposed to eternal victims'.[3] Loy's manifesto for a new woman clearly draws upon contemporary scientific eugenic and sexological discourses, discourses which fed into avant-garde dreams of a new type. She was also interested, at this time, in the campaigning of the American sex radical Margaret Sanger, though she remained resolutely uninspired by Sanger's emphasis upon birth control. Loy's championing of sexual freedom at this point did not embrace nonreproductive sexualities. She was more in tune with Havelock Ellis, whom she was reading, and to whose case studies she attributed the inspiration for her idea of the surgical destruction of virginity. In Ellis's work, the erotic rights of women are always articulated in terms of a biologically reproductive heterosexuality and Loy, too, conceived female sexuality to be inherently procreative. (Indeed, what appears, today, quite startling about her manifesto is its yoking of individual sexual freedom to an eugenicist assertion of race-responsibility.) The manifesto championed an active powerful female (hetero)sexuality freed from parasitic attachments to men. To this end it demanded the rejection of all those degraded emotional weaknesses associated with love – 'honour, grief, sentimentality, pride & consequently jealousy' – and that 'sex or so called love' be stripped of its mythological layers and ideological values, 'reduced to its initial element' (*LLB II* 156). Yet, as at least one critic has observed, this feminist and apparently naturalistic call 'to strip love of its cultural dress' might be seen to signal an alignment with a longstanding, but also, in 1914, very contemporary, 'misogynist critique of love as a feminine and sentimentalizing cultural façade'.[4]

Despite the confidence of the manifesto's belligerent declaratives and denunciations, its negotiation of femininity is not unambiguous. There is the surprising closing assertion that: 'Woman for her happiness must retain her deceptive fragility of appearance, combined with indomitable will, irreducible courage & abundant health.' (*LLB II* 156) It is not immediately clear why this emergent autonomous and individualist modern subject should retain such a mask of vulnerable femininity. The new woman is to be feminine, after all, but this femininity is to be fictitious, a deceit. More intriguing still is the manifesto's projection of an alternatively conceived femininity in a formulation which recalls Loy's description of Dodge as a singular avatar of new womanhood: 'The women who adapt themselves to a theoretical valuation of their sex as **relative impersonality**, are not yet **Feminine**' (*LLB II* 154). Femininity is precariously situated in this manifesto. It is clearly that which is being repudiated, but it is also that which is not yet achieved. Loy's manifesto hovers between an antagonism towards the feminine that violently denounces it as an empty and degraded male tool, and an aspiration towards a radical resignification and refashioning of the feminine (women are not yet feminine).

A strong contempt towards the feminine, particularly as it is construed in terms of an adherence to fictitious values, runs throughout Loy's early writing. Yet this contempt, which in a poem such as 'Virgins Plus Curtains Minus Dots' borders on revulsion, is offset by inscriptions of sympathetic identification. Indeed, what is striking about the early poetry is its blend of compassion and uncompromising satire. The effect is frequently one of disconcerting oscillation and powerful hesitancy. As in the manifesto, there appears to be a failure or a refusal to resolve an ambivalence. What is clear is that for Mina Loy in the early teens 'woman' as an appellation was being experienced as profoundly debilitating, even wounding, and that femininity was to a considerable degree conceived as a mark of degradation. She articulates a profound antipathy towards the demands made by the identity category 'woman' upon the individual, an aversion which corresponds well to that which Denise Riley has described as gender 'claustrophobia'.[5] This claustrophobia manifests as a kind of femme-phobia. In the 'Feminist Manifesto', for instance, the emancipatory move would seem to necessitate a vilifying refusal of femininity. A repudiation of femininity and a *derision of women* become crucial to the effort to forge a feminist position.

Of course a disdain for women and for femininity – the two are not always so easily disentangled – has in no way been anathema to feminist politics, indeed for many feminists a critique of the social and psychological formations characteristic of conventional femininity has been the essence of such politics. Nor was such a repudiation and distrust of femininity in any way exceptional amongst women of the early avant-garde. Emily Apter has recently discussed Natalie Barney in this respect and, indeed, mentions Loy's manifesto. Apter has endeavoured to propose a feminist 'gynophobic subject', predicated upon repudiation and expressing a 'life-preserving "aversivity" in rendering femininity the phobic object'.[6] This gynophobia implies a form of female or feminist fetishism: 'not unlike her male counterparts, a woman may equally well (though perhaps for significantly different reasons and stakes), comprehend femininity as an object of dread'. Articulating an account of selfhood forged out of foreclosure and flight, Apter regards Melanie Klein and Joan Rivière's deployment of a logic of negation and interiorized anxiety as crucial to 'understanding the complex motivations of femininity's turn away from itself'.[7] Yet somewhat remarkably, considering these references, Apter pays very little attention to ambivalence in her effort to claim gynophobia for feminism and queer theory. An issue which she elides, though clearly troubled by it, is that of at what point feminist gynophobia becomes collusion with a long history of degrading women and, moreover, whether it is possible to enact a disidentification with femininity which does not involve its simultaneous degradation.

It is through an understanding of Loy's 'gynophobia' that we can account for the way in which *Sex and Character*, Otto Weininger's hugely influential pernicious misogynist treatise on the ontological nullity of the female sexological type, haunts her early body of feminist writing. Her manifesto attack on the division of women into two classes appears as a direct rejoinder to Weininger's division of Woman into two fundamental types: the Prostitute and the Mother. Yet, despite moments of critique, it is evident that Loy's attack on a femininity conceived in terms of fictitious values finds an echo and even a source in Weininger's account of the 'organic mendacity of Woman'.[8] Like Loy, Weininger too saw women's purity as a fictitious value engendered by and originating with men. Indeed, for him, all the apparent attributes of femininity were simulation, false-selfhood constructed in unconscious response to male expectations, and thus, in actual fact, a projection of male sexuality. Women 'have no intrinsic standard of value', and so 'because they are nothing in themselves, they can become everything'.[9] Beyond the fictitious values assumed in order to ensnare men there is only pure undifferentiated sexuality. Femininity (along with Jewishness) implied a 'psychological constitution' corresponding to a degrading servile condition, a negation of independent selfhood and the antithesis of individual genius.

Substantial extracts from *Sex and Character* were published by the former suffragette Dora Marsden in the *Freewoman* in 1912, much to the alarm of many of its readers. Loy was in London throughout the autumn of 1912, by which time the *Freewoman* had become hugely controversial. It is almost certain that she read it, a fact which would begin to account for the strong affinity between her manifesto and

Marsden's *Freewoman* editorials. Like Loy, Marsden espoused an anar-
chist evolutionary feminism that attempted to imagine and will into
being a radically new woman in opposition to the mass of ordinary or
typical women. Through the term 'bondwomen' she poured scorn
upon the latter, condemning a configuration of womanhood she
conceived as the opposite of individual self-determination:
'Bondwomen are the women who are not spiritual entities – who are
not individuals.'[10] Hailing the freewoman as a higher countertype
who 'must have the essential attribute of genius', Marsden criticised
the Suffragist movement for taking its stand 'upon the weakness and
dejectedness of the condition of women'.[11] Virulently denouncing the
'stupefying influence' of protection, and conceding the misogynist's
argument that women have shown only '"servant" attributes', she
blamed women's subjugation on their own psychological make-up: 'If
they were not "down" in themselves – i.e. weaker in mind – no equal
force could have crushed them down'. Contempt for such women, for
women generally, is thus not only 'the healthiest thing in the world'
but a condition for the emergence of the freewoman.[12] As with Loy,
female emancipation is to be achieved through a strenuous effort of
repudiation.

Despite editorial criticism of Weininger's sexualised account of
Woman, it is clear that Marsden found much that was compelling in
the work of her 'favourite misogynist', and much that seemed
commensurate with her own hard feminism. Without doubt
Marsden – and Loy – would have conceded that '[t]he ultimate opponent of the emancipation of women is woman'. Weininger's scorn for
woman's acquiescence in her objectification echoed Marsden's own:
'She is willing to be used by others as a tool, as a "thing"'.[13] Marsden
appears to have been energized by a rhetoric that implied that emancipation was to be achieved through women vanquishing their femininity:

> Femaleness, as Weininger defined it, is the Thing to be Destroyed. It is
> the Great Denial – the thing to be overcome. But this "femaleness"
> has no special kinship with the females of the human species . . . It is
> the Foe of Life whom men and women alike have to meet and have to
> overcome, or perish.[14]

Marsden, then, applauds and endorses Weininger's affirmation of the
cosmic separateness of the individual personality, accepting his

account of femaleness as the degrading negation of personality she had herself identified in bondwomen. This embroilment with *Sex and Character* gave momentum to what Bruce Clarke has traced as Marsden's defensive reaction against the discourse of types, commensurate with her reaction against social-democratic politics, which led ultimately to the eclipsing of the gendered figure of the freewoman by the anarchistic antitype of the egoist.[15] For while Marsden's ultimate insistence that 'Woman' has no existence[16], signalled a refusal of types indebted to the anti-democratic philosophy of Max Stirner, it also echoed Weininger's rendition of Woman as cosmic negativity. Her egoism was to be powered by a repudiation of the feminine which would owe much to Weininger. In Marsden's defence, Judy Greenway has made the case that: '[t]hose readers who ignored the unpalatable aspects of Weininger's work were not endorsing them; they were taking what they needed in order to construct their own version of the world'.[17] Yet we must attend to the fact that what was useful to Marsden's feminism was precisely some of the most unpalatable aspects of his work: a vision of femininity as pathological and pernicious, and a demand that it be overcome.

Marsden and Loy were supreme feminist gynophobes, though the trajectory of Marsden's feminism seems to have led less towards Apter's nonconformist queer feminist ontologies than towards spiritual absolutism. Both imagined emancipation in terms of a refusal of womanliness and an active (hetero)sexual self-expression. In this respect they are wholly at odds with Weininger for whom the repudiation of femininity is continuous with a repudiation of sexuality. My point in highlighting the influence of *Sex and Character* upon their thinking is not to condemn feminist gynophobia, though I admit to greater unease than Apter regarding its capacity to utilise the most vicious misogyny, and I trace a corresponding unease in Loy's writing. Expressions of avant-garde feminist gynophobia appear to acquire something of a critical mass with the emergence of sexology at the turn of the century. The importance of gynophobia, as Apter describes it, is that it theorizes femininity as something to be repudiated and as something that *can* be repudiated: it makes reconfigurations of the feminine subject conceivable even as it demands that the feminine be vilified and abjected. Gynophobia rejects the status of femininity as an immutable essence of self. In contrast to the misogyny it appropriates, it has the potential to radically undermine the stability of femininity. In 1912 and 1913 feminist gynophobia appears to have offered an alternative to political feminism's efforts to valorize female difference.

Whereas Dora Marsden left behind, or went beyond, the issue of how to identify or disidentify as a woman, for Loy it remained central to the act of writing. Her political identification was equivocal: in correspondence she claimed to feel 'hopeless of devotion to the woman cause', and declared, elsewhere, that 'what I feel now are feminine politics'.[18] Aside from the way in which this latter formulation complicates gynophobia, I am struck by her preference, here, to designate her feminist identification in the adjectival form. Though the privileging of 'feminine' over 'woman' inverts the dominant preference of twentieth-century feminism, it seems Loy chooses 'feminine' as a more flexible designation: it is the name that induces claustration, whereas the adjective leaves a little room for manoeuvre.

2. The Futurist Woman

There is evidence in Loy's writing of a wariness about the gynophobic refusal of femininity, wariness of the ways in which it could be turned against women and exacerbate the punishments which accrue to femininity. Her poetic satires show that she was a formidable critic of the rabid and anxious misogyny of the Futurists. Loy's erotic and intellectual entanglement with the two protagonists of Italian Futurism, F. T. Marinetti and Giovanni Papini, has by now received considerable critical attention though there remains resistance to acknowledging the positive debt Loy owed to their thinking. It is not possible, however, to understand Loy's formidable defence against the Futurist discourse on Woman without understanding her investment in it. Italian Futurism was an obvious influence upon Loy's gynophobia: an attack on femininity continuous with an attack on fictitious values emerges as a leitmotif in Futurist rhetoric, specifically in the attack on Love. In fact, Loy's ambivalence towards women was exacerbated in *both* directions by Futurist misogyny – it antagonized her phobic response to femininity while provoking her defence of women.

'Aphorisms on Futurism', a series of aggressive imperatives construed as 'primary tentatives towards independence' and psychic expansion, appeared in Alfred Stieglitz's *Camera Work* in 1914 and marked Loy's first and last open identification with the movement in print. Its derisive address is strikingly similar to that of the 'Feminist Manifesto', expressing contempt towards a current mode of identity in an attempt to project an ideal modern (Futurist) subject:

THROUGH derision of Humanity as it appears –

TO arrive at respect for man as he shall be – (*LLB II* 152)

There is, however, an insistent expression of compassion in amongst these early aphorisms that will assume greater prominence in Loy's writing: 'OPEN your arms to the dilapidated, to rehabilitate them' (*LLB II* 149). It will trouble her hard feminism, as it troubles her Futurism here.

Futurism offered Loy the exciting vision of a transformed culture and spoke to her own desire for a 'renovated consciousness'[19]. This avant-garde dream of the meeting of art and praxis – arguably, first expressed by the Futurists[20] – was hugely relevant to Loy's desire to imagine a radically new woman. Such an aspiration brought her up against the question of how a woman could be a Futurist. Yet in Futurist discourse the Futurist woman is, in fact, inconceivable – as Loy was abundantly aware. The reliance of Futurist rhetoric upon a vilified femininity needs little documentation. Its most concise articulation is the legendary 'scorn for women' of the 1909 'The Founding and Manifesto of Futurism'.[21] Woman was associated with all things condemned as 'passatista': sentimentality, nostalgia, pacifism, symbolist poetry, auratic art, psychology and nature. As Peter Nicholls has formulated it, Woman in the manifestos denoted a 'particular psychological formation which is in some sense resistant to the new'.[22] A belligerent repudiation of Woman identified with resistance to modernity, was the bedrock of Futurism's power fantasies. Woman was, in Marinetti's own words, 'the eternal enemy that we would have to invent if it didn't exist'.[23]

Though Marinetti was not in the habit of quoting his sources, the influence of Weininger is easily traced in his writing: the notion of genius as perfected masculinity, the desire for a world in which (the threat of) Woman had been annihilated, and the representation of women as both inferior animals and the cause of man's degradation. It is even more evident in the philosophical writing of Giovanni Papini. He called for the (inevitable) liquidation or 'massacre' of the female sex in an article which directly acknowledged its debt to *Sex and Character.*[24] In this respect it is worth noting that Weininger's text expressed the same distaste for decadent art and its feminized 'fops' or aesthetes as Futurism would, blaming women (and Jews) for a degraded 'coitus culture'. Marinetti's response was a totalizing affirmation of the strong male ego through the annihilation of the feminine other.

A considerable number of women were nonetheless attracted to the 'beautiful freedoms'[25] that Marinetti proffered in the name of an invigorating modernity, compelled no doubt by a rhetoric which advocated individual transcendence and liberation from the taboos and institutions of bourgeois morality. His militant discourse against the shackles of the past even chimed with that of the suffragettes in London, with whom he on one occasion marched. Marinetti advocated a sex radicalism of sorts, demanding women's emancipation from 'marriage as legal prostitution' and echoing Weininger in condemning women's 'state of intellectual and erotic slavery'.[26] Some women even achieved a modicum of visibility in the Futurist movement. It has been argued that it was through a notion of exceptionality that such women sought Futurist recognition, where the exceptional woman was one conceived as possessing virility of spirit. Exemplary was Valentine Saint-Point's assertion that 'What is most lacking in women and men alike is masculinity'.[27] Marinetti applauded the masculine woman, drawing upon a punitive sexological linking of feminism, lesbianism and masculinity: he hailed the suffragettes as allies in their quest for rights and powers that he believed would masculinize women thus diminishing their capacity to ensnare men. Unsurprisingly, no Futurist woman appears to have been able to positively appropriate this categorization. Cinzia Sartini-Blum's reading of Enif Roberts and Rosa Rosa suggests that the 'exceptional' identification more often produced a contemptuous antagonism towards other women, a loathing, easily turned back on the self, that accepted and reinforced the identification of women's bodies with sexuality and pathology.[28] What is clear is that in Futurist discourse the Futurist woman would not emerge in anything like the magnificence of the projected metallised and multiplied Futurist New Man.

A letter which Loy wrote from Florence around 1915 makes clear that gender was very much at stake as she sought to comprehend her own reaction to Futurism, a reaction she conceived to be exceptional:

– the vitality I learnt from Marinetti to use – has not abated – in some mysterious way that inimitable Explosive – rejuvenates his familiars – though I am the only female who has reacted to it – exactly the way I have noticed men do – Of course being the most female thing extant – I'm somewhat masculine.[29]

This is not a claim to androgyny but to an excessive femininity which undoes itself, for this, curiously, is a masculine identification consequent upon a full possession of femaleness. Elsewhere, in a manuscript from this period, Loy describes a woman who appears to seek in Futurism an escape from her female self:

She had got into the Flabbergast world where everything seemed to be worked by a piston – hiding away from her self in this man's jacket, she was caught in the machinery of his urgent identification with motor frenzy; and dropped consciousness of everything but Rush.[30]

The woman inhabits the Futurist world by means of a masculine identification which is not masked but a masquerade. There is equally, however, a sense that she inhabits this world as a spy.

Loy wrote several poems in which she presented female figures caught up in Futurism and ironized their desire for Futurist recognition (though the primary target of her satire was the posturing and anxious misogyny of the Futurists themselves). In 'Lions' Jaws' an aspirant female Futurist appears as a groupie petitioning for the honour of bearing the Futurist child:

These amusing men
discover in their mail
duplicate petitions
to be the lurid mother of "their" flabbergast child
from Nima Lyo, alias Anim Yol, alias
Imna Oly
(secret service buffoon to the Woman's Cause) (*LLB II* 49)

In this poem, which can be read as a retrospective negotiation of her own investment in the movement, Loy explicitly poses the question of female solidarity and its betrayal:

.   .   .   Manifesto
of the flabbergast movement
hurled by the leader Raminetti
to crash upon the audacious lightning

of Gabrunzio's fashions in lechery
.   .   .   and wheedle its inevitable way
to the "excepted" woman's heart
her cautious pride
extorting betrayal
of Woman wholesale
to warrant her surrender
with a sense of   .   .   .   Victory (*LLB II* 47–8)

Female Futurism is a risky business. The title of the poem itself, of course, emphasises a perilous positioning. That the aspirant female Futurist is a spy for the 'Woman's Cause', however, suggests that she may maintain her allegiance – albeit ambiguously – as a 'buffoon'. The question of female solidarity is further complicated by the radically indeterminate identity of the female figure. Loy inscribes her own name into this poem by means of a proliferation of mutating anagrams which converge on the elusive figure of the speaker. Moreover, Imna Oly, the first of these aliases, is, we are later told, 'not quite a lady', exacerbating the unstable semantic gap between 'lady' and 'Woman' to undermine the stability of the latter.

Indeterminacy inscribes resistance equally in 'Giovanni Franchi'. Here, another woman is presented caught up in 'Flabbergastism'. She emerges as a foil to the eponymous young acolyte and is his rival for the attention of the philosopher Giovanni Bapini. Her exhibitionism and extravagant fashionably femme 'ferny flounces' find an alliterative echo in Franchi's spectacularly exceptional trousers which 'flapped friezily' ('Were they not the first / No others could ever be the first again') (*LLB II* 27). A comic presentation of female erotic pursuit, the poem foregrounds female sexual curiosity. The female figure is described as a fetishist and a voyeur, her pursuit of the philosopher determined by a desire to know the number of his toes: 'They fluttered to her fantasy' (*LLB II* 31). The knowledge she seeks is both transparently sexual and absurd, opaque. For all the mockery, there is a sense that this desire is potentially disruptive. In the face of Bapini's denunciation of women – irrevocably designating them 'those pernicious persons' (*LLB II* 30) – female difference is both exaggerated and destabilized. As 'threewomen who all walked / In the same dress', the female figure dissembles (*LLB II* 27).

Loy's satirical treatment of Futurist rhetoric foregrounded its invocation of 'sex war', a formulation which conceived of sexed identities as antagonistic immutable binary opposites and which was also invoked by some in the Women's movement in Europe. Loy rejected this formulation, finding more feminist mileage in destabilizing the monumental category of Woman (which is not necessarily to repudiate it). She was also alert to, and amused by, a current of disavowed anxiety in the Futurist attack on Woman. In an early unpublished short 'play' Loy comically collapsed the 'sex war', heterosexual seduction and the Futurist attack on Love into one farcical spectacle: a ludicrous fixed boxing-match between Love, who is also Woman, and Futurism who delivers his 'psychological' blows with heart-shaped boxing gloves.[31] The play opens with a group of men discussing the modern woman's preference for a man as a shopping companion rather than as a lover, with one even lamenting 'being born in an age when it is unnecessary for me to live'. 'Futurism' bursts onto the scene to announce his virility and denounce this defeated decadent as 'pastist'. The originary moment of Futurist declaration is thus located, here, in an anxious and defensive response to the changing desires associated with modern womanhood. Cinzia Blum has convincingly argued that despite its extravagant celebration of modernity, Futurist rhetoric betrays an unarticulated anxiety about modern reality, specifically about the emergence of new feminine identities. She reads Marinetti's Futurism as a defensive response to a radical sense of crisis: a 'masculinity crisis' (exacerbated by modern war) which is the emotional underside of its fiction of power. In this reading, the feminine threat stands not for all things 'passatista' but for the disempowerment of modern man in a rapidly changing new world.

The modern woman, conceived in her affinity to capitalist goods, emerges, in fact, as a figure of acute ambivalence for Marinetti. With her new desires and erotic prerogatives she is regarded as both by-product and catalyst of a celebrated modernity. In a 1913 manifesto which charts and champions those modern phenomena which have become the key elements of the new Futurist sensibility, the modern woman's narcissistic disdain for love in favour of commodities is seen to concur with the depreciation of love so desired by Marinetti:

> Depreciation of love (sentimentalism or lust), produced by the greater freedom and erotic ease of women and by the universal exaggeration of female luxury. Let me explain. Today's woman loves luxury more than love. A visit to a great dressmaker's establishment, escorted by a paunchy, gouty banker friend who pays the bills, is a perfect substitute for the most amorous rendezvous with an adored young man. The woman finds all the mysteries of love in the selection of an amazing

ensemble, the latest fashion, which her friends still do not have. Men
do not love women who lack luxury. The lover has lost his prestige.
Love has lost its absolute value. A complex question; all I can do is to
raise it.[32]

The woman of fashion who prefers shopping to love must be seen as
a primary agent of desirable change. Yet she generates a distinct
unease, with Marinetti tripping himself up rhetorically over the inti-
mation of male devaluation, even redundancy. Her lack of interest is
threatening – the Futurist cult of virility depending on women as
objects of erotic consumption even as it aspired to a world without
women. In fact, this new woman with a perceived erotic autonomy
inextricable from a love of commodities, appears far more unsettling
for Marinetti than that other modern woman, the suffragette.

By 1920, the woman of fashion would become, in Marinetti's writing, unequivocally pernicious, her investment in commodities now
construed as a 'morbid mania', her corrupt appeal threatening to
turn men into feminized fetishists in *their* taste for artifice: 'The man
gradually loses the power to sense the female flesh and replaces it
with a faltering, totally artificial sensibility, that responds only to silk,
velvet, jewels and furs [. . .] The naked woman is no longer pleasing.'[33]
The modern woman's perversion is contagious, she threatens the
natural value of masculinity. For Futurism the 'true' object of virile
desire is the 'natural' woman – 'carne', flesh or meat.[34]

Futurism, nevertheless, did not at all repudiate fashion. It actually
sought to appropriate its spectacular dimension. Fashion and
Futurism were perceived as fellow conspirators in the cult of the new,
both privileging 'the perishable, the transitory, and the ephemeral'.
The 'Founding Manifesto' had announced Futurism as a response to
Italy's desperate need for new clothes: 'For too long has Italy been a
dealer in second-hand clothes'.[35] By 1913 fashion was already being
celebrated as a Futurist phenomenon. Balla's 'Futurist Manifesto of
Men's Clothing' derided men's dismal, uniform attire and prescribed
spectacular 'Futurist Clothes' that would produce a 'merry dazzle' in
the city streets, making everything 'sparkle like the glorious prism
of a jeweller's gigantic glass-front'. Such clothes would be coloured
in the same violent colours that were emerging from Paris at that
moment in women's fashion. The Futurist man was to wear Futurist
clothes to declare his allegiance to Futurist modernity and to mark
his extreme individualism. These clothes were to become quickly
obsolescent: 'they must be made to last for a short time only in order

to encourage industrial activity and to provide constant and novel enjoyment for our bodies'.[36] While Balla's manifesto concluded by promising an equivalent manifesto on women's clothes 'shortly to appear', it did not materialise for another seven years. This was not simply another instance of women's exclusion from the Futurist brotherhood. The irony was that women's fashions *already were Futurist* in the manner prescribed by Balla: he was haranguing men to dress more like women in order to achieve modernity.

When the 'Manifesto of Futurist Feminine Fashion' finally did appear in 1920, a significant shift of emphasis was evident. While openly conceding 'Women's fashion has always been more or less futurist', and declaring fashion to be the 'feminine equivalent of Futurism', it did not at all conceive of women as creative agents in the way the earlier manifesto had imagined fashionable men. It represented an effort to reassert male authority through a privileging of the autocratic Futurist fashion designer: 'It is absolutely necessary to proclaim the dictatorship of artistic Genius over feminine fashion against interferences'. The manifesto produces fashionable women as objects not agents of fashion. The bizarre Futurist feminine fashions it proposes reveal a Futurist fantasy of domination and humiliation, whereby women are turned into fetishized technological objects:

> In woman we can idealize the most fascinating conquests of modern life. And so we will have the machine gun woman, [the tank woman], the radio-telegraph antenna woman, the airplane woman, the submarine woman, the motorboat woman. We will transform the elegant lady into a real, living three-dimensional complex. [37]

As a futurist machine spectacle the modern woman's potential autonomy is negated.

Loy's archives contain a considerable body of prose writing from the Florence years which draws directly upon her creative wrangle with Futurism and her affairs with Marinetti and Papini. The tendency of Carolyn Burke's important biography of Loy to read this material as transparent memoirs has resulted in a failure to appreciate not only its fictionality but also its status as some of Loy's earliest experimental writing. For it is in this writing that we can see Loy beginning to experiment with forms of irony, ventriloquy and indeterminacy in her effort to mediate both a defence against and an investment in Futurist rhetoric.

The narrative of Loy's unpublished novel, 'Possessions'[38], traces the encounter of a female protagonist with the compelling excesses of 'Flabbergastism'. Here again, we encounter the 'sex war' collapsed sadomasochistically into heterosexual seduction by the Futurist-Flabbergast leader. Jemima or Sophia – the names are interchangeable – emerges as an Alice in a Futurist wonderland, embarking upon a 'psychic adventure' in her search for a way of being in a disorientating world whose absurdities she confronts as her fascination intensifies. Like Caroll's Alice, her own identity is elusive, her physical presence registered in the text by scattered accoutrements – a 'silken ankle', a 'leopard collar', 'glossy skirts'. In her first exchange with the Marinetti figure, 'Brontolivido', Jemima confronts him with the way his rhetoric excludes her from the Futurist cosmos and attempts to foreclose her own potential for modernity. She inquires of him: 'why in your reconstruction of the universe, leave woman out?' His reply is that 'Woman [. . .] Is never going to change' and, in any case, 'The Flabbergasts will finish her off'.[39] Brontolivido is the Humpty Dumpty of this wonderland, ('This is a beautiful word – that means what I say'), assuming a dictatorial relation to language and difference: 'Woman he blazed is a wonderful animal – and when I print any part of her body that I choose – it is in purist of appreciation'. ('This is a beautiful word – that means what I say'.)[40] Claiming a technologically reinforced domination over representations of the feminine, he seeks to violently negate otherness.

In her first meeting with Brontolivido the heroine experiences both a sense of derivative scripted scenarios – his 'florescent gallantry' 'gave her a silly sensation of irruption into a D'Annunzio novel' – and a sense of something truly new, an unprecedented performance: 'Sophia was watching a spectacle she had never seen acted quite that way before'. (In all of Loy's poetic representations of Marinetti, she presents him as some kind of performer.) She describes Brontolivido, in his obsession with a prosthetically reinforced virility, as an overblown hyperbolic cliché: he is 'the man I too easily understand grown to proportions I cannot apprehend'.[41] His exhibitionism and parading generates a hypertrophied masculinity which by its very excesses is rendered radically unstable. Indeed, in Loy's rendition of the Futurist world, aggressively proclaimed sexed identities seem to literally topple over, with Flabbergast male posturing persistently slipping into feminized spectacle. Loy becomes a kind of camp reader of Futurism, outrageously indicating that Brontolivido, being the most masculine thing extant, appears somewhat feminine. There is deliberate humour too in the presentation of Marinetti's Futurist antics as seductive performances aimed at audiences of women fans. Although Brontolivido declares, 'I'm a healthy man – there's no sentimentality about me – I don't pander to women's pretentions', he nevertheless harangues the Flabbergasts to follow his example and 'stir women's lust with glitter and glare'.[42] In order to prove his 'healthy' virility he must 'pander' to, produce himself as commodified object of, a desirous female gaze.

Jemima/Sophia emerges at particular moments in the text as a perfect illustration of the Weiningerian articulation of femininity as non-identity, formlessness and dependent being:

> I have the honesty to admit anything I'm aware of – so here goes. Woman is omniplastic – she can mould herself to the vision of any man stronger than herself – She is merely potential prior to her impact with man – it would be for her an economy of time could she invoke the oracle.[43]

Here, the heroine flamboyantly performs and laments an abject, empty femininity, professing to painfully experience herself as an ontological void. Yet the extravagance of her rhetorical performance serves to render it absurd, mask-like. The same can be said of her plea: 'Tell me what sort of man will choose me so I will know what sort of woman to become'.[44] Brontolivido's excesses seem to render his identity as elusive and protean despite his loud assertions of a strong ego. He variously appears as a martinet, a 'bicephalous spider-tiger', 'a juvenescent panther', a 'sea lion in training', an electric battery, and a 'bombastic superman'. Indeed, his selfhood comes to illustrate a derivative dependent mode of being which has all the ontological inconsistency of Weininger's conception of Woman's mendacious self: the narrator describes how in 'his inconsecutive spontaneity – he became the thing he sensed in its requiredness'.[45] Brontolivido even comes to mirror the female protagonist 'in her amoral feminine fluidity – feeling for a protoform to crystallize to'. Trying to seduce her he appears to become 'flabbier and flabbier – his physique seeming to convey – it was for her to mold him'.[46] This mirroring of hyper-male and hyper-female subjects is crucial to the comedy of 'Possessions'. Brontolivido approximates to fictitious values, and it is to this capacity that the narrator attributes his success: 'And it was this ability to crystallize to any absolute form whatsoever – that he blindly and brilliantly progressed on'.[47] His genius is seen, ultimately, to reside in his femininity. So, confronting him with his utter dependence on an audience, the heroine almost applauds the way in which he draws 'something' out of this audience 'in order to give it back to them in your superb pretentiousness as yourself'.[48]

Through Jemima/Sophia, then, the Futurist-Weiningerian configuration of Woman is displayed, dissected and ridiculed. Further – and it is here that Brontolivido's mirroring of Jemima/Sophia's performative mode of being acquires its most radical significance – Loy's narrative seems to expose this ontological void that Weininger attributed to Woman as the void that defines subjectivity itself. Slavoj Žižek has noted how Weininger in *Sex and Character* cannot approach such an insight: 'In this endeavour of nothing to become something, he fails to recognise *the very striving of the subject for a substantial support.*'[49] Bronty and Jemima emerge as model subjects in a narrative which suggests that their 'female shapelessness' might be the constitutive feature of subjectivity.

In Loy's rendition of the Flabbergast world, its forms and performances radically destabilize established 'authentic' values, generating an exhilarating sense of new, liberating possibilities. Yet these possibilities are betrayed. In taking up with Flabbergastism, Loy's heroine seeks escape from the inertia of a debilitating femininity: she is described as having initially 'thrown her-self desperately on the inimical male force – for harbour from her suffused femininity'.[50] Yet the pernicious representations of the feminine viciously reasserted by Flabbergastism/Futurism are not so easily shaken off. Thus in a formulation that establishes both solidarity and a degree of distance, the heroine declares: 'the way you talk about women has made you repulsive to me – I have quite a few sympathies with my sex'.[51] Jemima/Sophia comes to inhabit the Flabbergast world less through masculine identification than through feminine ventriloquy. She undermines Futurist constructions of Woman by taking them on ('I am a woman and you are the man who has annihilated me'[52]), oscillating between a professed vacuity and a formidable wit and superior disdain in deflating Bronty's hyperbole. Jemima's abject femininity is thus rendered highly equivocal by a narrative apparatus which, operating different levels of irony, generates fundamental problems of attribution.[53] While there is a clear distinction in the text between the knowing aloof sophistication of the narrator and the heroine's bewildered naivety, it is recurrently undermined by an implied identification between the two. The sophisticated linguistic artifice of the narrator generates a knowingness which inflects Jemima/Sophia's abject rhetorical performances: she emerges, in the narrative and in the Flabbergast world, in her superb pretentiousness as herself.[54]

A similarly unstable distinction between narrator and female figure is deployed to comparable effect in Loy's most acclaimed early poem 'The Effectual Marriage or The Insipid Narrative of Gina and Miovanni'. Here, the wifely female figure occupies a space designated or owned by the man – she resides in his kitchen, amongst 'his pots and pans', 'where he so kindly kept her' (*LLB II* 36). Gina apparently aspires to a wholly feminine identity: 'Gina was a woman / Who wanted everything / To be everything in woman / Everything every-way at once' (*LLB II* 38). Her 'value' resides only in her utility as a material springboard for the spiritual departure of male genius. She corresponds to the pulpy formless materiality which male genius repudiates in a constitutive reaction:

> So here we might dispense with her
> Gina being a female
> But she was more than that
> Being an incipience   a correlative
> an instigation of the reaction of man
> From the palpable to the transcendent
> Mollescent irritant of his fantasy
> Gina has her use   Being useful (*LLB II* 36)

Her being, her identity, is depicted in the poem as illogical, inconsistent ('Diurnally variegate') and insubstantial, while her husband Miovanni who is 'magnificently man' remains 'Monumentally the same' (*LLB II* 38, 37, 39). Gina exists in a state of utter dependency, her existence wholly circumscribed by the fictitious values of love which determine her relation to Miovanni, the 'axis' upon which her being revolves.

The poem presents a superficially functional or effective marriage between a genius and his wife. The romantic, devotional and dutiful Gina appears to have secured what Loy referred to caustically in her manifesto as that 'most advantageous bargain'. Both live out their existence in their separate spheres under one roof, acting out the

complementary parts of the domestic script like clockwork dolls. Yet
things are clearly not what they seem, either in this house or in this
poem. Most obviously this is a relationship devoid of meaningful intimacy as is hinted at in the clearly sexual reference to the door that
is 'quotidianly passed through' (*LLB II* 36). Miovanni's genius is slyly
exposed as a mere posture, an empty pose. He dismisses Gina's
inquiry as to supper time with the declaration 'I am / Outside time
and space' (*LLB* 37). There is a suggestion that Gina refuses an intuition, which at some level she already possesses, that Miovanni's
strong creative ego might be illusory and no less insubstantial than
her own:

> While Miovanni thought alone in the dark
> Gina supposed that peeping   she might see
> A round light   shining   where his mind was
> She never opened the door
> Fearing that this might blind her
> Or even
> That she should see   Nothing at all (*LLB II* 38)

Thus while on one level the poem presents Gina as a stupidly happy
well-mated animal woman, there is much which hints otherwise. Her
'audacious happinesses' are deeply suspect: this 'effectual' marriage is
a ghost marriage. Gina may have 'devotional fingers' with which to
minister to Miovanni's needs but her patience is no constitutional
virtue, simply an 'attribute', something external and dispensable
(*LLB II* 39, 37). Her faithfulness may even be provisional: she is 'Gina
who lent monogamy' (*LLB II* 38).

The poem generates a sense of claustrophobia and of an insurgent
tension barely concealed by the surface of things, as well as a sense of
elaborate knowingness in which Gina is implicated and which works
against her apparently contented naivety. Thus a blasphemous image
of the Madonna on the parlour wall as a male operated puppet or
even as a transsexual (the stiffened, crinolened man another of Loy's
simultaneously lewd and opaque references) produces a corrosive
dissonance which resonates throughout the poem:

> anybody could see it
> Shimmered a composite effigy
> Madonna   crinolened   a man
> hidden beneath her hoop (*LLB II* 37)

Primarily, however, it is less through image than through language that the poem's, and even Gina's, knowingness is generated. Indeed, the elaborate syntax and diction of the poem generates a resistive knowingness through which Gina is partially redeemed from her state of insipid, dependent being. As in 'Possessions', a clash of registers in the poem sets up a distinction between the speaker and Gina, which is also undermined. The simple vocabulary and nursery rhyme rhythms associated with Gina ('so kindly' and 'so wisely', 'Ding dong said the bell') and her poem written on the milk bill ('Something not too difficult to / Learn by heart'), are held in tension with the erudite cerebrality and linguistic artifice of the speaker and her decidedly more difficult poem (*LLB II* 37, 39). Yet, at moments, the two are slyly implicated. Gina's cuisine is positively literary, her dish 'appropriately delectable' (*LLB II* 37). Certain words, the most magnificently pretentious of which is the noun 'sialogogues' (Gina's culinary creations) accrue such a materiality as to appear in the poem as objects that resonate a special power, signalling points of resistive knowledge.

Such moments are also clearly the moments when Gina is revealed as Mina. Of course, the most obvious way in which Gina and Mina's identities are mutually implicated in this poem is through the name. Loy simply swapped the initials of her own and Giovanni Papini's forenames (thus inserting the possessive pronoun 'my' ('mio') into Papini's name). So when Loy inscribes herself into her poem, as she frequently does, she does so by way of producing the name as a cryptogram or a puzzle, pointing up the linguistic artifice of the name and unsettling, even ridiculing, its presumed transparent referentiality in relation to personal identity. We saw this in the mutating anagrams of 'Lions' Jaws'. In 'At the Door of the House' Loy writes herself into a sympathetic identification with the deluded women whose predicament the poem laments, its melancholy rhythms echoing a collective yearning. The poem concludes with a litany of Italian women's names into which Loy slips her own:

> Those eyes
>
> Of Petronilla Lucia Letizia
>   Felicita
> Filomina Amalia
> Orsola Geltrude Caterina Delfina
> Zita Bibiana   Tarsilla
> Eufemia

> Looking for the little love-tale
> That never came true
> At the door of the house (*LLB II* 34–5)

'Filomina' is a curious hybrid of Loy and Marinetti's forenames (Filippo and Mina) and 'Geltrude' is a perversion of Loy's middle name Gertrude. What is striking about this list is the strangeness of most of the names, bestowed as they are upon common Italian women. The effect is to foreground the strangeness of the name itself, its materiality and its opacity. Each individual name invites scrutiny, demands, and frequently defies, interpretation. Loy confers the dignity of poetic artifice upon these women in names which appear as jewel-like poem-objects: complex linguistic constructions in their own right.

Loy deploys irony in this early writing to undermine the stability of femininity as a natural sign. Denise Riley has recently insisted that: '[irony] is not antithetical to solidarity — it is not my detachment from my attributed condition that leads to my irony, but on the contrary my deep involvement in it'.[55] The achievement of Loy's most successful early writing is precisely to illustrate this contention. She produces an ironic treatment of feminine identity that does not preclude feminist solidarity. Perhaps we can say that she rescues gynophobia (if we still wish to use the term), sometimes by a hair's breadth, from its potential collapse into misogyny. Her experiments in writing reconfigure gynophobia, female fetishism, and masquerade, as forms of affiliation.

3. Sexology, irony and love

Loy's correspondence frequently alludes to gendered perspectives and experiences which she regards as having been excluded from literary representation. She notes that while plenty of acclaimed books have been written about prostitutes, 'nobody tries to find out how or rather express — what they react to things'.[56] Over and over in her letters to Carl Van Vechten, moreover, she expresses a preoccupation with the difficulties and the risks, but also the *necessity*, of being truthful: 'I am writing a book — the purest — most truthful and personally imaginative book that could be written — it's very hard to be truthful'.[57] This professed effort to write about herself truthfully was also construed, by Loy, as an effort to express some truth about women, and this 'truth' was sexual insofar as sexuality was perceived to be key to the 'difference' of women's interiority.

Such a conviction would have been wholly confirmed by the sexology in which Loy had immersed herself in the pre-War years: she had been reading Freud, Ellis, Weininger and Krafft-Ebing. There are moments in her correspondence when Loy herself refers to women as a 'type' to be investigated: 'I think women are wonderfully interesting when they are not "intellectual" — and being truthful!'[58] The imperative to tell the truth about women's sexuality, to confess sexual truths, was a sexological imperative. (And writers such as Ellis and Krafft-Ebing depended utterly on the confessions of patients and correspondents, which they frequently published.) Loy's 'Love Songs', published in New York in 1915, answer to this imperative, though they also parody, frustrate and challenge it.

The scandal of 'Love Songs', for many of its first readers in New York, was that it appeared to confess the (new) desires and sexual secrets of a very particular type: the modern *new woman*. More recent readers of the sequence have frequently commented upon its overall stance of clinical and analytic detachment and in this respect the sequence indeed mimics a sexological stance, reinforced by the poem's appropriation of the vocabulary of sexual and biological science. If the effect is to suggest that a sexological will to know the secrets of the type drives the self-scrutiny of the sequence, this scrutiny is performed with a devastating irony, is itself a masquerade. It produces no consistent scientific elucidation, but rather a disaggregation of voices, emotions, poses, declarations and vocabularies. It seems that it was precisely the aspiration to 'express' a gendered interiority that led Loy, here, to a poetics of surface, irony, and ventriloquy. The scientific language interrogates and ironizes but is also interrupted by the debased sentimental language of romantic longing. At times these languages converge: 'And spermatozoa / At the core of Nothing / In the milk of the Moon' (*LLB II* 56). The extreme obscurity of some of the vocabulary, which frequently teeters on the edge of the ridiculous, also works against the transparency of scientific language. Scientific terms become ornaments. John Collier, in his contemporaneous review of the *Others* anthology, objected to the 'quasi-scientific pomposities'[59] he read in Loy's poetry, and expressed exasperation with a terminology 'so stilted, so consciously artificial'. Yet these hilarious 'quasi-scientific pomposities', so succinctly and accurately described by Collier, are crucial in creating the sense of deliberate posturing which emerges in 'Love Songs'. They are thus crucial to the ironizing of the stance of clinical detachment. To be sure, the speaker flagrantly indulges in precisely the kind of cerebral posturing she mockingly attributes to her male lover — and the language of 'Love Songs' contains echoes of the erudite philosophical 'voice' of Papini.

The female object of scrutiny in 'Love Songs' persistently recedes from view. We glimpse her traipsing through the poem in her 'silly shoes', or passively keeping devotional vigil, sentimentally hoarding discarded remnants of her lover's genius: 'I am the jealous storehouse of the candle-ends / That lit your adolescent learning' (*LLB II* 56). Several critics have read the sequence as charting the failure of the aspirations of Loy's 'Feminist Manifesto'. Rachel Blau DuPlessis has argued that Loy's poem 'violated the terms of her own brave Feminist Manifesto', and it is certainly the case that the extirpated emotions associated with Love and femininity in the manifesto resurface in the sequence, as do fragments of 'the conventional narrative of passion and loss, thraldom and aftermath'.[60] The sequence is littered with confessional declaratives which suggest 'feminine' dependencies and vulnerabilities in relation to the addressed beloved, but these are undermined, undone even, both by their proliferation and by their strangeness. Jeffrey Twitchell-Waas has provided one of the most satisfying descriptions of 'Love Songs' in his insistence that 'a number of the songs . . . are masks, seeming to pose as expressions of pain and betrayal, yet on closer inspection dissolving into a play of ironies which mock the sentimental trappings of romantic love'.[61] This mask-like quality actually achieves considerably more than what Twitchell-Waas reads as a ridiculing of romantic sentiment indebted to the Futurist attack on *Amore*. What emerges through the powerful ambivalence of the poem is an expression of resistance to the imperatives of an ideological femininity that simultaneously resists misogynist denunciations of the feminine.

The speaker of 'Love Songs' takes on an attributed femininity, her cultural dress, which is continually unsettled by a knowing sense of posturing as the sequence works to foreground this very taking on. In song xxii, for instance, the 'silly shoes' are held, through juxtaposition and alliteration, in close association with a 'flowered flummery', so that the fashionable shoes and the sickly floral sweetness inevitably combine to suggest a trivialized sentimental femininity. We almost hear *flim flam*:

> And flowered flummery
> Breaks
> To my silly shoes
>
> In ways without you
> I go
> Gracelessly
> As things go (*LLB II* 62)

We surely cannot fail to hear in the dismissive designation 'silly', a ventriloquizing invocation of the male lover's misogynist contempt. The speaker's own relation to this flim flam femininity is complicated. She tramples over the femme 'flowered flummery'- she breaks it underfoot; but she walks on into the future independently and stoically in her silly femme shoes. In negotiating her identification with the feminine, the speaker's gracelessness actually performs some nifty footwork. There are, moreover, echoes of Sappho's lyric fragments, here — allusions to the 'bright coloured sandals, / skilful Lydian work', 'the bride / whose feet are graceful', 'those who go ungarlanded', and to the purple flower trampled underfoot, 'staining the earth' — which work to confer dignity upon the manner of her going.[62] In Song xxiv the speaker again appears to take on a designated femaleness, though the tone here is starkly different. She lays claim to a female sexual essence located in the biological function of reproduction in a self-description which draws upon the Futurist-Weiningerian formulation of the woman's 'prurient womb':

> The procreative truth of Me
> Petered out
> In pestilent
> Tear drops
> Little lusts and lucidities
> And prayerful lies (*LLB II* 62)

Just as the speaker appears to lay claim to this reproductive essence as the truth of her identity, it is dissipated. It leaks from her body as wasted bodily fluids — whether abortion, miscarriage or menstrual blood. The bitterness in these particular lines is more sardonic than despairing.[63] The mask-like quality of the speaker's declaration displaces the sexological identitarian 'truth', as does the fact that it dissipates as it is named.

Indisputably the strong procreative new woman proposed in the manifesto does not emerge in this poem. Moreover, whereas the manifesto foregrounded the strong ego as a precondition for individual freedom, 'Love Songs' treats it with scepticism:

> Let us be very jealous
> Very suspicious
> Very conservative
> Very cruel
> Or we might make an end of the jostling of aspirations
> Disorb inviolate egos (*LLB II* 58)

The strong inviolate ego here seems predicated — and perilously so — upon a defensive recoil, a repudiation of any connection or solidarity with others. If Loy, in her manifesto, appeared to echo Dora Marsden's rejection of female non-identity, her poetic writing did not at all proclaim the strong originary ego of Marsden's gospel. Certainly, no coherent autonomous feminist subject or freewoman emerges in 'Love Songs'. Nor, incidentally, does a strong androgynous ego. It seems that, by this time, Loy's brush with Italian Futurism had made her deeply sceptical of the 'integral ego, sung . . . in its perpetual aggressive evolution'.[64] It should be clear by now that it had made her wary, too, of any easy feminist appropriation of the avant-garde / avant-guerre policy of open fire upon a 'parasitic' femininity.

The fully realised radical new woman proposed in the 'Feminist Manifesto' has, ultimately, to be held in tension with the commitment that emerges in Loy's poetic writing to an exploration of selfhood as constructed — and disrupted — through the artifice and fictitious values of language. There is a sense, in 'Love Songs', in particular, that writing undoes the coherent self. We might say that in the sequence the female self is disaggregated in the direction of what Denise Riley has helpfully termed a 'disintegrative liberty' in which contingency becomes a cause for hope rather than lament.[65] Experimental writing, for Loy, was a reaching beyond inherited conceptual structures: 'Behind God's eyes / There might / Be other lights' (*LLB II* 56). She was committed to avant-gardism for its continual struggle towards a 'new consciousness of things' and foremost amongst such 'things' were words themselves. In 'Love Songs' lyrical self-revelation *becomes* an exploration of the self's relation to and construction through language: words are ready made objects put on to 'express' the self and its desires, but also held aloft, inviting scrutiny and emerging in their full strangeness, their superb pretentiousness. This struggle with language, moreover, is accompanied by the sense of a struggle to imagine new erotic and relational possibilities. Binary sexual difference emerges in the sequence as an 'archetypal pantomime', a matter of incognitos and cryptonyms, masquerade and language, thus making a mockery of the Futurist imperative to unclothe sexuality, to reduce it to a biological moment. 'Love Songs' brings a productive hesitancy to bear upon the categorical imperatives of sexology, reaching out towards something considerably more radical than the manifesto's 'brave new world of heterosexuality'.[66] The perverse excesses of the sequence inscribe a yearning that is at once erotic and linguistic: this defiant yearning, which displaces romantic longing, contains within it an affirmation, one that is bound up with a riotous pleasure in the materiality and instabilities of language.

Notes

[1] Mabel Dodge Luhan, 'Mina Loy', n.d., Mabel Dodge Luhan Papers, Yale Collection of American Literature, Beinecke Rare Book and Manuscript Library, MSS 196. Subsequent references to the Yale Collection of American Literature abbreviated to YCAL.

[2] Mina Loy, Letter to Carl Van Vechten, n.d., Carl Van Vechten Papers, YCAL.

[3] Lucy Bland, *Banishing the Beast: English Feminism and Sexual Morality 1885–1914* (London: Penguin, 1995), 279

[4] Eric Murphy Selinger, 'Love in the Time of Melancholia', in Shreiber and Tuma, eds., 24.

[5] Denise Riley, *'Am I that name?': Feminism and the Category of 'Women' in History* (Basingstoke: Macmillan, 1988).

[6] Emily Apter, 'Reflections on Gynophobia', in Mandy Merck, Naomi Segal and Elizabeth Wright, eds., *Coming Out of Feminism?* (Oxford: Blackwell, 1998), 116.

[7] Ibid., 108, 116.

[8] Otto Weininger, quoted in Chandak Sengoopta, *Otto Weininger: Sex, Science, and Self in Imperial Vienna* (Chicago: University of Chicago Press, 2000), 105.

[9] Quoted by Dora Marsden, 'Sex and Character', *The Freewoman* 2 no. 30 (13 June 1912), 63.

[10] Dora Marsden, 'Bondwomen', *The Freewoman* 1 no. 1 (23 November, 1911), 1.

[11] Dora Marsden, 'Commentary on Bondwomen', *The Freewoman* 1 no. 2 (30 November, 1911), 1.

[12] Ibid., 2, 1.

[13] Otto Weininger, 'Woman and Mankind: Chapter XIV of Weininger's "Sex and Character"' (first extract), *The Freewoman* 1 no. 23 (25 April 1912), 454.

[14] Marsden, 'Sex and Character', 63.

[15] This trajectory is reflected in the name changes undergone by her journal from *The Freewoman* to *The New Freewoman* (in June 1913) to *The Egoist* (in January 1914). See Bruce Clarke, *Dora Marsden and Early Modernism: Gender, Individualism, Science* (Ann Arbor: University of Michigan Press, 1996). It was, however, during Marsden's Weininger phase that her journal made its first titular shift: *The Freewoman: a Feminist Review* became *The Freewoman: a Weekly Humanist Review*.

[16] See *The New Freewoman* 1 no. 1 and no. 2.

[17] Judy Greenway, 'It's What You Do With It That Counts: Interpretations of Otto Weininger', in Lucy Bland and Laura Doan, eds., *Sexology in Culture: Labelling Bodies and Desires* (Chicago: University of Chicago Press, 1998), 40.

[18] Mina Loy, Letter to Mabel Dodge, n.d., in Mabel Dodge Luhan Papers, YCAL MSS 196; Mina Loy, Letter to Carl Van Vechten, n.d., Carl Van Vechten Papers, YCAL.

[19] Umberto Boccioni, Carlo Carrà, Luigi Rossolo, Giacomo Balla, Gino Severini, 'Futurist Painting Technical Manifesto' (1910), in Umbro Apollonio, ed., *Futurist Manifestos* (New York: Viking Press, 1970), 29.

[20] Marjorie Perloff makes this case in *The Futurist Moment: Avant-garde, Avant Guerre and the Language of Rupture* (Chicago: University of Chicago Press, 1986).

[21] F. T. Marinetti, 'The Founding and Manifesto of Futurism', in Apollonio, ed., *Futurist Manifestos*, 22.

[22] Peter Nicholls, *Modernisms: a Literary Guide* (London: Macmillan, 1995), 89.

[23] F.T. Marinetti, 'Let's Murder the Moonshine' (1909), in R.W. Flint, ed., *Let's Murder the Moonshine: Selected Writings* (Los Angeles: Sun and Moon Press, 1991), 54.

[24] Giovanni Papini, 'Il massacro delle donne', *Lacerba* 1 (April 1914), 97–99.

[25] Quoted from *Come si seducono le donne*, by Barbara Spackman in 'The Fascist Rhetoric of Virility', *Stanford Italian Review* 8 no. 1–2 (1990), 90.

[26] F. T. Marinetti, 'Against *Amore* and Parliamentarianism', in *Let's Murder the Moonshine*, 81.

[27] Valentine de Saint-Point, 'Manifesto of Futurist Woman' (1912), in Mary Ann Caws, ed., *Manifesto: a century of isms* (Lincoln and London: University of Nebraska Press, 2001), 214.

[28] See Cinzia Sartini Blum, *The Other Modernism: F.T. Marinetti's Fiction of Power* (Berkeley: University of California Press, 1996), chapter 5.

29 Mina Loy, Letter to Carl Van Vechten, n.d., Carl Van Vechten Papers, YCAL.

30 Mina Loy, 'Brontolivido', Mina Loy Papers, YCAL MSS 6, fol. 2.

31 Mina Loy, 'The Sacred Prostitute', Mina Loy Papers, YCAL MSS 6, fol. 176.

32 F. T Marinetti, 'Destruction of syntax — Imagination Without Strings — Words in Freedom', in Apollonio, ed., *Futurist Manifestos*, 97.

33 F. T. Marinetti, 'Contro il Lusso Femminile' ('Against Feminine Extravagance'), quoted in Blum, 86–7.

34 The manifesto against luxury thus becomes a kind of reply to Baudelaire's decadent hymn to feminine artifice in 'The Painter of Modern Life'. Yet, in its association of women with a repudiated vulgar reality and materiality, or 'Nature', which the aesthete transcends through art, the difference between decadent and Futurist positions seems less substantial.

35 F. T. Marinetti, 'The Founding and Manifesto of Futurism', in Apollonio, ed., *Futurist Manifestos*, 22.

36 Giacomo Balla, 'Futurist Manifesto of Men's Clothing', in Apollonio, ed., *Futurist Manifestos*, 132–4.

37 Volt [Vincenzo Fani], 'Futurist Manifesto of Women's Fashions', in Caws, ed., *Manifesto: a century of isms*, 514–5.

38 Catalogued as 'Brontolivido', but referred to in Loy's correspondence with Carl Van Vechten as 'Possessions', Mina Loy Papers, YCAL MSS 6, fol. 1–6.

39 Ibid., fol. 2.

40 Ibid., fol. 7.

41 Ibid., fol. 2.

42 Ibid., fol. 6, 4.

43 Ibid., fol. 5.

44 Ibid., fol. 5.

45 Ibid., fol. 9.

46 Ibid., fol. 5.

47 Ibid., fol. 9.

48 Ibid., fol. 8.

49 Slavoj Žižek, 'Otto Weininger, Or, "Woman Doesn't Exist" ', *new formations* 23 (Summer 1994), 103.

50 Mina Loy Papers, YCAL MSS 6, fol. 2.

51 Ibid., fol. 5.

52 Ibid., fol. 9.

[53]Loy described her novel in process (to Van Vechten) as 'frank and irresponsible exposition of a very stupid woman's mind', arguing that 'it's quite time we psychologists realised the importance of the merely stupid'. Loy is herself of course, both stupid woman and psychologist, complicating the issue of whether it is Jemima or the narrator who is undermining Bronty. Mina Loy, Letter to Carl Van Vechten, dated Sep 6, Carl Van Vechten Papers, YCAL.

[54] Perhaps the most vivid instance of this superb pretentiousness is her impeccably faked orgasm: 'This urged the purist unabashed by the flesh — this is the reality of pleasure — on the altar of her self-sacrifice to artifice she gasped to his touch — hailing every consummation that eluded Her — with pretty little ripples of delight' (Mina Loy Papers, YCAL, fol., 8). The heroine's feminine performance and the narrator's irony and artifice are thoroughly implicated, at the expense of Futurism's 'healthy' virility.

[55] Denise Riley, *The Words of Selves: Identification, Solidarity, Irony* (Stanford: Stanford University Press, 2000), 172.

[56] Mina Loy, Letter to Carl Van Vechten, n.d., Carl Van Vechten Papers, YCAL.

[57] Mina Loy, Letter to Carl Van Vechten, post marked June 1915, Carl Van Vechten Papers, YCAL.

[58] Mina Loy, Letter to Carl Van Vechten, July 1915, Carl Van Vecthen Papers, YCAL.

[59] Quoted by Roger L. Conover, 'Introduction', in *LLB II*, xv.

[60] Rachel Blau DuPlessis, '"Seismic Orgasm": Sexual Intercourse and Narrative Meaning in Mina Loy', in Shreiber and Tuma, eds., 59.

[61] Jeffrey Twitchell-Waas, '"Little Lusts and Lucidities": Reading Mina Loy's Love Songs', in Shreiber and Tuma, eds., Mina Loy, 120.

[62] Sappho, *Poems and Fragments*, trans. Josephine Balmer (Newcastle upon Tyne: Bloodaxe, 1992), 41, 54, 35, 58.

[63] While it is true that the desire for a child is represented in 'Love Songs' as a sexual desire, a component of the sexuality the poem explores, I do not read the poem as one of mourning for a lost child. The loss the poem negotiates is not at all so specific.

[64] F. T. Marinetti, 'I Poeti Futuristi', cited with translation in Vivian de Sola Pinto and Warren F. Roberts, eds., *The Complete Poems of D. H. Lawrence* (New York: Viking, 1971), 9.

[65] Denise Riley, *The Words of Selves*, 175.

[66] Blau DuPlessis, 53.

Obscene Modernism and The Wondering Jew: Mina Loy's 'Anglo-Mongrels and the Rose'

Rachel Potter

Shedding our petty pruderies
From slit eyes

We sidle up
To Nature
— — — that irate pornographist (*LLB II* 63)

Mina Loy's poems are often read in relation to the 'pruderies' she sheds, the slits she puts into language, the obscenities she explores. Loy came to cultural consciousness in 1915 with the publication of the first four 'Love Songs', which were immediately greeted with excited wails about their indecency. Later, her poems were seized at the American border by customs officials on the grounds that they were obscene.[1] Subsequent discussions of these poems have often discussed the connection between their sexual explicitness, sometimes equated with vulgarity, and their modernity and experimentalism.

The word obscene is from the Latin obscenus meaning ill-omened, but it can also mean off-stage. The reasons for shoving certain areas of representation into the wings are always revealing. It is partly from the desire to test representational limits that obscenity plays such a central role in modernist writing. Modernist writers also often use obscene images to attack a combination of an unhealthily repressed attitude to the body and hypocritical cultural norms. This is a theme in novels from the late nineteenth century on. From Emile Zola's novel, *The Masterpiece* (1886), through to *Ulysses* (1922) and *Lady Chatterley's Lover* (1928) it is the sentimental cant of the moral majority that is labelled as obscene, not the explicit references to naked bodies or sexual interaction. These writers attempt to overturn dominant cultural and legal understandings of obscenity.

It was partly because of the literary inclusion of sexualised flesh in realist novels that prosecutions for obscenity in Britain and America rose exponentially from the 1870s through to the 1933 *Ulysses* trial in America and the *Lady Chatterley's Lover* trial in Britain in 1960. At the same time, this literary drive coincided with a new kind of desire to stamp out sex in literature. What became known as the New Puritanism in America, and 'comstockery' by those on the other side of the argument, was energized by Anthony Comstock who boasted two years before his death in 1915, 'In the forty-one years I have been [in New York] I have convicted persons enough to fill a passenger train of 61 coaches . . . I have destroyed 160 tons of obscene literature.'[2] Much of what he destroyed seems innocuous now: the mere mention of prostitution, for example, was enough to send a book to the pulping machine. The emergence of literary modernism, then, coincided with the rise in legal prosecutions of literary obscenity.

Modernist and avant-garde writing, with its more deliberate flouting of moral conventions and exploration of sex and the language of sex, ratcheted up this confrontational dynamic. The period of modernist writing, then, is framed by an embattled context of legal censorship. Alongside the famous *Ulysses* trials in 1921 and 1933, and the banning of *The Rainbow* in 1915, as well as Lawrence's and Joyce's difficulties getting *Dubliners* (1914) *Women in Love* (1921) and *Lady Chatterley's Lover* (1928) published, there were a whole raft of modernist texts which were censored in this period, such as Ezra Pound being forced to alter poems in *Lustra* in 1915, and the postmaster general stopping the circulation of the *Little Review* because of its inclusion of Wyndham Lewis's short story, 'Cantleman's Spring Mate' in 1917.

Loy's first published poems tend to construct obscene images within a moral framework in a way that is similar to that explored in early modernist texts such as Joyce's *Dubliners*. In 'Parturition' (1914) 'Virgins Plus Curtains Minus Dots' (1915) and 'At the Door of the House' (1917) the obscene female body, in images of the woman in childbirth as a 'crucified wild beast' or female flesh as 'like weeds' which 'sprout in the light', undermines sentimental or religious constructions of femininity.

In 'Love Songs', she takes the exploration of obscenity further, shifting the aesthetic focus from an exploration of sentimentalism or religion to an engagement with the way that obscene-grotesque imagery challenges forms of mimesis and representation. In highly visual images, such as the famous 'rosy snout' of Loy's 'Pig Cupid' or love's 'skin-sack' Loy presents us with the undeniable fleshiness of sexual relations. She combines this dense imagery with an ironic take on the discursive ticks of love: the 'wild oats' of conventional adolescent experience are re-directed, and re-imagined, by being 'sown in mucous membrane'.

The most powerful moments in these poems, however, come when she shifts the focus of what is obscene, or unmentionable, from flesh to mind: it is not the 'trickle of saliva' that remains unspoken, but the 'subliminal flicker' of misunderstood drives. These drives lead the poet to places she does not want, or is not allowed, to go: the poems describe both the 'abominable shadows' of the self (*LLB II* 54) and the fact that she cannot get beyond the 'threshold' of her lover's mind. Her 'Love Songs' pose a series of questions about agency: who has erected this barrier on the mind's threshold? The narrator or her lover? Are these psychological places 'suspect', and thereby forbidden, because social guardians or legislators deem them to be so? Or, are they left unrepresented because language is limited in its ability to represent the most intimate dimensions of the self? Further, would such a journey into the self be, itself, a kind of obscenity?

In *Fantasia of the Unconscious* D. H. Lawrence insisted that there should be limits on the literary journey into the self: 'What was there in the cave: Alas that we ever looked! Nothing but a huge slimy serpent of sex, and heaps of excrement, and a myriad repulsive little horrors spawned between sex and excrement.'[3] Lawrence vigorously asserts a barrier to representation, insisting that the obscene interior is that which cannot, and should not, be put into language. In doing so he sets his work in opposition to a Joycean modernism of psychological scrutiny.

Loy's focus on the barriers between self and other in 'Love Songs' is fuelled less by a Lawrentian condemnation of the aesthetic exploration of psychology and more by an interest in the distortions of selfhood produced through a desire which is figured as obscene or unspeakable. Let's take the powerful lines of 'Love Song xxix', for instance:

Let them clash together
From their incognitos
In seismic orgasm

For far further
Differentiation
Rather than watch
Own-self distortion
Wince in the alien ego (*LLB II* 66)

While Loy is happy to put the impersonal physical orgasm into words, the self which is recognised through the wince of the other is disfigured. Desire, by making the poet psychologically reliant on the other, produces a self-undermining and distorted image of the self. The unspeakable effects of her relationship with the addressed man, which Loy calls the 'bird-like abortions' of love, produce the disarranged selves of these poems.

In a number of poems of the early 1920s, Loy shifts her focus, from this interest in the disturbing distortions of interpersonal misrecognitions, to a more politicised understanding of obscenity and censorship. She had formed part of the group cheering in support of the *Little Review* outside the Jefferson Market police court when the journal was prosecuted for publishing *Ulysses* in 1921 (*BM* 288). In her poem of the same year, 'Apology of Genius', she produces a subtle meditation on the relationship between avant-garde expression and authority. She begins by connecting the ostracised artistic 'us' of the poem with disease:

Lepers of the moon
all magically diseased
we come among you
innocent
of our luminous sores (*LLB II* 77)

The disease in these lines is not so much an affliction which is internal to the body as something which others see. These diseased artists are greeted by the 'smooth fools' faces' of the authorities, faces as unblemished as 'buttocks bared in aboriginal mockeries'. The magic obscenities of the avant-garde compete here with the uncomprehending, blank obscenities of the censors. Both use their arses to make a point, but it is the 'censor's scythe' as she calls it at the end of this poem, which seems to have the final word. This poem represents the attempt to police the aesthetic obscenities Loy and other writers and artists had explored in the 1900s and 1910s. If the artists are 'innocent' of how they appear mutilated or diseased, a more official and legal language sees them, and positions them, as 'criminal'. Loy stages a battle over words, and the ownership of words: the artists' claim to innocence competes with the litigious authority of the censor to decide the meaning of innocence.

In the rest of this essay, I will turn to a discussion of Loy's long poem, 'Anglo-Mongrels and the Rose' (1923–25), as it is here that Loy produces her most sustained attempt to bring together the psychological obscenities examined in 'Love Songs' with the exploration of the ideological power which attaches to particular kinds of languages in early 1920s poems such as 'Apology of Genius', 'O Hell', and 'The Dead'. Despite the construction of the censor's scythe as an externalised entity in 'Apology of Genius', Loy's work is often at its most powerful when it reveals the self-enforced barriers, or internalised limits, that control artistic expression. The 'pruderies' she mentions in 'Love Songs' and quoted at the beginning of this essay, for instance, are constraints in both a legal and psychological sense. Above all, I will argue that this poem is acutely sensitive to the question of how the self is formed through a complex identification with and dissociation from existing discursive structures and limits. This is a poem which produces a subtle meditation on the nature of limits; bodily, discursive, psychological, legalistic and aesthetic.

1. A mongrel text: 'Anglo-Mongrels and the Rose'

Loy's poem, 'Anglo-Mongrels and the Rose' is one of the most remarkable descriptions of the evolution of selfhood in modernist writing. Deliberately mixing sordid biological imagery with spiritual registers, religious cant with commodity fetishism, civic discourses with racial language, Loy traces a child's development from a grotesque birth to a young adulthood in which she is imprisoned by 'every discomfort / that proceedeth out of / legislation' (*LLB I* 130, 172). At each stage of this development, Loy brutally violates the discursive conventions attached to ideas of familial, religious or civic life.

Loy wrote a number of unpublished prose pieces, including 'The Islands in the Air' and 'The Child and the Parent', in which she uses some of the images and lines central to 'Anglo-Mongrels and the

Rose', so that it is clear that she worked over this material throughout her life.

The poem has a complicated and interesting publishing history, as it came out in sections in separate journals and books in different geographical locations during 1923–1925. Initially under the title 'Anglo-Mongrels and the Rose', Loy published the first section 'Exodus', in the Spring, 1923 'Exiles' edition of the New York magazine the *Little Review*.[4] She went on to publish a separate poem called 'English Rose', which consists of the first three stanzas of section two of the final poem, in her first collection of poems, called *Lunar Baedecker* [sic], published in Dijon in 1923. Then, under the title 'Anglo-Mongrels and the Rose', she again published 'English Rose', but this time in New York in the Autumn – Winter (1923–1924) edition of the *Little Review*.[5] The final sections of the poem, 'Enter Esau Penfold', 'Ova Begins to Take Notice', 'Opposed Aesthetics', 'Marriage Boxes', 'Psychic Larva', 'Christ's Regrettable Reticence', 'Enter Colossus', 'Ova. Among. The. Neighbours.', 'Ova Has Governesses', 'Jews and Ragamuffins of Kilburn', 'The Surprise', 'Illumination', 'Contraction', 'The Gift', 'Ova Accepts the Popular Estimate of Humanity', 'Religious Instruction' and 'The Social Status of Exodus', came out in Robert McAlmon's Paris based, *Contact Collection of Contemporary Writers* in 1925 under the title 'The Anglo-Mongrels and the Rose'.[6]

In the 1958 edition of Loy's selected poems, *Lunar Baedeker and Timetables*, edited by Jonathan Williams, a shortened version of the poem appears under the title 'Anglo-Mystics of the Rose'.[7] This includes the following sections: 'Enter Esau', 'Ova begins to take notice', 'Ova has governesses', 'Christ's regrettable reticence' and 'Religious instruction'. The poem was only published as complete under the title 'Anglo-Mongrels and the Rose: 1923–1925', in Loy's collected poems *The Last Lunar Baedeker* edited by Roger Conover in 1982 (*LLB I* 109–75).

The slippage between Anglo-Mystics and Anglo-Mongrels is highly suggestive, as the former poem edited by Williams focuses far less on the issue of Jewish paternity. We do not know why Williams wanted to change 'mongrel' to 'mystic'.[8] It is possible that he wanted to underplay the eugenicist, and racial undertones of the word mongrel. In this he would not have been alone, as the racial register of this word has troubled readers ever since.

There has been disagreement about the nature of Mina Loy's engagement with the idea of Jewish paternity as it gets played out in 'Anglo-Mongrels and the Rose'. Marjorie Perloff argues that 'in her portrait of her father Sigmund Löwy Loy seems to accept all the anti-Semitic stereotypes of her time and place.'⁹ Elizabeth Frost, in contrast, sees 'Anglo-Mongrels and the Rose' as attacking racial and gender 'typing'. In particular, she argues that despite seeming to employ a eugenicist language of racial superiority, a key part of the 'anti-Semitic stereotypes of her time and place', Loy actually rejects the 'eugenicists' emphasis on racial difference and focuses on the potentially determining power of culture'.¹⁰ We know that Loy had been interested in eugenicist arguments, such as those put forward by Francis Galton from early in her career. Frost persuasively argues, however, that Loy ironizes, rather than endorses this eugenicist language of racial difference, putting the word mongrel in quotation marks: 'The title links the eugenical notion of "mongrelization" — a 'term used for miscegenation — to national symbolism and literary tradition (the "rose" of England, and of courtly love).'¹¹

Despite disagreeing with Frost about whether Loy ironizes or reproduces the 'anti-semitic prejudices of her time', Perloff also insists that Loy's mixture of different registers and discourses disrupts any straightforward representation of identity. Perloff claims that it is language itself which is 'mongrelized' in Loy's poem: 'what is entirely Loy's own poetic signature is that her rose images, far from producing an imagist or symbolist landscape, jostle with conceptual nouns, puns, and aggressive rhymes, in a 'curious "mongrelization" of linguistic registers.' Perloff helpfully suggests that in response to her Jewish and Christian parentage, Loy invents an 'intricately polyglot language — a language that challenges the more conventional national idiom of her . . . contemporaries'.¹²

Keith Tuma, in a different reading of the poem, argues that it describes religious, rather than racial, forms of difference. He insists that it should be 'read as a "religious" poem', but that 'nearly all forms of "orthodox" religious doctrine — Jewish and Christian — are renounced by Loy on behalf of an experience beyond intellect which she believed to be a direct sensual and intuitive apprehension of divinity.'¹³ Tuma's interpretation would support Williams's change of 'Mongrel' to 'Mystic', although interestingly Williams cuts out the section 'Illumination' which Tuma reads as central to the poem.

Frost's account helpfully situates Loy's poem in relation to a wider discourse on eugenics, and I do not want to repeat her argument here. Instead, I want to pick up on Perloff's claim about Loy's creation of a mongrelized language in 'Anglo-Mongrels and the

Rose', and consider it further. The word mongrel had become central to certain debates in 1923 around censorship and freedom of speech. The ongoing battle between the censor and avant-garde literature in the US had become particularly fierce by 1923. John Sumner, the head of the New York Society for the Suppression of Vice, had lost a number of high profile obscenity cases in the courts during 1918–1922, although one of his few successes was the prosecution of Margaret Anderson and Jane Heap in 1921 for publishing sections of *Ulysses* in the *Little Review*. In response, conservatives and Vice Crusaders had mobilised and spearheaded a 'Clean Books' bill which aimed to tighten up censorship legislation in New York. It was in this atmosphere that Henry Walcott Boynton, a well-known editor and anthologist of the standard English classics, declared in March 1923 that most of the 'offensive', by which he meant obscene, recent American and British novels were 'mongrels' written either by 'persons with alien names and frankly alien standards' or by their native-born emulators.[14] Three months later, the novelist Mary Austin, in an article discussing 'Sex in American Literature' warned against literary expressions of the Anglo-American love tradition being 'asphyxiated in the fumes of half-assimilated and fermenting racial contributions.' She was particularly worried about the unhealthy eroticism characteristic of 'Semitic' authors.[15]

This anti-Semitism was energized by the fact that a number of the new and important publishers of obscene texts in the 1920s were Jewish immigrants, or of recent immigrant background, such as Horace Liveright, Thomas Seltzer, Bennett Cerf and Donald Klopfer. Not only were these publishers the products of a process of emigration which was seen to be somehow corrupting US publishing, they were also disseminating mongrel texts which threatened the purity of a tradition of American literature.

Frost is right, then, to see Loy's use of the word mongrel as tapping into eugenicist arguments about racial purity. With this publishing context in mind, however, it is also possible to read the poem itself, as well as the character Ova, as a mongrel. Perloff's observations about the internationalism of Loy's mongrelized writing style take on a different meaning in the light of this historical context. Loy's polyglot style is perhaps more oppositional than it at first appears, as her very use of language, even her use of the word mongrel, can be seen to disarrange racist attempts to produce and protect a pure and asexual American literary language.

The poem, in its original scattered form, and with its combination of sexual, scientific, religious and spiritual languages can be read as a kind of homeless, wandering mongrel, popping up in different formats from New York to Paris to Dijon. The poem is not only about racism; its very formal properties are concerned with a political context of linguistic nationalism, and its disruptive opposite.

2. The wondering Jew

The dumb philosophies
of the wondering Jew
fall into rhythm   (*LLB I* 117)

'Anglo-Mongrels and the Rose' collects together a number of different images of Jews: a Hungarian Jewish patriarch; the Jewish father, misunderstood by his racist English wife; the poor Jews of Kilburn, spurned by Ova's nurses; the mongrel child, Ova, caught between two faiths and cultures; and the Jewish tailor, who is figured as a weird kind of modern deity at the end of the poem.

The key motif of the poem, however, is its depiction of Jewish wondering, in particular its reinterpretation of the infamous legend of the Wandering Jew, the punished figure doomed to wander in the wilderness forever for his crimes against Christ. The Wandering Jew is the tale of a 'man in Jerusalem who, when Christ was carrying his Cross to Calvary and paused to rest for a moment on this man's doorstep, drove the Saviour away, crying aloud, "Walk faster!" And Christ replied, "I go, but you will walk until I come again!"'[16] The legend had undergone many interpretations, some anti-Semitic, seeing the Jew as antichrist and the diaspora as the punishment of the Jews for their refusal to recognise the divinity of Christ. Other readings produced a more positive evaluation of the Jew as outcast. This latter version had gained a certain currency in the mid-nineteenth century. Most famously, Eugene Sue's serialized novel, *Le Juif Errant* (1844–5), saw the Jew as a reflection of his Fourierist and Saint-Simonian socialist beliefs, a champion of the working man able to articulate the protest of all labourers against their oppressors. Courbet's painting *The Meeting* (1854), in turn, represents a portrait of the artist-as-Jew, whose social homelessness reflects that of working men in general. As George Anderson documents, by the end of the nineteenth century the Wandering Jew became a 'symbol of the

Jewish people'. He summarises the situation: 'Along with the rise of Zionism, near the close of the nineteenth century, one finds Ahesuerus [the Wandering Jew] identified with all Jews deprived of their homeland; on the reverse side of the coin, because of this identification, he becomes a target at which the anti-Semitic element of the world's Gentile population can aim its missiles.'[17]

The fate of the figure of the Wandering Jew mirrors wider historical shifts in constructions of the Jewish people. By the end of the century, for instance, the image of the Wandering Jew had recovered a more literal significance because of the striking phenomenon of large numbers of Jews wandering across Europe. The Russian pogroms of 1881 had produced a swathe of East European Jewish emigrants who travelled to Paris and London for refuge and economic prosperity. A benevolent nineteenth century liberalism, which culminated in the right to sit in Parliament in 1858, had produced a period of security and prosperity for British Jews. With the influx of emigrant Jews in the 1880s and 1890s, however, a new tide of anti-Semitic propaganda emerged, alongside a feeling of hostility amongst British Jews themselves.

The spectacle of wandering Jews fed into the cultural imagination in significant ways. Jan Goldstein has documented how the images of wandering Jews connected to the emerging discourses of psychiatry and psychopathology at the end of the century to produce an entirely new discursive subject: the psychopathological Wandering Jew. This figure rested on the claim by psychiatrists such as Jean-Baptiste Charcot and Henry Meige that Jews had a propensity for neurosis, and in particular travelling neurosis, or what was called 'travelling insanity'.[18] These connections originated in claims about the pathological nature of vagabondage, but were quickly extended to provide an explanatory model for the behaviour of migratory Jews after the Russian pogroms. Henry Meige, in a pseudo-medical thesis of 1893, argued that it was in the character of the race that the Jews were 'at home nowhere and everywhere', and were able to change 'their location with extreme ease'. He went on to make extreme claims connecting Jewish identity and a pathological urge to travel: 'Jews were especially vulnerable to all manifestations of nervous illness' and were therefore 'apt to take the intrinsically rational, goal-directed idea of travel to irrational, absurd or pathological lengths, feeling compelled at the end of one voyage to start another.'[19]

Loy's family history shares features with that of mid-to-late nine-teenth-century Jewish emigrations. Loy's father, Sigmund Löwy, had been born in 1848 into a once wealthy but declining Budapest Jewish family. When Sigmund's father died his mother married a working-class man who forced Sigmund to learn the tailoring trade. Despite the fact that Jews were granted political rights in Hungary in 1867, they were still denied religious equality. Many emigrated, including Sigmund, who, once he had attained his apprenticeship, decided to travel to liberal England to make his fortune (*BM* 17).

Like the pseudo-medical discourses of late nineteenth-century psychiatrists Loy has a propensity to construct Jewish wandering as both an enforced and a pathological condition. In connecting wander-ing to wondering she also emphasises the psychological causes and dimensions of homelessness. She extends this dual register into her depictions of Ova's inherited urge to travel and the structure of the poem. Not only are the key characters in 'Anglo-Mongrels and the Rose' inclined to movement, the poem itself is profoundly restless:

> An insect   from an herb
> errs on the   man-mountain
> imparts   its infinitesimal tactile stimulus
> to the epiderm   to the spirit
> of Exodus
> stirring   the anaesthetized load
> of racial instinct frustrated
> impulse   infantile impacts with unreason
>   on his unconscious (*LLB I* 113)

I have quoted at length here to reveal the effects of Loy's precarious balancing act between racial and psychological vocabulary. We here have displayed Loy's typically insistent alliterative and assonantal style. This highly formalistic surface foregrounds the very physical-ity of words, seemingly prioritizing 'physic' over spirit in a way which is mirrored in the content of these lines: 'tactile stimulus' energizes Exodus's 'racial instinct' to wander. The word 'impacts' echoes into the 'pack' which he shoulders a few stanzas later.

Yet, Loy's style allows her to keep the lines ambiguous, so that she does not simply refer to skin rather than spirit, the body rather than the mind. The line 'to the epiderm to the spirit' sits in the middle of these images, insisting that the 'stimulus' that stirs Exodus to movement is both tactile and psychological. Similarly, the 'racial instinct' that is referred to here, is presented as a 'load' with both sensory and psychic content: it is both 'anaesthetized' and 'unconscious'.

Loy is careful to maintain this dual focus throughout the poem. Later in the poem the new-born Ova is described as a 'mysterochemico Nemesis'. Fleshy or chemical registers, the inimitable 'clotty bulk of bifurcate fat', are juxtaposed with psychological and/or religious vocabularies throughout (*LLB I* 131, 130). The extreme discordance of these juxtapositions distances the text from any one overriding discourse. It is as though all the words in this poem are ever so slightly in quotation marks. If Loy is keen to sever words from the power of the authorities, she also wants to dislocate them from their conventional meanings, what she describes in an article on Gertrude Stein as freeing words from the canonical 'frame or glass case or tradition' (*LLB I* 298).

This produces a kind of restless linguistic wandering. Take the word 'insect' in the quotation above. It seems to buzz around the page, touching other alliteratively connected words: 'imparts', 'infinitesimal', 'instinct', 'infantile', 'impacts'. The word flies away from the line 'An insect from an herb', and locates itself elsewhere. The alliteration is also so insistent that Loy does not allow the word to settle into any one specific new connection. Insect is in all of these related words; and in none of them in particular. Like the restless Jew, Loy's words often land in one new place, only to move instantly on to the next. The result of this, however, is to refuse any new conceptual synthesis in which insect would somehow inform and be informed by an idea of imparting something. The effect is both to isolate words from their original poetic context (insect ceases to be connected to 'from an herb') and create language which is restlessly elusive in form and meaning.

Just as Loy lifts words out of their conventional contexts, so Ova's journey from pre-birth to adulthood involves a dislocation from established discourses of the self, here the 'destinies' of 'traditional / Israel and Albion'. Human displacement involves an inevitable alienation. Exodus experiences this in the foreign streets of London, lifting 'his head / over the alien crowds / under the alien clouds'. Ova is inherently (both racially and spiritually) homeless: she is 'the mongrel-girl / of Noman's land'. Always in motion, 'this child of Exodus / with her heritage of emigration / often / "sets out to seek her fortune"' (*LLB I* 131, 117, 143, 170–1). The 'often' is signifi-

cant. If she must repeatedly set out, these intermittent starts never
seem to find an end. These fragmented images of Ova are helpful in
considering the structure of the poem as a whole, which consists of
a number of starts, Exodus's, Ova's, Esau's, Colossus's, which do
not conclude. The geographical homelessness that Loy captures in
her depictions of Exodus transmutes into a more general picture of
a series of fragmented and inconclusive modern lives.

Wandering, displacement, alienation, wondering: of words,
humans, and books. By prioritizing wondering/wandering Loy
emphasises the importance of psychological as well as physical kinds
of dislocation, something which she attempts to capture in her focus
on rhythm:

> The dumb philosophies
> of the wondering Jew
> fall into rhythm   with
> long unlistened to   Hebrew chants (*LLB I* 117)

Exodus's philosophies are mute both to others and to himself, so that
the knowledge he possesses, and passes on to his daughter, is
contained in an idea of rhythm. Loy's poem might be said to 'fall into
rhythm', less in terms of chanting ('Anglo-Mongrels and the Rose' is
not a particularly musical poem), and more in the sense of the
rhythms of the body or the alliterative connections between words.
The product of Ova's physical and philosophical inheritance is not a
specific body of textual knowledge. Instead, it is an unconscious state
of mind, or a condition of the body; it is in the gait of the wanderer,
the contours of the mind's rhythm. Here an idea of Jewish or female
restlessness, a restlessness that I think Loy wants to extend to all of
the alienated subjects of modernity, is figured as a physical, mental
and literary quality.

3. The politics of 'Anglo-Mongrels and the Rose'

Loy's images of containment and escape, and the particular focus on
wandering and wondering Jews and women as figures of modernity,
feed into an important strand of modernist thought and culture; the
importance of global mobility to the writing of the early 1920s. As
Michael North has documented in his book *Reading 1922*, D. H.
Lawrence, Claude McKay and Charlie Chaplin, to take three exam-

ples, have in common 'a shared experience of restless travel so relentless that citizenship ceases to have any meaning, as does the difference between home and abroad.' For North, this mobility, which he
sees as central to the cultural formation of modernism in the 1920s,
produces the 'polyglot' language Perloff discusses in relation to Loy.
As he puts it: 'formalist experimentation becomes its own international language and the medium, of paint and letters, an alternate
homeland quite separate from any real country or community.'[20]

North's reading of 1922, and his questioning of the meaning of citizenship and internationalism in the language of modernism is
extremely helpful for understanding Loy's poem. If she sets the scene
of the beginning parts of her poem in the late nineteenth century, its
publication in 1923–25 locates it firmly in this post-war period; and its
images of wandering connect at least four constituencies of homeless
individuals: the emigrating Jews of the late nineteenth century, the
Jewish immigrants of the 1920s, the modern woman and modernist
artists.

The idea that homelessness leads to the production of a new kind
of linguistic home in the international language of modernism is also
of interest when considering Loy's poem. Loy's 'polyglot' poetry
conforms to this model, but there is also a struggle in her writing to
provide a more politicised account of the difficulties of homelessness,
particularly in light of her understanding of a Jewish history of
enforced migrations and racist exclusion. Is discarding the bonds of
citizenship more or less difficult for somebody who has never been
made to feel comfortable with claiming this label in the first place?
Is embracing homelessness more or less complicated for somebody
whose home was never very homely?

The politics of 'Anglo-Mongrels and the Rose' come into focus when
Loy puts pressure on the power structures which underlie particular
words or ideas. I want to suggest that not all the words in Loy's lexicon are allowed to be equally promiscuous or restless. She seems, in
other words, quite keen to pin some of them down. Her writing
becomes particularly vicious and cutting, for example, when she
applies what Djuna Barnes described as Loy's 'scalpel' to an oddly alienated English home.

Throughout her life, Loy was interested in the conflicts of
Jewishness and Englishness, and the wider politics of this, as they had
played themselves out in her parents' marriage. In her writing, she
charted the collision between a father's fantasies of cultural inclu-

sion, and a mother's brittle resistance to such fantasies. Often a child is caught between these opposed fantasies of racial and religious identity. Variously named Ova, Mina or Goy, the child is presented as both alienated from the securely Jewish girls of her Hampstead School and from the stern and hypocritical Christianity of her mother.

Loy does, however, tend to see the Jewish father as a source of intellectual ambition, and the Christian mother as the mouth-piece for moral hypocrisy. In a series of unpublished notes, Loy captures the child's peculiar role of family mediator:

> For while she climbs down from her-self to placate the
> matriarch, her father is imposing the pinnacles of ambition . . .
> "BE ashamed" says the Christian
> "Think," says the Jew
> "Before or after" queries the confused brain anyhow it is
> impossible for this cloven ego to concentrate[21]

Here, the public conflicts of British Imperialism and the colonised are mapped onto the private relationships of a family: more generally the mother often becomes 'The Christian', the father 'the Jew' and the parents 'Mr and Mrs Israels', in her writing. The product of these conflicting religious and ideological messages is the confused child, caught between the injunctions of intellect and shame. In this description, we can already see where Loy places the child and where she will end up: she has to 'climb down from her-self' in order to placate her mother and conform to the edifice of Christian morality. Selfhood is already directed towards the more lofty fatherly intellect.

The mother's emphasis on being ashamed captures a central conflict in women's position at the end of the nineteenth and beginning of the twentieth centuries. Women attempting to assert their freedoms found themselves held by the idea that intellectual endeavour was shameful.

Loy does not simply connect the Jewish father with intellectual freedom, however. In some other unpublished notes, she tries to unpack the contradictions in a father's secular Judaism: 'Having relinquished judaism, this father could give his girls the freedom of the intellect historically witholden from the jewish woman. "Advanced" of him at this period in a class where women who "did anything" were still unwomanly.'[22] Despite the father insisting that his daughters be allowed to develop themselves intellectually, however, he stops short of assigning them the sexual freedoms enjoyed by men:

On the other hand, to this jew, woman is somewhat of the nature of impurity — something that must not be let out of sight lest it confirm itself. / The Christian era is the Woman's period. Nature may continue to impose upon her; but there its no doubt about it the Christians have cleaned her up.[23]

Here, the woman cannot be let out of sight in case she reveals herself. Despite the fact that the father is an enlightened and secular Jew he has a residual belief in women's impurity and places an extremely high value on female virginity. A belief in women's shame, it seems, extends across the Judeo-Christian traditions.

Like Nietzsche, Loy was interested in those beliefs that have their origins in religious traditions, and re-emerge in a secular context in a different guise. Throughout her life, she was focused on how female purity, and the shame that was seen to accompany its violation, had outlasted its Christian origins. Here she discusses how both the Judaic and Christian traditions attempt to police a female body they position as obscene.

Loy suggests that despite the ideological battles and cultural differences between her mother and father, they concur in their belief that women are somehow impure. This parental insistence on the significance of women's impurity became a central plank in Loy's resistance to the tyranny of the past. It also focused her belligerent attempts to put the obscene biological body into poetic language.

Loy also ties this sense of the obscene body to a consideration of another kind of obscenity: that of the shamefulness of English racism. In some unpublished notes, Loy extends her attack on a mother's sense of obscenity to a description of her domestic Imperialism:

The point of view of Mrs Israels is that of the British colonist often sadistic always disdainful; This mother is a Briton colonising the alien attributes of her marriage; her marriage the appropriation of an alien property. / . . . Is this an unhappy home? Is it neglected — an ugly home? It is Mrs Israel's Empire; all the world she knows, and it must be administered — charitably — . . . To the protestant Morality is always an assault upon something.[24]

There is something painful in Loy's depiction of the sadistic nature of domestic forms of Imperialism and her attempt to put into language the combination of racism and financial speculation (alien property) which comprises this ugly home. We here have a different instance of Loy's engagement with the obscene. There is a linguistic masking at the heart of Loy's descriptions of 'Mrs Israels', or 'The Christian', rather than 'my mother', and 'The Jew', rather than 'my father'. This obfuscation seems to suggest something about Loy's difficulties with autobiographical descriptions of her home as unhappy or in acknowledging that she has been positioned as ugly, shameful and obscene by her parents. But we also have a desire here and in 'Anglo-Mongrels and the Rose' to explore what can and cannot be said about family life. This is an instance in which Loy grapples with the obscene in a different way: not the 'suspect places' of one's lover's mind, as in 'Love Songs', nor the artistic representation of the sexualised body; but the sadistic elements of an English home.

4. The obscene 'Paradox-Imperial'

Home and homelessness, Englishness and Jewishness, colonialism and alienation, shame and intellect, the language of the spirit and the obscene body; these are some of the focal points around which Loy structures her meditation on the nature of modern selfhood in 'Anglo-Mongrels and the Rose'.

Ova, a word which obviously insists on the biological core of identity, becomes a person through her resistance to a number of discursive structures. Above all, Loy is interested in the ideological construct of what she calls the 'paradox Imperial'. Our initial view of this powerful paradox comes through Exodus's foreign eyes. Having nothing else to believe in, he finds himself trying to understand the mystery of Englishness. He pursues this ideal by chasing after an English 'Rose'. Ada is attractive because she is adorned with a whole array of ideological constructs. In its decorative form, for example, the English Rose adorns the ceilings of houses:

> herd-housing
> petalling
> the prim gilt
> penetralia
> of a luster-scioned
> core-crown (*LLB I* 121)

The heart of the English home is likened to the penetralia, the most holy place of a temple. By extension, Loy locates the innermost mysteries of Englishness in the decorative roses of Victorian ceilings.

In these houses, however, individuals gaze upwards at their mass-produced ceilings, rather than at God. This is a curtailed form of wonder, then, a prim and proper spiritualism which stops short at the domestic frontier and does not ascend to the skies. Even the monarchism, the 'core-crown' of the rose, is a limp one.

The combination of qualities symbolized by the rose offers a telling insight into Ada's beliefs. She is also a rose with 'arrested impulses'; her heart is a 'tepid' one. She cannot see beyond the frontier of the home. Nevertheless, she believes in 'the divine right of self-assertion' which will not only determine her marriage to Exodus, but which wipes its 'pink paralysis / across the dawn of reason'. Ada's repressed understanding of the self, then, has disastrous wider effects, both on enlightenment ideals and world politics: her blushes form part of a 'World-Blush / glowing from / a never-setting-sun'. The Imperial stance, the 'Conservative Rose', is composed of the beliefs of the 'dry dead men' of tradition, a 'shrivelled collectivity'. This ideology relies on the 'puff of press alarum', and in particular on 'whirling itself deliriously around' a puffed-up enemy, 'the unseen / Bolshevik' (*LLB I* 122).

Loy's damning images of English conservatism determine her description of Exodus's floundering attempts to penetrate the mystery of England. It is significant that, in his own way, he is as spiritually bereft as Ada, finding in 'the Anglo-Saxon phenomenon / of virginity' a kind of mystery he can believe in. When he encounters, then, the repressed Ada in the English hedgerows, a village maid in a sunbonnet 'simpering in her / ideological pink', he is seduced by his own fantasies of her sexualised mystery despite the fact that she 'scowls at the heathen' (*LLB I* 124, 123). Her barricaded virginity becomes the focal point of his fantasy.

The fantasies, ideological contradictions and misunderstandings which produce the stultifying box of Ada's and Exodus's marriage, are torn apart by the poem. Exodus does give Ova something vital, however; the Jewish brain. This intellectual gift must battle with the anti-Semitic prejudices of her mother, and various nurses. In the section of the poem called 'Jews and Ragamuffins of Kilburn', Loy depicts her nurse gingerly lifting her nose 'because / in Kilburn there are so many Jews // She fears to find them crawling up her socks' (*LLB I* 158). Ova ends up passionately at odds with these hypocritical prejudices and her mother's brand of Christianity. Instead, she embraces the figure of Christ as an outcast and finds herself in empathy with the alienated of society.

Ova's isolated upbringing is contrasted with that of her contemporaries, who seem to have an uncomplicated connection to the 'navel-cord of the motherland' (*LLB I* 154). At other moments in the poem, particularly when describing Ada's nationalism, Loy suggests more complex identifications. Ova's mother is also alienated, but this estrangement is a product of a mis-match between an ideological construct, the 'Rose' and the self: 'an impenetrable pink curtain / hangs between it (the Rose) and itself' (*LLB I* 128). Ada is unable to read or penetrate, as Loy puts it, this pink curtain, which perhaps signifies femininity, or a more bloody, obscene physicality. The body, in it sexual or procreative functions, is both a shameful thing that needs to be administered, and the thing, like the 'unseen Bolshevik', around which Ada's fears can circulate.

The paradox-Imperial rests on an idea of shame which fears and polices the disruptive energies of Bolshevism and modern forms of subjectivity. It also, by implication, relies on particular kinds of language: official, legal and familial. As in the racist attempts to pin down a pure American literary tradition in the early 1920s, Loy's poem disrupts the ideological nationalism of the paradox-Imperialism, both thematically and stylistically.

Ova, as the site of a modern form of female subjectivity also produces a new kind of language. Facetiously, Loy creates this new language out of obscene excrement: 'in her ear / a half audible an / iridescent hush / forms "iarrhea"'. Not only does the physical consistency of diarrhea allow us to visualise baby Ova's corresponding 'cerebral / mush', but the syllables of 'Iarrhea' suddenly reveal something central about the nature of language: the 'fragmentary / simultaneity / of ideas' which embody 'the word'. Further, the very vocables of 'iarrhea' are transposed into to the child's visionary new experience of language: 'A / lucent / iris / shifts / its / irradiate / interstice' (*LLB I* 140, 141).

This principle of language acquisition becomes a basis for aesthetics: 'moon-flowers' are made 'out of muck' and Ova begins to 'coerce the shy / Spirit of Beauty / from excrements and physic' (*LLB I* 142, 143). This shy modernist beauty, however, is distinct from Futurist attempts to incorporate waste by gulping down the 'nourishing sludge' of factory waste or the dadaist embrace of a 'huge mouth filled with honey and excrement.'[25] While Marinetti, Tzara and Eliot create an avant-garde or modernist aesthetic by incorporating or embracing the fragmented waste products of modernity, Loy's interest in excrement is connected also to a meditation on the physical nature of modern selfhood. Excrement is significant because it disturbs our sense of boundaries, not simply because it is aesthetically shocking to gulp or immerse oneself in shit, but because as an entity it is not entirely free of the body which produced it. Loy seems interested in this, its position on the margins of the human. As a substance and a word, it does not belong.

Lawrence is concerned in *Fantasia of the Unconscious* that the modern literary turn inwards had produced a grotesque aesthetic encounter with the physical realities of sex and excrement. Loy, in contrast, uses excrement as a key metaphor for the relationship between past and present. Ova is a product both of her 'forebear's excrements' as Loy puts it in 'O Hell', and of her break away from that past. In 'Anglo-Mongrels and the Rose' Ava constructs her child as a 'vile origin', and manages to 'erode' Ova's sense of self through 'psychic-larva', a phrase which synthesizes images of psychic violence and flow (*LLB I* 147). The obscene, that which by definition cannot or should not be put into language, is located in this toxic relationship between two things: the 'larva', in other words, that flows from one generation to the next.

Loy's poem attempts to bring into being this poisonous relationship between conflicting ideologies and generations. Ada's Christian beliefs construct the origins of life as vile and obscene and modernist subjects break from this ideology through the embrace of sexuality. Loy's poetry, by encompassing both of these moments, has become something very different to Ova's imagined poetry of 'moon-flowers'. Instead, it is a language which is able to accommodate both excrement and illumination, family violence (psychic larva) and speculative wonder. Modernity, which by definition is concerned with what it means to break from the past, is found here, in an obscene relationship between past and present.

The poem maintains this focus on obscene conflict throughout. For all Ova's attempts to escape her family it is significant that 'Anglo-Mongrels and the Rose' radically fails to produce a positivistic description of modern female autonomy. Instead it concludes by sceptically ironizing any such straightforward image of individual freedom. The final section focuses on a new kind of modern god: the Jewish tailor: 'And there arose another / greater than Jehovah / The Tailor' (*LLB I* 173–4). A number of new gods were proclaimed in the immediate post-war period: D. H. Lawrence offered up the spectacle of a mannequin in an Oxford Street shop-window, seeing this as the new deity towards which the masses abase themselves.[26] Like Lawrence, Loy, in her image of the Jewish tailor god, suggests that in his ability to dress and remake us, he is the appropriate deity for an age of radical self-fashioning: 'And man / at last assumes his self-respect' (*LLB I* 175).

If collective ideals of British Imperialism, religious doctrine and moral law are attacked in the poem it is also critical of the commodified individualism that underlies this collective worship of self-fashioning.

Loy's writing is powerful because she is always alert to the dialectical pressures of liberation or alienation. The idea of modern freedom is always seen from at least two angles so that impulses of empathy and critique jostle with each other. In her 'Feminist Manifesto' (1914), for example, she describes both the political factors which curtail women's freedoms and women's self-imposed prisons of fantasy and desire. She insists that if women want to liberate themselves from the 'entrails' of the past they must destroy their own desires to be loved. Our desires, represented as obscene in 'Love Songs', are capable of imprisoning us just as securely as traditional patriarchal structures. In 'Anglo-Mongrels and the Rose' Loy meditates on the troubling nature of biology, both as an undeniable aspect of the physical and sexual self, and as the inescapable fact of one's relationship to the past. In terms of this poem, Ova's wanderings, as well as Loy's lead back to the home, even though the home has been transformed into something different in the process.

5. Writing the past: modernism and memory.

On an unpublished strip of paper, written in the 1920s, Loy produced an arresting image of the nature of memory: 'our personality or destiny / is like a roll of negative film — already printed But unrevealable [sic] / until it has formed a camera / to project it — and a surface to throw it upon.'[27] A half-revealed roll of negative film: this seems like quite a good description of 'Anglo-Mongrels and the Rose', with its inconclusive hints at Ova's breaks from the past. Loy goes on to describe the negative film of personality as something which pre-dates birth:

> To discover the hidden influences that affected my childhood, I have had to seek further and further back until, coming to the prenatal, I must inevitably imagine events that took place before I was born. / For this I have to use a little hearsay, a few confidences, some personal observation, and above all, evoke that voiceless converse I held in my infancy with the souls of entrails.[28]

In her search for herself Loy produces a highly biological image of pre-natal personality or destiny. It is not only that Loy saw her relationship to the past as the key to understanding the present. It is also that the biological body is depicted as a peculiarly weighty repository of cultural and individual memory. These images are arresting because of the way in which Loy synthesizes biological and mystical registers. As she admits, capturing her past involves an impressive imaginative leap into the 'souls of entrails'. Not only does she imbue a fragment of the human body with a soul, she suggests that this piece of biology holds the key to her personality. This interest helps explain the emphasis in 'Anglo-Mongrels and the Rose' on the 'hidden influences' of pre-birth and childhood on Ova's identity.

Loy puts the obscene into modernist poetic language in a number of senses: the sexualised body, the hidden parts of the self, the traumatic image of one's lover's mind, the power dynamics of an English home, the racist aspects of a culture, the hybrid languages of modernity. By exposing the unrepresentable aspects of a culture, however, one does not escape different kinds of mimetic barriers. As she puts it, the entangled 'souls' of entrails which structure Loy's identity, are 'already printed But unrevealable'. Her work generally stops short of providing us with a camera and a surface; in trying to describe in a positivistic sense a continuous entity of modern selfhood. Many modernist writers explore how new ways of representing selfhood are entangled in existing discursive traditions. Loy also specifically avoids presenting an Ova free from the familial and cultural constraints explored in the poem. For Loy a positivistic depiction of such a female is as unrepresentable as the 'suspect' psychological 'places' explored in 'Love Songs'.

Notes

[1] See Roger Conover, 'Introduction', *LLB I*, xxiv.

[2] Quoted in Felice Flanery Lewis, *Literature, Obscenity and the Law* (Carbondale & Edwardsville: Southern Illinois University Press, 1976), 11.

[3] D. H. Lawrence, *Fantasia of the Unconscious/Psychoanalysis and the Unconscious* (Harmondsworth: Penguin, 1971), 203.

[4] Mina Loy, 'Anglo-Mongrels and the Rose', *Little Review* 9 no. 3 (Spring, 1923), 10–18.

5 Mina Loy, 'Anglo-Mongrels and the Rose: English Rose', *Little Review* 9 no. 4 (Autumn-Winter, 1923–24), 41–51.

6 Mina Loy, 'The Anglo-Mongrels and the Rose', in Robert McAlmon, ed., *Contact Collection of Contemporary Writers* (Paris: Contact Editions, 1925).

7 Mina Loy, *Lunar Baedeker and Time-Tables*, ed. Kenneth Rexroth (Highlands: Jonathan Williams, 1958).

8 The circumstances around the shift are hard to unravel. Huge thanks to Roger Conover who pointed out to me in an email exchange that Loy was still alive when the 1958 selected poems were published, and evidently looked over the proofs, 'JW told me she looked at the proofs, but from the correspondence it appears to me that her daughter Joella actually signed off on them, so it is difficult to know how involved ML was.' Email, Roger Conover to Rachel Potter.

9 Marjorie Perloff, 'English as a "Second" Language: Mina Loy's "Anglo-Mongrels and the Rose"', in Shreiber and Tuma, eds., 139.

10 Elisabeth Frost, 'Mina Loy's "Mongrel" Poetics', in Shreiber and Tuma, eds., 152, 157.

11 Ibid., 157.

12 Perloff, 140, 133.

13 Keith Tuma, 'Mina Loy's *Anglo-Mongrels and the Rose*', in Shreiber and Tuma, eds., 184.

14 Henry W. Boynton, 'Native vs. Alien Standards', Independent CX (17 March, 1923), 192. Quoted in Paul Boyer, *Purity in Print: The Vice Society Movement and Book Censorship in America* (New York: Charles Scribner's Sons, 1968), 111.

15 Mary Austin, 'Sex in Literature', *Bookman* LVII (June 1923), 391. Quoted in Boyer, 111.

16 See George K. Anderson, *The Legend of the Wandering Jew* (Providence: Brown University Press, 1965), 11.

17 Ibid., 248, 332.

18 Jan Goldstein, 'The Wandering Jew and the Problem of Psychiatric Anti-semitism in Fin-de-siècle France', *Journal of Contemporary History* 20 no. 4 (October 1985), 539.

19 Quoted in Goldstein, 541.

20 Michael North, *Reading 1922: A Return to the Scene of the Modern* (Oxford: Oxford University Press, 1999), 12, 15.

21 Mina Loy, 'Goy Israels', Mina Loy Papers, YCAL MSS 6, fol. 28, typescript, 64.

22 Ibid., 46.

23 Ibid., 46–7.

24 Ibid., 52.

25 F. T. Marinetti, 'The Founding and Manifesto of Futurism', and Tristan Tzara, 'Dada Manifesto', in Vassiliki Kolocotroni, Jane Goldman and Olga Taxidou, eds., *Modernism: An Anthology of Sources and Documents* (Edinburgh: Edinburgh University Press, 1998), 250, 278.

26 D. H. Lawrence, 'Democracy', in Edward D. McDonald, ed., *Phoenix: The Posthumous Papers of D.H. Lawrence* (London: William Heinemann, 1936), 703.

27 On a strip of paper headed Mina Loy, 52 Rue du Colisée, 52, Paris, 192_ [1920s]. Mina Loy Papers, YCAL MSS 6, fol. 10.

28 Ibid.

Mina Loy's 'Unfinishing' Self: 'The Child and The Parent' and 'Islands in the Air'

Sandeep Parmar

The presumption that the cause of life is biological will appear ridiculous—when it becomes evident that the body is for operative convenience the 'island in the air' to which the Electrolife is anchored—or in which—focused. For the 'spiritual' religion teaches us the body is a peaceful instrumentation over which it being a microcosm a <u>man</u> has dominion—for the materialist allows it to become a parasite of most various destructive resources, if not being dominated by the self-realising electrolife.[1]

The above quotation is from an undated notebook page archived among Loy's unpublished papers under the heading 'Notes on Metaphysics'. Each of these notes meditates on related themes: religious faith and twentieth-century science; the creative power of man and god; the spiritual experience of being alive; and the principles of Christian Science. Loy describes bodily existence in terms of mechanical and atomic forces, such as electricity. However, she partly removes these forces from their scientific context; electric energy is deified, as in the case of the 'electrolife'. The 'electrolife' is an essential, universal current that connects the mortal body to its creator by means of conduction.

Loy also reworks religious ideas in scientific terms or the quantitative formulae of physics. Another of these 'Notes on Metaphysics' offers the 'equation': '[t]he universe=absolute presence. All dimension time space contract to the hereness of one Being, and this hereness [is] identical with the hereness of all beings of all time.'[2] She quantifies absolute presence, or 'hereness', as an algebraic constant. 'Hereness' is indivisible and no coefficient alters its value. Simply put, Loy argues that in the universe, individual life and all of creation are one and the same. It follows then that any one life has the same value as that of the entire universe.

For Loy, such revelations appear to be central to the joint acts of perception and artistic creation. If a shared divine force permeates an individual's existence then the value of art is also universal. The making of art becomes a religious calling, one that unites people not only with their creator but also with mankind. Loy writes that 'only creative men are activated by anything but apprehension' and argues that historically religion has incited that 'aboriginal fear of being clubbed on the head while implanting the seed indispensable to human succession'. Activating that 'seed', which is bodily, sexual and creative, is the responsibility of the creative being. Another note develops this idea further:

> Jesus Christ availed us the concept of love [sic]—the cohesion of the individual to plurality—Love the deific juncture of the creator and the created—of the individual with plurality—and of these created one with another—the universal intercommunication. The creative impetus [. . .] is the recognition of the individual's collective identity in God.[3]

Indirectly, Loy equates an individual's creative act with Christ's 'love' of humankind. In another notebook page, she paraphrases John 10:10 in the Gospels: 'I am come that they might have life and that they might have it more abundantly.' Loy identifies herself with Christ as the 'good shepherd', who leads man into salvation. By following Christ's example, the artist redeems humanity and unites the creator with the physical world. The artist is both man and god, and he or she channels the universe through the communication of a collective identity.

Possibly dating from the late 1920s to the 1940s, Loy's notes are radical and often self-aggrandizing texts that sometimes lack coherence. Her treatises are attempts to answer 'the great question' of 'how and where does man's creativity begin'.[4] Her 'failure' to arrive at a definite conclusion can be seen as reflecting an ongoing and unresolved search for her own creative origins. Religion, God and her critiques of both are axiomatic to the creation of artistic identity in both her poetry and unpublished prose of this period. Scholars have written about Loy's engagement with Christian mythologies in her long poem 'Anglo-Mongrels and the Rose' (1923–1925). It often references the Old Testament especially in sections about Exodus, a character who is partly based on Loy's father (*LLB I* 111, 112, 116).[5] Many of Loy's later poems, such as 'Revelation' (n.d.); 'Hilarious Israel' (ca. 1944); 'Transformation Scene' (1944); 'Show Me a Saint Who Suffered' (1960) and 'Portrait of a Nun' (n.d.) focus on religious topics. Interestingly, an early draft of 'Hilarious Israel' also appears on the verso of fragments of notes for her 'History of Religion and Eros'.[6] Loy's notes also provide an ideological backdrop for a series of unpublished prose texts with autobiographical content written during the same period: *Islands in the Air, The Child and the Parent* and *Insel*.[7]

In this essay, I will consider how Loy's juxtaposition of religious and scientific languages impacts on her construction of selfhood in her prose works of the 1930s and 40s. Loy's ongoing refashioning of the autobiographical 'I' in these texts, as well as her attraction to acts of impersonation, suggests that she saw selfhood as unfixed and provisional. In this essay I show how this understanding of the self relates to her claims elsewhere that the individual is connected to a unifying divine force.

1. Notes on religion

Loy's 'Notes on Metaphysics' might just as easily be labelled 'Notes on Religion'. As Carolyn Burke has detailed, Loy converted to Christian Science in 1909 and shared her beliefs with Joseph Cornell, Julien Levy and her daughters. In letters she wrote of the healing power of 'C.S.' or the 'Science' (*BM*, 117). Two pages from what appears to be an undated letter in Loy's hand reveal her apprehension about the traditionally anti-materialist nature of Christian Science practice:

> I am bothered by what materialists call escapism such as smoking and crossword puzzles—whereas I want to feel calm enough to work steadily. I am sure my work is better than it was ever—and I enjoy it— when I am not worried by the past—my husband I loved was murdered in Mexico—my son kidnapped by a divorced father and died of ill-treatment—I have struggled with poverty and almost died of real starvation—But all the time I have tried to understand faith—Mrs. Bayer [Joella, Loy's daughter] told an acquaintance that she wondered if I had cancer—and this has depressed me—because of the constant harping on this fear—surrounding humanity—and one wonders what might happen if one is not a good enough Christian Scientist [. . .] I have found in C.S. as my first wonderful healer explained one cannot in the least iota admit any other law into one's consciousness—one had to give up all reliance on material [sic] [. . .] But dear friend it is so easy to

understand intellectually—I find—it is funny I had not a religious
nature . . . [8]

It is unclear to whom her letter is addressed. Presumably, her 'dear
friend' is unaware of the exact biographical details of her life, and is
acquainted with Loy's daughter, Joella Bayer. It does not appear at
least that she knew the letter's intended recipient intimately, though
it may be possible that Loy is reiterating her personal history as a
series of contributing factors for her present condition. It seems
reasonable to assume that this letter dates from Loy's residence in
Aspen late in her life, after Joella had married Herbert Bayer, roughly
between 1953 and her death in 1966 (*BM* 425–40).[9] Her letter betrays
an unease with the Christian Science doctrine 'to give up all reliance'
on material, which she associates with a refusal to dwell on the past,
and the bodily experiences of starvation, poverty and death. Loy's
vision of the electrolife and her writings on mysticism reorient the
body as a strong, central aspect of faith and creation.

It is likely that her choice of electric force as a metaphor for the
divine spirit draws from Christian healing practices that involved
electricity. In the mid-eighteenth century, John Wesley founded the
Methodist Church based on his belief in the 'compatibility between
electricity and divine power.'[10] According to Amanda Porterfield's
historical account of Christian healing practices, Wesley 'viewed electricity as a subtle form of fire pervading and animating the universe,
enlivening the air, and running through the blood and nervous
system, making the human body "a kind of fire machine".'[11] The early
Methodist Church promoted the use of electricity as a form of
disease-countering therapy. Science and faith healing was taken up by
the Pentecostal Church and Seventh-day Adventists, and the combination of divinity, the body and death was implicit in mesmerist
experiments (the founder of the Seventh-day Adventist Church
worried over becoming a channel 'for Satan's electric currents').[12] By
negotiating a spiritual link to the soul within the body, Loy redirects
the materialist's focus on bodily suffering. In doing so, she investigates the divine potential of the body as it sees, feels, perceives, and
most importantly, creates.

In her twenty-page long, unpublished treatise on faith, 'History of
Religion and Eros', Loy returns to the idea that 'man is a covered-
entrance to infinity', a line which also appears in 'Being Alive'.[13] It is
possible that these archived 'Notes on Metaphysics' were the basis for

'History of Religion and Eros' (hereafter referred to as 'History'); sections share similar language and ideas about spiritual evolution. In the archive folder of 'History', handwritten fragments allude to the text's possible influences. She writes that in '1920 Havelock Ellis told me that, in England [,] women were becoming suspicious of marriage'. She describes a conversation with Ellis in which he surmised that ninety percent of English women found no physical pleasure in sex. Her response was to refer to an article on 'atomic theory' that claimed the energy in one 'little finger' could blow up the whole of Boulevard Montparnasse. Ellis's 'clear blue youthful eyes' hardened and he hissed 'you're mad!'[14] In another fragment Loy argues that initially Freud's 'contribution lay in ridding people of the blind shame veiling biological function'. She later credits Freudian psychoanalysis as having equated God with the unconscious, and religious mysticism with confession.[15]

Certainly evolutionary theories and scientific advances in genetics contributed to her crossbreeding of religion and science. Loy's involvement with Italian Futurism would have exposed her to F. T. Marinetti's equation of man's body with the mechanics of the machine. In *War, the World's Only Hygiene* (1915), Marinetti envisioned a future in which human bodies would merge with machines, anticipating much later debates about modern societies and the figure of the cyborg. Alluding to the Darwinian principle of natural selection, Marinetti imagined that eventually a mechanical evolution would refine mankind's bodies and minds for the 'omnipresent velocity' of modern life.[16]

The specific features of Loy's merging of spirituality and scientific ideas might also be traced to her engagement with Frederic W.H. Myers's *Human Personality and its Survival of Bodily Death* (1903). Myers contended that 'the question for man most momentous of all is whether or not he has an immortal soul [. . .] whether or no his personality involves any element which can survive bodily death'. Myers's ideas about the infinite existence of the human soul are based on the premise that individual lives have a foundation of 'ancestral experience'; the individual's evolutionary consciousness scientifically proves that the soul is immortal. He championed the methods of 'modern science' and claimed that his study followed 'that [scientific] process which consists in an interrogation of Nature entirely dispassionate, patient, systematic; such careful experiment and cumulative record as can often elicit from her slightest indications her deepest truths'. According to Myers, science is the purveyor of 'indisputable truth'; it refuses to 'fall back upon tradition' and therefore offers an alternative to the subjectivities of religious faith or superstition.[17]

Loy criticised aspects of Myers's work, particularly focusing on how his discussion of literature revealed the limits of scientific ideas. She wrote to Mabel Dodge that Myers's book was an example of how 'scientific dissertations fall flat because they lack the element of taking risks—that art and life have'.[18] He tended to treat literary texts as psychological case studies. William Wordsworth's *The Prelude*, for example, is a 'human document': 'there can be no doubt as to [Wordsworth's] conscientious veracity as an introspective psychologist' and the poem 'is a deliberate, persistent attempt to tell the truth, the whole truth, and nothing but the truth, about exactly those emotions and intuitions which differentiate the poet from common men'.[19] Certainly, the systematic truth telling in which Myers claims Wordsworth engaged aligns itself with his scientific method of determining man's essential nature. It reflects the expectations of a scientific readership for the 'whole truth' about the internal workings of creative genius.

Loy's conviction, in contrast, was that it was impossible for the writer to represent the 'whole truth' of the creative self. Instead, she implied that the kernel of artistic 'intuition' was the work itself. Her method of self-analysis refuses the dispassionate scientific method by which Myers generates his theories on personality and the soul. Instead, Loy constructs the body as simply an 'island in the air', an 'operative convenience' to which the soul is anchored, a construction which can be read against studies that suggest personality or character is biologically determined.[20]

On the verso of her description of the electrolife she handwrote the phrase 'notes for Book'.[21] Loy's references to her 'book' can be found in prose drafts and her correspondence. It is unclear to which text she is referring. However, her use of the phrase 'island in the air' suggests that her notes on the electrolife are related to her later autobiographical draft of the same name. Although it is impossible to determine which came first—the quotation about the electrolife or the title 'Islands in the Air'— in this latter text she frames human life as superior to mere bodily existence. It is difficult to reconcile this with other parts of her autobiographical narratives, and indeed her poems, which detail bodily sensations and physiological phenomena.

Carolyn Burke and Roger Conover have suggested that her 'book' is an amalgamation of her many autobiographical narratives, composed over a period of many years. It is striking that Loy's notes link the artist with divinity through a specific kind of artistic act. In order for the artist to 'universal[ly] intercommunic[ate]' with others, Loy argues that he or she must transcend the physical body to unite with the 'divine force' that is common to all mortal beings.[22] She sets out to achieve this by writing about a self. In doing so, she navigates the universal within the limits of her own perception.

In 'History of Religion and Eros' Loy claims:

> It is not prohibitive to man, as the complete microcosm, to train his intelligence on his components and gain control of their potentialities. To avail himself of his resources, akin to the atomic, electronic etc. in order to transcend the restrictions of his overt senses.[23]

Man has the ability to harness his resources and, in doing so, to transcend his mortal, sensual body. We also learn that man's dominion over his own being is akin to God's control over the universe. By 'avail[ing] himself of his resources' he can transmit God's essence creatively to his fellow man. In 'Being Alive' Loy elaborates on the purpose of divine, artistic creation:

> Being alive is the loneliness of the multitude, similar in the helpless parasitic lascivity [sic], distinct as each one crying alone and forever—-"I — I!" That individuality which like a phialed [sic] viable explosive, is conditioned by each man having, as label, a face which he alone among his fellows can never see; even as he has to compose his own psyche with the experience of the human race. He exists to the extent of the general understanding of his unless he can make a personal contribution to add to this human experience of which he is composed.
>
> He has no concrete proof of being other than a soft machine that moves in a landscape, and thus we see him, when looking from long distance, where he first appears as a pale creature stirring against a wall of green and later as a clothed creature surrounded by erected stone. But taken from close-up, as if he formed a covered entrance to infinity, he would seem to include something as illimitable as the universe external to him.[24]

An individual's 'personal contribution' to the 'multitude' is his or her own 'human experience'. Shared experience is 'proof' of the

'I's existence and it saves him from 'loneliness'. This transmitted experience brings the individual closer, and reveals the 'illimitable' universe within him. This universe could be the infinite force common to all individuals: Loy's electrolife. Her description of the individual as a 'machine' or an 'explosive' who harnesses 'atomic' energy is similar to her anecdotal conversation with Ellis. It also bears a likeness to Wesley's own writings on electric forces within the body and the human machine.[25] She elaborates on the idea of man's 'face' or 'label':

> If being alive is having a face, that window which is identical with the being who looks out of it, one can imagine a man who had never seen his own reflection even in a pool as remaining one with the air, or being stuck in an impersonal scenery as part of a back-drop from which he was incapable of making a conscious advance.[26]

Through writing her autobiographical novels Loy formulates a 'face' in order to depict an individuated self in process, one that is 'making a conscious advance'. Therefore it would appear that the value of being alive rests in self-realisation through scrutinized experience. Loy's novels exhibit an ever-increasing investment in sharing proof of having existed. But overall her notes for her 'book' imply that she does not claim to explain, historicize or unify her life. Her prose sets up deliberate textual barriers in order to defy the reader's expectations of a life that is rooted in a coherent selfhood. Loy's narrative voice mimics the communication of a universalized being and in doing so keeps her reader at a distance. While her ideas about the possible function of art seem to unite her with her audience, they also dilute the personal implications of her confessional statements into something more general and abstract.

2. 'The Child and The Parent' and 'Islands in the Air'

In this section I will compare Loy's 'The Child and the Parent' and 'Islands in the Air', two linked texts written roughly twenty years apart, and show how their narrative voices manipulate the seemingly polarised ideas of the universal and of the personal. 'The Child and the Parent' and 'Islands in the Air' (hereafter referred to as 'Child' and 'Islands') include similar chapters. A note from Joella Bayer, appended to the archive manuscript of 'Child', suggests that 'Child' is an earlier draft of 'Islands'.[27]

The archived manuscript of 'Child' consists of nine chapters, numbered III-XII. It shares Chapters Four and Five with 'Islands'. Chapters Six to Twelve are not carried over into 'Islands' and do not appear in any other drafts. The final typescript of 'Islands' has ten chapters but is significantly longer than 'Child'.[28] The close similarity between parts of these two drafts poses an obvious problem. How might one differentiate between the two if they contain only slightly varied wording? How can one typescript or handwritten note be definitively attributed to one manuscript or the other? Each folder contains multiple typescripts of the same chapter, which makes it difficult to determine which draft is earlier or later. Most of these typescripts bear the typed title 'Islands in the Air', but two that are untitled are included in the 'Islands' manuscript folder. Based on the physical appearance and on the altered order of the chapters shared by the two versions, it is arguable that these untitled chapters are the misplaced first two chapters of 'Child' and not drafts of the first chapters of 'Islands'. An examination of the change in narrative voice Loy employs in the twenty years between the drafting of the two texts depends on the separating out of these intertwined versions. The erroneous placement of these two chapters of 'Child' only becomes apparent with a close reading of the first chapter of 'Islands', entitled 'Hurry'.

'Hurry' is the only published section of the 'Islands' manuscript.[29] Although this chapter was published as 'Chapter 1', this contradicts Loy's own handwritten note on the back of the first manuscript page that 'Hurry' was to be 'an experimental introduction'.[30] Loy's narrative voice in 'Hurry' claims that her introduction was written after the main text of 'Islands' was finished. 'Hurry' navigates the interface between Loy's experience of the present and her accumulated memories of the past. The events of the introduction are fairly straightforward. Though unnamed, the female narrator recounts her arrival home late one night to find her apartment in disarray. Several objects, including lipstick-soiled tissues are described; each reflects the narrator's sense of discomfort at having erupted into a kind of divine psychic mess. The first of these is a black pair of shoes. Each shoe points in a different direction; one points straight at her and the other is set out at a right angle. Loy writes: 'Something remarkably sinister in their imperusable vagrancy brought me up short. That dead-lock gait come to the parting of the wayfarer took shape as a sign-board on my private road. Mine had been a dislocated journey, every step I had taken resulted in a jam.'[31] The awkward placement of the shoes represents the narrator's psychological impasse in which a lack of focus and direction has prevented her from completing something yet unmentioned by the narrative. It is not long before she compares the accumulated debris around her to the abandoned writing of her 'book'. Loy writes of this project:

> The book I had felt impelled to write! Tentatively assuming that what seemed likely to me would seem likely to others. Intermittent . . . unfinishing, I saw how this Book in itself constituted my inhibition.[32]

Loy explains that her 'inhibition', an inability to complete her book, results from a lifelong tendency to allow detail to distract her by flooding the senses with a kind of entrancing beauty. The Hurry, which appears in Loy's story of the same name as a kind of supernatural force, interferes with moments of contemplation — the narrative consciousness skips between intense concentration on something seemingly miniscule like a cockroach in the sink in one instance, and a row of windows across the street in another, and then breaks off into a fury over the loss of time and the nearing of her own mortality. The introduction ends with the narrator running to the closet to dig the chapters of her book out of a valise and concludes with her offering it to her reader so that she might compare her life with her own.

On the surface, Loy's introduction reveals the narrator's desperation to be heard and for her existence to be validated by the act of assembling a life story for an audience. At times her self-effacements reach a martyr-like pitch, as in the following: 'No longer in touch with the world at all I was left to bear the undistributed weight of my communication [. . .] Two generations have evolved while I stood at the cross-purpose of the roads, my mouth open to speak or rather my pen dipped in air.'[33] The story which Loy presents reveals her problematic relationship with the Victorian and religious ideologies of her upbringing and their impact on her attempt to become a modern woman. While the narrator's childhood self rejects the indoctrinations of her conservative childhood, she also explores her complicated relationship to modernity. 'Child' and 'Islands' reveal the difficulty of overcoming the shame and inhibitions of early life. Loy focuses her attention on the incipient consciousness of an artistic self.

Even though it may at first appear that Loy is addressing her own inability to complete 'Islands', 'Hurry' is not solely an author's self-indictment for not producing. 'Hurry' and the body of Loy's 'Book' must be considered together in order to understand their joint significance to Loy's work. If several years elapsed between the writing of 'Hurry' and the abandonment of her hidden 'Book', then the two pieces also differ in the 'self' they construct. The time delay gives us a sense of the difference between the speaking voices in both sections as well as of the later Loy's impression of her earlier self. Yet this book in the 'valise' is not 'Islands' as Francini suggests, but an earlier version: Loy's 'unfinishing' 'Child'.

In the archive folders that contain Chapters Two and Three of 'Islands' there are very similar additional typescripts that are labelled 'Chapter I' and 'Chapter II'. These typescripts are on the same mimeograph paper as the incomplete typescript of 'Child' that is missing its first two chapters. In the typed title for 'Chapter I, The Bird Alights' Loy has, at most likely a later date, pencilled in an additional numeral and changed it by hand from 'I' to 'II'. This alteration confirms that 'Child' is the 'Book' to which Loy refers in 'Hurry'.[34]

In 'Hurry' she writes:

> ... I ran to the closet & dragged out that valise. It was easy to pick the first chapter: 'The Bird Alights'. Here is no mysticism. I have simply used a well known symbol as an aid in describing a unique registration of consciousness in infancy. When I became aware of what was then my state of Being.[35]

It seems likely that 'The Bird Alights' is the first chapter of 'Child', not 'Islands', and is part of the manuscript that Loy pulls out of the valise. The 'intermittent . . . unfinishing' 'Book' that Loy agonizes over in 'Hurry' predates 'Islands' and is her earlier narrative 'Child'.[36] The Hurry hastens Loy to uncover the 'Child' manuscript and to revise it into 'Islands':

> ... Bring into view! . . A lot of foolscap in a closed valise. . . . . . The Hurry catching up the tail end of time as a lash to drive me to a last exertion, was upon me again . . . To gather up, to put together, to elucidate! . . . To what end?

Perhaps the relief of a not uncommon anxiety to produce proof of
having, oneself, existence?

Moreover, discerning in these tenants of a sheet of glass a public to
my contact I must hasten to complete a message orally impossible.[37]

Loy insists that the Hurry embodies a vital anxiety that compels her
to write her life story. It opposes her inhibition while torturously
driving her to prove her 'existence'. Much of Loy's introduction
focuses on her own inability to 'gather up' and preserve in writing
her 'orally impossible' message. Loy suggests that the Hurry specifically presses her to write; it is as though this force psychologically
and artistically generates the will to create. The Hurry disrupts the
present by urging Loy to document her experience of 'being'.
However, intermittency is essential to Loy's product. It provides the
backdrop against which finally she frees herself from the shame and
fear of her upbringing.

In Loy's rewriting of the 'Child' manuscript into 'Islands' she
removes the original manuscript's 'Parent' section. The focus of
'Islands' is squarely on the child consciousness and the parents are
only part of the narrative through their involvement with their
daughter. At the top of the first page of the 'Ladies in an Aviary'
typescript, Loy has handwritten the words: 'These chapters come in
as attempts of a woman constantly interrupted to begin a book she
is too shy to write.'[38] The 'chapters' to which Loy refers are the five
remaining chapters of the 'Parent' section that begins with Chapter
Seven, 'Ladies in an Aviary', and ends with Chapter Eleven, 'The
Outraged Womb'.[39] Read with these words in mind, it would appear
that the shame Loy claims she inherited from her mother's surveil-
lance prevents her from being able to complete these chapters
which dissect a parental sex life and the mystery of female sexual
pleasure. A child's shame, a mother's 'Voice' and the Hurry
combine in her novels to create an anxiety to write in spite of these
forces. Together they shape her intermittent narrative of simultaneous confession and concealment. Perhaps Loy's removal of her
parents from 'Islands' is a final casting off — a necessary step
towards planting her narrative in the modern era. How successful
Loy felt she was in doing so can in part be gauged by her persistent anxiety about her manuscript and her audience's reception of
it in 'Hurry'.

Loy's opening sequence is, as I mentioned earlier, fairly straight-forward. She begins: 'As I arose from the twisting staircase to the landing a door stood open. On the floor in abandon, black as hearses, lay a pair of shoes. Thrown in the pattern of a tee square one walked straight toward me, the other set out on its own right angle.'[40] The general feeling of these lines is mixed. The 'twisting' staircase and the unexplained open door in addition to the hearse-black shoe that points ominously at her are all undeniably forbidding. But, as is the case throughout 'Hurry', the significance of objects is manipulated by an excess of detail. How do shoes 'lie' if they are at once 'in abandon' but also drawn into 'the pattern of a tee square'? In a manuscript draft of this page Loy has illustrated her description by drawing in a triangle; the specificity of the image is central to her message. The lines that follow this section are even more overwritten. Describing the scene before her as she returns home, Loy writes:

> The scenic dry-goods surrounding the foot-wear presented the cubis-tic hay-stack of a recent school. Countless segments set at a various subtlety of degree and a wild diversity of direction piled to overlapping strata in the centre of the room and started from corners to spear the eye at every point on the ocular periphery.[41]

Rather than repeat the word shoes, Loy writes 'foot-wear', and instead of waste paper, 'scenic dry-goods'. The terms 'foot-wear' and 'dry-goods' are curious choices as they have commercial meanings; one might expect to find such names on a mercantile sign, as they are general categories under which a variety of individual items can be classified. The intentionally scientific terms 'ocular periphery' and 'overlapping strata' do what science does best. They classify phenom-ena with great specificity, but in doing so take the thing being described out of the normal world of relative meaning and render it foreign. The appeal of using scientific terms is that words borrowed from physics, mathematics and chemistry have a particular authority, a claim to truth which ties Loy's largely metaphysical and spiritual meditation on the nature of being and perception to reality and fact. Loy's authorial presence in her introduction is also injected with a fair amount of control by the language in which she chooses to set out her vision. She orients the narrative self in terms of measure-ments and, as though she were part of a reproducible experiment, uses phrases like 'misanthropic readjustment of the comparative' rather than a simpler statement like 'mulled over'.[42]

Another example of Loy's meditations on the essence of the soul comes from the slightly later autobiographical novel 'Goy Israels' (hereafter referred to as 'Goy'). Goy is a pseudonym for Loy's bi-spirited childhood self, half Christian, half Jewish. The word 'Goy' comes from the Hebrew for 'people' and in common usage refers to non-Jews, while the surname Israels betrays Goy's Jewish heritage. In 'Goy' Loy writes:

> If a murderer denies his guilt long enough he is telling the truth; in the time elapsed since the crime his entire atomic volume (or cellular structure) has been renewed. The one with the desire to kill has disappeared in the ether, leaving a fresh body that prefers to play Pinnochle. The affair of justice, then, is prosecuted upon memory.[43]

In the margin Loy has handwritten the question 'Which is correct' next to 'atomic volume (or cellular structure)'. Either way the effect is the same; regardless of whether the body is renewed in terms of volume or individual cells, Loy's (incorrect) hypothesis that the body's matter is replenished is unchanged. The authority of scientific data, of quantifiable measurements and of systems of classification lends Loy's narrative voice an air of objectivity. Surely if one can trace and add up the causes of one's present life through scientific analysis then whatever outcome results must be a form of hard evidence, a counteraction to the more amorphous self which results from guilt, shame or a sense of loss.

Is Loy's autobiographical voice really 'intermittent' and 'unfinishing' or is there an element of disguise to her 'inhibition'? And if so, what might her inhibition be hiding? If Loy's book, that is the supposedly unfinished draft of her autobiography hidden in a suitcase, constitutes her inhibition, then why does its unearthing and the description of its states of decay take up so much of her introduction? Is Loy confronting her reader with a kind of private archive, her abandoned book, and performing for the reader her 'failure' to publish and preserve a life story? Loy's valise, presumably a travelling case, concealing the proof of her existence is suggestive. Her closed suitcase could be seen to symbolize her underlying narration of self-exile and the boundaries of personal and national identity. The valise is not forgotten; it has been hidden away and left to age and decay.[44] On the surface, it appears to represent the mind's gradual loss of memory. However, the valise and its contents also stand in for Loy's simultaneously ailing body, which in death will be superseded by the life of her archived autobiographies. Loy means to escape her reader's scrutiny by hiding behind the incompleteness natural to the archive. Yet how do we reconcile the simultaneous concealment of Loy's manuscript with the painfully descriptive, near-forensic examination of it she provides? Loy herself offers a clue. She writes: 'Had early precep-tor's insistence on unconditional confession complicated by the shame they had heaped on all forms of self-expression brought me to the conscientious pass of a woman anxious, under the onus of revealing her whole absurdity, to preserve her incognito?'[45] 'Preceptors' refers to her mother specifically and to her mother's generation more generally. In 'Goy' Loy depicts her zealously reli-gious mother's belief that her daughter was immoral. She writes:

> 'Be sure your sins will find you out, I hope you feel ashamed of your-self' jeers Mother. What is this nervous concussion that answers to the call of shame. How can an inexperienced child perceive that the preceptors are planting a blade in her to turn among the subliminal roots of her faculties to lop off the green shoots of initiative, while they sow shuddering seeds — of silence and shift. The protestant harvest shall not fail. And so adolescence receeds [sic] behind a pride-like mask of one who has received the mortal wound before the battle of life has begun.[46]

Planted by 'preceptors', silence is bred by shame and the fear of being found out. The result is that the child hides behind an impenetrable 'mask' of defeat. According to Burke, Loy's mother also repeatedly tore up her drawings and childhood poems for their supposed licen-tiousness (*BM* 42). In the quotation from 'Hurry', she suggests that the urge to confess is complicated by the ensuing shame so that the anxi-ety of telling makes her anxious to maintain her 'incognito'. The word incognito appears in Loy's later poems attached to the spectral figure of the vagrant (*LLB II* 143). The unknowable quality of Loy's homeless incognitos stems from their being overlooked; they are saint-like in their suffering but the shared tragedy of their invisible lives is invisible, unlike the saint who is canonised. During the 1930s, at the time Loy was most likely writing early drafts of her autobio-graphical novels, a rumour circulated in Paris that Loy was not in fact a real person but a forged persona, a hoax of critics of modern poetry. According to Roger Conover, Loy turned up at Natalie Barney's salon on the rue Jacob and said 'I assure you I am indeed a live being. But it is necessary to stay very unknown. . . to maintain my incognito, the hazard I chose was—poet.'[47] In 'Hurry', Loy figures herself as one of her common anonymous saints. She bares her wounds in an appeal for canonisation; much in the same way that she turned up at Barney's salon to reveal that she was a real person in hiding. Loy fully exploits the reader's sympathy and by giving the impression of what Francini calls 'a desire to pin down one's own essence', she is in reality providing yet another version of an authorial self cloaked as an unassailable autobiographical 'I'.

She artfully manipulates her audience into believing in the voice in 'Hurry' as with all of the late novels—to paraphrase the American poet Anne Sexton, she fakes it up with the truth, meaning that a believable mask is one that is too true, too personal, too willing to shame itself before an audience. Loy refers to her audience near the end of her introduction: 'Apparent only in a primary effulgence of Being as bare of troubled incidence as the area of perfectibility I would point out to them, this audience at a distance would wear whatever transparencies I chose to clothe it in.'[48] The audience, both psychologically and temporally removed from the narrative voice, will accept Loy's construction of self because it will be hidden in a seemingly transparent cloth, though it will not be transparent at all. She is masking not only herself but also her audience—whom she masks in her own authorial fantasy.

Again, Loy is hiding by emphatically confessing some version of the truth. The artfulness of the transformation of human life into fiction dressed as fact is not lost on Loy—she writes: 'But listen to me, O Islands in the Air, I have made even of your biology—a lily.'[49] Rightly, Francini has suggested that Loy chose the 'lily flower' because it represents beauty and that her purpose was to raise human life above mere biology. Another possible reason for the image of the lily could be to invoke its religious symbolism. The lily appears in Matthew as a symbol of spiritual purity; it is antithetical to the bodily toil of mortal man. It also stands for oneness and impregnability, which is why the lily so often appears in medieval paintings alongside the Virgin Mary. Yet, the Virgin also stands for fertility, this is the dual nature of her divine conception: she is at once both chastely intact and fecund. Though on one level Loy's evocation of the lily might represent a transmutation of the living being into something beautiful and divine it also suggests a potential multiplicity of the 'self'. Another of Loy's many autobiographical pseudonyms is Ova—we

again see that Loy plays with the idea of one representing and changing into many varying but connected narrative selves. As in her writings on the electrolife and 'Being Alive', she suggests that human
biology cannot fix a spiritual self. Loy's engagement with the process
of becoming modern engages with a past, real or imagined, and
expresses the dilemma of living in the present moment yet being
rooted in the influence of memory.

The first five chapters of 'Islands' vary only slightly from the first
four corresponding chapters of 'Child'. Both versions begin with Loy's
earliest childhood memories. The opening metaphor of the bird in
'The Bird Alights' represents the infant mind's first 'registration of
consciousness'.[50] This 'winged perception' 'snared' by the body's flesh
comes into contact with objects in her childhood environment, such
as a mesmerising row of glass bottles described in the second chapter.[51] Loy frequently offers such examples to highlight the intensity of
the infant consciousness's response to the human world:

> The afternoon sun shone through the bottles, through the fanlight,
> firing the drastic reds and yellows in a triple transparency—the blaze
> exploded in me. I was riddled with splinters of delight.[52]

Loy's memory of the bottles suggests that she experienced a saint-like
ecstasy. Although she observes the phenomenon externally, the
perception of colour and beauty originates inside the body as it is
manifested in her mind. In these first few chapters Loy imagines that
the infant consciousness sees itself and other objects as materially the
same. Her portrayal of perception, as a kind of ecstatic immolation,
likens consciousness to religious devotion. Loy's idea of the divine
electrolife is revisited:

> Quickened by that fundemental [sic] excitement combined of worship
> and covetousness which being the primary response to the admirable
> very likely composes the whole human ideal, my arms like antennae
> waved towards the glitter of those bottles & through a sort of vibra-
> tional extension, came into as good as bodily contact with them as if I
> were capable of a plastic protrusion beyond my anatomical frontiers.
> Infants are always attaining to things they cannot touch.[53]

The child wishes to meld with the admirable, or beautiful, object in
the same way as Loy's mystics and artists want to unite with god and
humanity. External objects adapt to the infant's desires. As the child

physically reaches for the bottles, space connects the two through a 'vibrational extension' that, like the electrolife, inhabits all matter. It is only when the child unintentionally commits its first punishable act that it begins to differentiate between the body and the mind, and between action and thought. Loy's introduction to the dynamics of good and evil takes place in the fourth chapter of 'Islands' (the third chapter of 'Child'). By accidentally throwing a domino through a glass window, Loy first incurs her mother's wrath and is scolded for her innate wickedness—an accusation her mother repeats in subsequent chapters.[54] However, the accident symbolizes the grounding of Loy's infant bird consciousness in the reality of the moral, and the mortal, world. Loy makes very few changes to the 'Child' chapters in 'Islands'. However, the most poignant omission is the following sentence from 'Child':

> If life is a promise made to be broken, such is the voice that shouts down fulfillment [sic], being a very echo of the Accident in which all trends or idea, rushing from opposite sources within the same confines, crash into one another and splinter to bits.[55]

Why is the above passage from 'Child' not carried over into 'Islands'? Loy's association of childhood self-expression with punishment dominates both chapters and remains largely unchanged. Yet this quotation hints at a subtext that she chose not to revisit in her later version. It is possible that Loy compares the loss of childhood 'innocence' with the loss of her second husband, Arthur Cravan. Cravan's disappearance in 1918 preoccupied Loy's poetry from the 1920s.[56] Her writings about their short time together depict a similar naïve spontaneity in their married life. Part of Loy's interest in staging her life possibly arose from a desire for continuity and meaning, especially in the face of her husband's fatal accident. By removing the above lines from 'Islands' Loy appears to regain control. Instead of giving herself the role of the fated victim, she maintains 'Hurry''s factual, quasi-scientific tone. The first chapters of 'Islands' explain her dual fascination and fear of destiny with more subtlety. However, the reader is still given no alternative but to see the course of the author's life as pre-determined by signs like the pair of hearse-black shoes in Loy's introductory chapter.

Both 'Islands' and 'Child' seek to explain the nature of modern consciousness, but both cite different causes for the formation of a

modern self. 'Child' looks backwards toward the Victorian era and
details how it stifled emerging modern thought at every religious and
moral opportunity. 'Islands' diverges from this perspective after
Chapter Five. Part II of 'Child', which describes sexual and moral
repression within Victorian society, is omitted in 'Islands' and
replaced with sections from 'Goy'. 'Islands' combines the two previous accounts into one text and in doing so includes Loy's anxiety over
her bi-racial identity in inter-war Europe. 'Islands' looks into the past
as well as the future, albeit fearfully: at what the danger of rooting
out sources of immorality and evil would mean for European Jews
during the 1930s and 1940s. Loy appoints herself as a prophet and
saint figure in 'Islands' by uniting her Jewish and Christian heritage
and by combining her critique of pre-war society and a post-war
context. In an early handwritten copy of 'Hurry', Loy indicates that
the 'precious knowledge' she had wished to communicate to her
'fellow man' is a kind of prophetic warning. The frustration she
expresses in 'Hurry' stems from not having offered 'advice' to her
'companions' or 'good news' when it was needed.[57] Written during
and after World War II, 'Hurry' demonstrates Loy's belief that had she
successfully finished 'Child' or 'Goy' she would have been able to
offer such warnings. Artistic and historical failures come together in
Loy's revisions and writing of 'Islands'. The artistic failure of not
being able to formulate and present a single narrative combines with
a lament about a history which seems destined to repeat itself. As she
puts it in 'Islands': 'Nothing has more amazed me than the idiotic
apprehension of the moralists that the world during recent decades
has lapsed from the purity of the pre war era.'[58]

3. 'Unfinishing' autobiographies

'Goy Israels' and 'Child' can be read in light of ideas about shifting
literary traditions of biographical writing. Laura Marcus argues that:
'In the early twentieth century in Britain, the desire of the literary
'moderns' to mark their absolute difference from their Victorian
predecessors finds one expression in the construction of "the new
biography".'[59] According to Marcus, the 'new biography', a term
coined by Woolf in her essay-review of Harold Nicolson's *Some People*,
was closely linked to simultaneous concerns over the possibility of
truthfulness in recorded lives and the partiality of biographers.[60] The
tendency of Victorian biographers to memorialise their subjects in

the form of hagiography, combined with concern about the biographer's own conscious involvement in the writing process are evidenced by Edmund Gosse's autobiographical *Father and Son* (1907). Published anonymously at first, the book alludes to the age's concern over 'accurate' self-representation.[61] Much like Loy's own fictional autobiographies, *Father and Son* narrates Gosse's pre-adult life, focusing mainly on his formative struggle with his deeply pious Christian father. Consciously throughout his retelling, Gosse equates his father's character and principles with an ideologically vanished and morally disowned generation, while portraying his own rebelliousness and aesthetic beliefs as reflective of a more modern era.

Interestingly, it was not until Gosse was assured of his book's warm reception and popularity that he assigned his name to a fourth edition, published within twelve months of its initial printing.[62] Such anxiety over his reputation was presumably the result of the potential effect personal revelation might have had on his public persona. In addition to this might also be Gosse's own uneasiness with his individuality, as his final lines suggest:

> . . . and thus desperately challenged, the young man's conscience threw off once and for all the yoke of his 'dedication', and, as respectfully as he could, without parade or remonstrance, he took a human being's privilege to fashion his inner life for himself.[63]

The distance offered to his subject (himself 'the young man') as well as his defiant tone (in an otherwise polite and even narrative) is resonant of Loy's own pseudo-scientific language and detached formation of her autobiographical self. Such language, coupled with his awareness of an imminent shift from conventional formations of public figures to the wilful instability of modern biography, is also revealed in his introduction. Gosse writes:

> At the present hour, when fiction takes forms so ingenious and so specious, it is perhaps necessary to say that the following narrative, in all its parts, and so far as the punctilious attention of the writer has been able to keep it so, is scrupulously true. If it were not true, in this strict sense, to publish it would be to trifle with all those who may be induced to read it. It is offered to them as a *document* . . . (Gosse's emphasis)[64]

As a preface to his book, this is a remarkably firm statement. Gosse declares the factuality of his autobiographical 'document', not only for his readership but also for himself as the writer. At work in Loy's early autobiographical texts are anxieties over the division between literary and scientific modes of writing. By narrating the life of the nascent and undifferentiated child, the autobiographer gauges and projects the development of the authorial adult personality. The child is pure and depicted as always within yet slightly beyond the narrated moment, displaced by the intervention of the author's hindsight. The sometimes ordinary and everyday quality of Loy's and Gosse's childhood narrations might mean to attest to the factualness of their writing—even though each author has chosen moments that are emblematic of a vital stage of development in their life. The porous boundaries between the written subject and the author are mediated by the concern of a modern generation: consciousness and fluidities of the self.

In 'Hurry' Loy's claim that she is unable to complete her book is heightened by an aesthetic of failure within the text. Obstacles appear such as physical breaks in the form of ellipses or dashed lines, as well as moments in which the present breaks through her narration of the past. This technique is not unique to Loy's writing; for instance, Gertrude Stein throws up similar narrative obstacles in *Everybody's Autobiography*. Loy's and Woolf's autobiographical writings also merit comparison in the ways both authors construct and subsequently reflect on their selves. It is unclear whether Woolf intended to publish her memoir 'Sketch of the Past', which she began writing in April 1939. The narrative breaks off after her last entry, which dates from November 1940, four months before her death.[65] 'Sketch' recounts her family life, childhood and early adolescence in Victorian London society. Memories of the Stephen family's residence in Hyde Park Gate, of the deaths of Woolf's mother and half-sister figure centrally in her reminiscences. Beyond this, Woolf addresses the problematic nature of memoir writing as she attempts to formulate her own life story. A childhood memory of St Ives and of 'hearing the waves breaking, one, two, one, two, and sending a splash of water over the beach . . . ' gives way to Woolf's self-interrogation, 'Who was I then?' The writing self intercedes:

> I could spend hours trying to write [the memory of St Ives] as it should
> be written, in order to give the feeling which is even at this moment
> very strong in me. But I should fail (unless I had some wonderful luck);
> I dare say I should only succeed in having the luck if I had begun by
> describing Virginia herself.
>
> Here I come to one of the memoir writer's difficulties—one of the
> reasons why, though I read so many, so many are failures. They leave
> out the person to whom things happened. The reason is that it is so
> difficult to describe any human being.[66]

At the beginning of 'Sketch', Woolf states that she is in the process of
writing a biography of Roger Fry. The difficulty of describing another
human being and potentially failing to compose a life story therefore
shadows Woolf's self-conscious treatment of her own transcribed
memories. She begins her narrative by being unable to 'describ[e]
Virginia', and subsequently draws attention to this failure by
concluding that she does not know how much the details of her birth
and parentage 'made [her] feel what [she] felt in the nursery at St
Ives'. Failure diverts the narrative from its recollections and 'Sketch'
obsessively questions the accuracy of those feelings that it brings into
the present:

> 2nd of May . . . I write the date, because I think that I have discovered
> a possible form for these notes. That is, to make them include the
> present—at least enough of the present to serve as platform to stand
> upon. It would be interesting to make the two people, I now, I then,
> come out in contrast. And further, this past is much affected by the
> present moment. What I write today I should not write in a year's
> time.[67]

In 1939–40, Woolf's critique of Victorian society, couched in exami-
nations of the character of family members, is more evident than in
her earlier memoir, 'Reminiscences' (1908). Most likely at the time
'Sketch' was written the popular image of a strictly regimented
moral and social Victorian order had solidified. By the late 1930s,
Woolf's conception of the past has been categorized by the present
moment and a gradual historicizing of the Victorian and Edwardian
eras in the public imagination.[68] It appears that the success of
memoir relies partly on sensing the differences between one's identity within the moments of one's life, of contrasting the 'I now' and

the 'I then'. Woolf elaborates on sorting through the experiences of past selves:

> Perhaps this is the strongest pleasure known to me. It is the rapture I get when in writing I seem to be discovering what belongs to what; making a scene come right; making a character come together. From this I reach what I might call a philosophy; at any rate it is a constant idea of mine; that behind the cotton wool is hidden a pattern; that we—I mean all human beings—are connected with this; that the whole world is a work of art; that we are parts of the work of art.[69]

'The cotton wool' refers to the unremembered, mundane daily activity that makes up what she argues is most of one's life. She contrasts this nondescript living with 'moments of being' that are intensely felt, and intensely recalled exceptional moments, which give one a 'sudden violent shock'.[70] If we compare Woolf's idea of a connective 'hidden pattern' with Loy's unifying concept of the electrolife it becomes evident that it is not one's uniqueness that matters to Loy and Woolf. Instead, it seems that memoir shows how one conceives of (and indeed lives) his or her own life according to a common human model. In fact, it would be impossible to discern which is imposed on the other, whether it is the idea of a life that shapes experience or if all lives have inbuilt their own pattern through which they come to exist. Yet the idea of a continuum, of a consistent pattern, is ruptured within and by Woolf's and Loy's acts of writing. Reaching for the work of art that is humanity alternates in these memoirs with the intensity of personal reflection. This tension for Loy was the force of the Hurry—validating existence through writing, fighting death through proving existence, and postulating historical selves.

Loy suggests that in composing her own story she is improving the course of human history, and she contends in a letter to Mabel Dodge dated February 1920:

> I have seen and experienced so much and such hitherto undiscovered kinds of people and circumstances—that I can see nothing but the world as a whole—and the only thing that counts is the psychology of the whole thing—and everyone is framing polite fiction about it.[71]

Again Loy depicts herself as the modern saint whose responsibility is to recount her sufferings for the benefit of the world. She reduces the broadness of her world vision and its psychology to the individual in the same way that she reinterprets Christ's love and sacrifice. Yet she cannot avoid the fact that her message is too late. By the late 1940s, when 'Hurry' was most likely written, Loy had dropped out of the artistic circles of New York and more or less ceased to publish poetry. Her only published novel *Insel* (ca. 1936–1940s), a Künstlerroman based on Loy's friendship with the German surrealist painter Richard Oelze, was at one time meant to be part of 'Islands'.[72] Published posthumously in 1991, *Insel* is a meditation on the failure of the avant-garde to prophesy or prevent the approaching reality of war. As a potential end to 'Islands' it challenges Loy's tense optimism in 'Hurry'. If she is not arguing that art is the most essential form of intercommunication then why did she revise and edit out her autobiographies into one narrative? Why bring them together in the late 1940s? Loy suggests that it is to relieve 'a not uncommon anxiety to produce proof of having, oneself, existence'.[73] However, each of Loy's revisions dismisses and refigures prevailing conceptions of the modern, not simply in terms of the future (the modern as prophetic) but in terms also of the past. Loy's evocation of modernity is not limited to a rejection of the past; rather, she sees the modern autobiography as an unfinished project, and one that must remain 'unfinishing' and 'intermittent'. For Loy, revising the voice of the past, and thereby signalling a break into which the modern can be temporarily ascribed, is part of the process of modernity.

Notes

[1] Mina Loy, 'Notes on Metaphysics', n.d., Mina Loy Papers, YCAL MSS 6, fol. 191, unnumbered pages.

[2] Ibid.

[3] Ibid.

[4] Ibid.

[5] Scholarly work that has addressed Loy's use of Jewish mythology includes the following: Rachel Blau DuPlessis, *Genders, Races and Religious Cultures in Modern American Poetry* (Cambridge: Cambridge University Press, 2001); Amy Feinstein, 'Goy Interrupted: Mina Loy's Unfinished Novel and Mongrel Jewish Fiction', *Modern Fiction Studies* 51 no. 2 (Summer 2005).

[6] Mina Loy, 'History of Religion and Eros', n.d., YCAL MSS 6, fols. 158–159, unnumbered handwritten pages.

7 After the 1930s Loy published fewer poems and began to write voluminous versions of autobiographical prose. Only one of the seven complete and semi-complete drafts she wrote has been published in its entirety. This novel *Insel*, published in 1991, was written during the late 1930s and 1940s. The other texts exist in multiple manuscript versions and are contained in six of the eight boxes of Loy's papers at Yale University's Beinecke Rare Book and Manuscript Library. The other two boxes hold her poems and drawings, and many of her prose manuscripts are missing whole sequences of pages.

8 Loy, 'Notes on Metaphysics', n.d., YCAL MSS 6, fol. 191. Loy has drawn a diagram of the 'materialist' and the 'mystic' bodies. In her drawing of the 'materialist', 'rays of awareness' descend from above and are absorbed within the body. In the 'mystic' drawing, these rays projected back up and outwards from the body, as if it were a mirror of the divine. Her drawings suggest that the 'mystic' receives and reflects creative forces from God and thereby becomes god-like. Loy's figure of the 'materialist' merely consumes and destroys these forces.

9 Joella and Herbert Bayer were married in 1944.

10 Amanda Porterfield, *Healing in the History of Christianity* (Oxford: Oxford University Press, 2005), 163.

11 Ibid. Porterfield's book provides an extensive account of electric healing practices within Pentecostalism and Mesmerism.

12 Ibid., 177.

13 Mina Loy, 'Being Alive', n.d., YCAL MSS 6, fol. 20, typescript.

14 Mina Loy, 'History of Religion and Eros', n.d., YCAL MSS 6, fol. 158, handwritten page.

15 Mina Loy, 'Conversion', YCAL MSS 6, fol. 153, typescript, 1.

16 F. T. Marinetti, 'Multiplied Man and the Reign of the Machine' (1915), in R.W. Flint and Arthur A. Coppotelli, eds., *Marinetti: Selected Writings*, trans. R.W. Flint (London: Secker & Warburg, 1972), 91.

17 Frederic W.H. Myers, *Human Personality and its Survival of Bodily Death* (London: Longmans and Green, 1903), 1.

18 Mina Loy, Letter to Mabel Dodge, February 1920, Mabel Dodge Luhan Papers, YCAL MSS 196, fol. 664.

19 Ibid., 109.

20 Loy, 'Notes on Metaphysics', n.d., YCAL MSS 6, fol. 191, handwritten page.

21 Ibid.

22 Ibid.

23 Loy, 'History of Religion and Eros', YCAL MSS 6, fol. 159, typescript, 3.

24 Loy, 'Being Alive', YCAL MSS 6, fol. 20, typescript, 2.

25 Porterfield writes: '[John] Wesley viewed electricity as a subtle form of fire pervading and animating the universe, enlivening the air, and running through the blood and nervous system, making the human body "a kind of fire machine" ', 163. She cites John Wesley, 'The Desideratum: or, Electricity Made Plain and Useful' in *The Works of the Rev. John Wesley* (Bristol, 1773), 24: 284–396.

26 Mina Loy, 'Being Alive', YCAL MSS 6, fol. 20, typescript, 7.

27 I quote Bayer's prefatory note to Loy's manuscript of 'The Child and the Parent' in the Introduction. YCAL MSS 6, fols. 11–19.

28 Throughout my discussion of 'Child' and 'Islands' I have referred to what appears to be the most revised typescript as the 'final' draft. In the case of 'Child' this is simpler, fewer drafts exist. 'Islands' however has multiple typescripts. I have followed the archivist's suggestion in choosing the draft that seems most finished, and indeed some of these scripts have Loy's notations to support this.

29 Antonella Francini, 'Mina Loy's *Islands in the Air*: Chapter 1', *Italian Poetry Review* 1 (2006), 236–244.

30 Loy, 'Islands in the Air', 'Hurry', YCAL MSS 6, fol. 58.

31 Mina Loy, 'Islands in the Air (Chapter 1)', *Italian Poetry Review*, 236.

32 Loy, 'Hurry', *Italian Poetry Review*, 238.

33 Ibid., 240.

34 Space does not permit a detailed description of 'The Child' and 'Islands' manuscripts. However, paper comparisons and close reading of both texts indicate that 'The Child' predates 'Islands' and that 'Hurry' is a re-reading (and 'Islands' is a re-writing) of 'The Child' manuscript.

35 Loy, 'Islands in the Air (Chapter 1)', *Italian Poetry Review*, 242.

36 It is also possible that 'Child' subsumed sections of 'Goy Israels', though there is no definitive archival proof of this. These two books might have been joined together at one time, and like all of Loy's novels, they describe similar scenes. Even if this is the case, the 'book' of 'Hurry' is not 'Islands', which means that 'Islands' was drafted after 'Hurry' was written.

37 Loy, 'Hurry', *Italian Poetry Review*, 241.

38 Loy, 'Child', 'Chapter Seven, Ladies in an Aviary', YCAL MSS 6, fol. 15, typescript, 15.

39 This is based on a handwritten draft of a chapter outline for 'The Child and the Parent' in Loy's Papers, YCAL MSS 6, fol. 10.

40 Loy, 'Hurry', *Italian Poetry Review*, 236.

41 Ibid., 236. Loy's drawing on the MSS version of 'Hurry' can be found in YCAL MSS 6, fol. 58, typescript, 1.

42 Ibid., 238.

43 Mina Loy, 'Goy Israels', YCAL MSS 6, fols. 27–29, typescript, 37.

44 According to Burke's biography, Loy used a 'show valise' in the 1940s to carry her designs for window displays to various companies in New York. In a sense, Loy's 'valise' in 'Hurry' has two layers of artifice, one is the design within and the other is the valise itself, which appears to be fashionable and belong to a woman of business and fashion. *BM*, 390.

45 Mina Loy, 'Hurry', *Italian Poetry Review*, 238.

46 Loy, 'Goy Israels', YCAL MSS 6, fols. 27–30, typescript, 63b.

47 Roger Conover, 'Introduction', in *LLB II*, xii.

48 Mina Loy, 'Hurry', *Italian Poetry Review*, 241.

49 Ibid.

50 Mina Loy, 'Hurry', 'Islands in the Air', YCAL MSS 6, fol. 70.

51 Mina Loy, 'Chapter Two, The Bird Alights', 'Islands', YCAL MSS 6, fol. 59, typescript, 9. Also 'Chapter One, The Bird Alights', 'Child', YCAL MSS 6, fol. 59, typescript, 1–5.

52 Mina Loy, 'Chapter Three, The Beginning of the World', 'Islands', YCAL MSS 6, fol. 60, p. 12.

53 Ibid.

54 Mina Loy, 'Chapter Four, The Accident', 'Islands', YCAL MSS 6, fol. 61, 18–22. Also 'Chapter Three, Arrival on the Scene of an Accident', 'Child', YCAL MSS 6, fol. 12, 18–24.

55 Mina Loy, 'Chapter IV, Arrival on the Scene of an Accident', 'The Child and the Parent', YCAL MSS 6, fol. 12, 23.

56 After Arthur Cravan's disappearance in 1918, Loy wrote several poems about her loss: 'The Dead' (1919), 'Mexican Desert' (1919–1920), 'Perlun' (1921) and 'The Widow's Jazz' (1927), among others.

57 Mina Loy, 'Hurry', YCAL MSS 6, fol. 58. (See the verso of the handwritten draft page).

58 Mina Loy, 'Islands', n.d., YCAL MSS 6, fol. 71, page fragment.

59 Laura Marcus, *Auto/biographical Discourses: Theory, Criticism, Practice* (Manchester: Manchester University Press, 1994), 90.

60 Ibid., 106–7.

61 Edmund Gosse, *Father and Son*, ed. Peter Abbs (London: Penguin Books, 1983). Originally published in 1907.

62 Peter Abbs, 'Introduction', in *Father and Son*, 9.

63 Gosse, *Father and Son*, 251.

64 Ibid., 33.

[65] Jeanne Schulkind, 'Sketch of the Past, Editor's Note', in Jeanne Schulkind, ed., *Moments of Being* (London: Pimlico, 2002), 176–8.

[66] Virginia Woolf, 'Sketch of the Past', in *Moments of Being*, 79.

[67] Ibid., 78, 79, 87.

[68] In 'Sketch of the Past', Woolf refers to the preceding generation as the 'Victorian age'; this suggests that temporally she is at enough of a distance from it to conceive of that time period as socially and historically distinct from the present. One example of this is: 'The patriarchal society of the Victorian age was in full swing in our drawing room'. See Woolf, *Moments of Being*, 154.

[69] Woolf, 'Sketch of the Past', 85.

[70] Ibid., 84.

[71] Mina Loy, Letter to Mabel Dodge, February 1920, Mabel Dodge Luhan Papers, YCAL MSS 196, fol. 664.

[72] Roger Conover's foreword to *Insel* states that this is the case. See *I*, 9. Marisa Januzzi also provides an extensive description of Loy's publication history, including details about her attempts to publish Insel as part of 'Islands in the Air'. See Marisa Januzzi, '"Reconstru[ing] Scar[s]": Mina Loy and the Matter of Modernist Poetics' [PhD diss., Columbia University, 1997], 124–5.

[73] Mina Loy, 'Hurry', *Italian Poetry Review*, 241.

Rhythm, Self and Jazz in Mina Loy's Poetry

Andrew Michael Roberts

In her book, *Autobiographics: A Feminist Theory of Women's Self-Representation*, Leigh Gilmore discusses the way in which the 'practice and criticism of autobiography' have become sites for 'the struggle for the meaning of both gender and genre'. She describes as follows the spectrum of theoretical positions in the interpretation of autobiography:

> At one end of the spectrum of interpretation, a poststructuralist position developed through deconstruction reads autobiography tropologically and construes the self as an effect of language, a textual construction, the figuration of what we call identity. At the other, a feminist position grounds autobiographical form and meaning in the experiences of the women who write autobiography and looks to women's lives for the framework to understand self-representational texts.[1]

Both ends of this spectrum are strongly represented in the critical debate about Loy's poetry, and both ends find much support in that poetry itself. Loy's modernist and avant-garde techniques, the foregrounding of textuality and materiality by her poetic texts, her pervasive irony of style and interrogation of subjectivity, all encourage us to adopt a deconstructive model of the subject in reading her work; indeed to see that work as a prescient precursor of the postmodern textualization of the subject. Yet we are also led, almost irresistibly, to read that work in term of her rich and fascinating biography, and to read her very manipulations of the poetic subject as strategies for asserting the voice of her own female experience against the numerous patriarchal or other domineering constraints on that identity which are apparent in the early part of that biography, from her

Victorian parents to her first husband and her Futurist lovers. More widely, her ironic manoeuvres around the idea of the self seem a form of resistance to the absence of certain aspects of women's experience from dominant poetic discourses of the time. Leigh Gilmore, it should be said, recognises that 'the analogy to a spectrum supports only one version of the debate', since 'feminist and poststructuralist critical positions [. . .] form, rather, open sets with some shared, or partially shared, figures', and interpretations of Loy are a strong instance of this overlap.[2] Nevertheless, it seems to me that there is an aporia, a potentially productive node of tension, at this point in readings of Loy, and it is this aporia that represents the impetus and starting point of my discussion. I want to explore the paradoxical quality of Loy's literary self-representations—the way in which what Maeera Shreiber and Keith Tuma call Loy's 'signature elusiveness' is created precisely through gestures of biographical and existential self-allusion.[3] Indeed, their phrase encapsulates the paradox neatly— since a signature is a mark of identity, a 'signature elusiveness' simultaneously identifies the self and evades such identification. This leads me towards the possibilities of a historically and biographically situated reading of Loy's poetry, in response to her representation of the self as intrinsically integrated with its cultural, personal and linguistic contexts, and its physical environment, even when that self is in a state of alienation or struggle. More specifically, I suggest that the idea of synchronization (and tension) between cultural, personal, and linguistic rhythms leads Loy to use jazz music as a model for the self. The direction that my argument takes is part of a dialogue with two other critics. An earlier, shorter version of this article was delivered as a conference paper in 2000 and was based around the antithesis of poststructuralist and feminist-autobiographical ways of reading Loy outlined above.[4] In discussion Rachel Potter suggested the need for a way of reading which was more responsive to Loy's own time and understanding, and less based on the imposition of theoretical positions. At the time I could not see how one could avoid such imposition, whether explicit or implicit, and to some extent I still take that view. However, by moving towards an interpretation of the self in accordance with Loy's fragmentary but highly suggestive formulations of rhythmic articulation, I hope to move in the right direction. Tim Hancock has argued for the importance of 'historicist elucidation' of Loy's work, based around attention to the biographical and cultural sources and context of Loy's work; a project which he links to Jerome McGann's championing of an understanding of poems as embodied processes, embedded in 'historical particulars'.[5] In my own previous work on Loy I have pursued the question of the highly embodied nature of her work and thought, as well as exploring its specific historical locations.[6] Hancock's connection between the physicality of her imagination and writing, and a focus on 'historical particulars' seems to me to carry forward the discussion of Loy in a valuable direction, responsive to embodiment in a way which avoids reification of 'the body' as theme, and responsive to historical / biographical details in a way which avoids reducing the meaning of the poem to its occasion.[7]

To read Loy's poems in terms of the practices and theory of autobiography might seem to beg the notorious key questions around the self, persona and impersonality in modernist writing—were it not that the theorizing of autobiography itself now embraces (as Gilmore's comment shows) issues of textuality and discursive construction, so that to read modernist poetry as autobiography is only to raise those questions in another, equally acute form (and, I hope, a form especially pertinent to Loy). As Laura Marcus comments:

> With the rise of deconstruction, autobiographical critics [. . .] could [. . .] reject the paths taken by post-structuralist and deconstructive critics, [and] reassert the essential irreducibility of subjectivity and the absolute value of subjectivism [. . .] [or] they could take the deconstructionist turn and use autobiography as an exemplary instance of the impossibility of self-presence, the radical split between the self that writes and the self that is written, and the crucial role of language in the constitution of the subject.[8]

As an instance of the way these interpretative dualities have introduced certain instabilities into the critical discourse around Loy's work, one might cite two comments from her biographer and interpreter, Carolyn Burke. In the introduction to her biography of Loy, Burke, who takes an early Loy memory of light seen through coloured glass as a sort of key to her psychology, suggests that '[i]n some ways, Mina put poems together as one would assemble a stained-glass window: her true self is found in the shimmer of light on color' (*BM* viii). Here, though the image (in a rather vague way) suggests collage and oblique self-representation, the conclusion implies the essentialist idea of the poem as home of the 'true self'. Yet elsewhere Burke contrasts the lyric poetry of self (consistently confessional, homogeneous, integrated, seeking wholeness) with the poetry of the subject (deploying a persona, fictive, unstable, taking up positions in language). She then argues that Loy is a paradigmatic case of female modernism, by virtue of her use of both, where near-biographical 'revelation' itself becomes one among several 'supposed persons'.[9] As a further instance of how Loy's work destabilizes critical discourse, Eric Murphy Selinger, in a discussion of Loy's satirical treatment of love in *Love Songs to Joannes*, points to 'the whittling away of the lover's selfhood [. . .] by modern psychologies', instancing William James's deconstruction of 'the self into four component selves'. Yet in connection with the possible allusion to an abortion in the poem, he claims that 'the impact of the loss is unmistakable: not a deconstruction of the self into Jamesian or Freudian component parts, but its evisceration, its hollowing into a "round vacuum / Dilating with my breath"', going on to interpret this loss as 'a deep wound to the speaker's sense of self'.[10] We have, in turn, the self as philosophically deconstructed, as physically eviscerated and as psychically wounded. The trajectory of Loy's poetry seems to require these disparate modes of explanation.

One might start to explore the question with that phrase 'signature elusiveness' deployed by Shreiber and Tuma, for Loy's name was a focus for her games of identity-shifting, which have been extensively discussed.[11] It is worth pointing out, though, how much Loy's name-changing (in life, but primarily in her poetry), point towards both ends of that spectrum. The 'Gina' and 'Miovanni' of 'The Effectual Marriage' are scarcely hard to decode as Mina and Giovanni Papini, even if the relationship portrayed may condense elements of Loy's relations with her first husband, and perhaps draw on aspects of her parents' marriage.[12] In other words, such transparent shiftings invite a reading as *roman a clef*; like the 'Lord S—' of Augustan satire, they invite recognition. Yet the cumulative effect of Loy's Ginas and Imna Olys, her Loys and Lowys, is to foreground the materiality of the name, making it part of what Marjorie Perloff describes as her poetry's structural principle, a 'network of rhyming, chiming, chanting and punning'.[13] Susan Gilmore, in her discussion of the anagrammatic elements of Loy's poetry, tends towards the deconstructive view of identity in that she draws on Jonathan Culler's account of Saussure's theory of anagrams, as resistant to logocentrism.[14] Susan Gilmore's conclusion grasps at one of those overlaps between the feminist and deconstructive positions outlined by Leigh Gilmore, when the former argues that Loy could not stand outside culture (because no one can), but could not happily rest her identity within the oppressive discourses with which she grew up, so that 'through anagrammatic tropes, Loy asserts the barely concealed secret-agency of one who can pass but who refuses to disappear'.[15] Gilmore suggests that Loy's poetic name-changings, 'point back to an earlier moment of erasure', relating to her troubled racial and psychological identification with her father in 'Anglo-Mongrels and the Rose', so that such changes may show subjectivity at risk as much as subjectivity reinvented. Certainly some theories of autobiography have given primal importance to the name. Laura Marcus cites Philippe Lejeune's claim, based on theories of language acquisition, that 'the individual person and his [sic] discourse are connected to each other through the personal name, even before they are connected by the first person', and that 'the deep subject of autobiography is the proper name'. Marcus notes Lejeune's inattention to questions of gender, and quotes Gilbert and Gubar's stress on the problematic nature of the proper name for women in Western culture, a consideration that certainly applied to Loy. Lejeune suggests that the acquisition of the proper name is 'as important as the "mirror stage"'. [16] If we accept the idea of the proper name as predating the 'I', then Loy's self-renaming as Ova in 'Anglo-Mongrels and the Rose' could certainly be read as a radical gesture of return, to an early moment where the risking of self and the reinvention of self would be hardly separable; a fictional self-reshaping 'ab ovo' or from the (missing) beginning. Since 'Ova' is the plural of the Latin word for egg, this infant version of Mina may partake of the multiplicity evoked in 'Giovanni Franchi', as:

> The threewomen   who all walked
> In   the same dress (*LLB II* 27)

The gaps in those lines (which cannot readily be heard, and need rather to be seen on the page) are as important to its textual dispersion of the self as the explicit idea of the multiple self. Leigh Gilmore refers to Gertrude Stein's discovery that 'representing oneself to oneself and to others creates enough discursive spacing to allow the autobiographer to see the discontinuities in "identity" and to construe its representation as a problem in writing'.[17] Loy's distinctive typography and layout creates such a discursive spacing in a very literal sense. Drawing the reader's attention to the materiality of the page, Loy's spacing foregrounds the signifier; it also interrupts the illusions of 'voice', that trope so closely tied to ideas of the poetic subject, precisely because the gaps cannot really be 'spoken'. The ending of 'The Effectual Marriage' displaces a reading grounded in Loy as speaking subject, though in a different way, with the comment in parenthesis: '(This narrative halted when I learned that the house which inspired it was the home of a mad woman).' (*LLB II* 39) Here the reader who has taken the poem autobiographically is wrong footed, left heading off in the wrong direction while Mina and Gina have both adroitly disappeared. The critical impulse to unification, to the generation of coherent readings, often leads us astray with Loy. Her discontinuities, instabilities and gestures of evasion are too radical to allow even of a consistently discontinuous self: her poetry occupies different points on that spectrum simultaneously. This radical discontinuity is also spaced out across genre difference: notably her various generic varieties of autobiography: 'Islands in the Air'; 'Anglo-Mongrels and the Rose'; 'Colossus'; fragments such as those collated by Roger Conover into 'Notes on Existence' and 'Notes on Childhood'; the lyric poems which give us glimpses of moments of her own life (*LLB I*, 111–75, 312–13, 314). A certain chronological pattern may be suggested, in which Loy's earlier work of 1914 to 1923, including poems such as 'The Effectual Marriage', shows the most radical and acerbic dispersals of self, while 'Anglo-Mongrels and the Rose' (1923) represents a transitional text (at once autobiographical and a critique of autobiography), following which works such as 'Modern Poetry' (1925) and 'The Widow's Jazz' (1927) show more interest in the self as locus of energy.[18] Any such suggestion remains very tentative, however, not least because of the uncertain dates of composition of many of these works.

I want to consider the way in which 'Anglo-Mongrels' represents the origins of the self, since the tracing of origins is so crucial to any unifying or 'authentic' discourse of the self. In going back before the birth of Ova, and beginning with 'Exodus', and in ending with 'The Social Status of Exodus', the poem, like *Tristram Shandy*, searches for an origin before the origin in a way which tends to unsettled the idea of origin rather than confirm it. This is especially so since, as Marjorie Perloff points out, the portrait of Loy's father 'seems to accept all the anti-Semitic stereotypes of her time and place'.[19] Certainly the narrative of Exodus and of Ada offers, as the title of the sequence implies, a potentially reductive narrative of identity as the product of racially-determined characteristics inflected by culture and experience. But Loy offers a discourse of racial identity *alongside* other, alternative discourses, of the unconscious, the soul, the body and the socially-constructed identity, in a way which ultimately does not privilege any one of these incommensurable narratives of the self. Thus, in 'Ada Gives Birth to Ova' we begin with the body as material object— 'A clotty bulk of bifurcate fat' (130)—followed by the body as mysterious fusion: 'A breathing baby / mystero-chemico Nemesis' (*LLB I* 130, 131). Then we get an abstract Cartesian self:

> The isolate consciousness
> projected   from back of time and space
> pacing its padded cell (*LLB I* 131)

This is followed by a Christian, ascetic and anti-corporeal rhetorical dualism of the soul trapped in the denigrated body:

> The soul
> apprenticed to the butcher business
> [. . .]
> A dim inheritor
> of this undeniable flesh (*LLB I* 131)

Then the discourse of racial determinism is evoked:

> The destinies
> Genii
> of traditional
> Israel and of Albion
> push on its ominous pillow
> its racial birthrights (*LLB I* 131)

In 'Ova Begins to Take Notice' we have a Winnicottian description of the infant self as 'A faggot of instincts' (*LLB I* 135), followed by a description of Ova's evolving sensibility in humanist / aesthetic terms:[20]

> Her consciousness
> [. . .]
> quickens
> to colour-thrusts
> of the quintessant light (*LLB I* 136)

Freudian and object-relations theories are suggested by the 'crimson
ball' which 'rolls / into non-being' and by the following lines:

> Her entity
> she projects
> into these sudden colours
> for self-identification (*LLB I* 137)

'Ova, Among the Neighbours' offers a mystical account of the self,
even if modified by the irony of tone:

> (The drama of)
> a human consciousness
> (played to the inattentive audience
> of the Infinite)
> gyrates
> on the ego-axis
> intoxicates
> with the cosmic
> proposition of being IT (*LLB I* 152)

But this cosmic fantasy is undermined by 'the inconsiderate /
competitional brunt / of its similars', before being followed by a
Foucauldian or Althusserian statement: 'personality / being mostly
/ a microcosmic / replica / of institutions' (*LLB I* 152, 153). The critical impulse to unification which have I mentioned leads to interpretations of the poem that privilege one or more of these
competing discourses. Carolyn Burke reads 'Ada Gives Birth to Ova'
in terms of a unified 'imaginative metaphysics' in which 'the soul
acquires individuation by being trapped in its body' (*BM* 351). Keith
Tuma argues that Loy uses the Freudian 'discourse of instinct' to
articulate her own brand of Christianity, and sees the sequence as
thereby 'transcending' autobiography.[21] Elisabeth A. Frost describes
Loy as 'sometimes seeming to subscribe to [. . .] social-radical eugenics', but as ultimately disavowing them to 'forge [. . .] her own idiosyncratic doctrines, merging the influences of psychology with
questions of race and gender'.[22] Perhaps all such attempts to read
Loy's self-representation in terms of her subscription to or modification of existing discourses of the self, however locally revealing,
risk occluding the very incommensurability of the models she
deploys, and her refusal to resolve that incommensurability into

any 'metaphysics'. Perhaps we need to read the spaces between these discourses, just as we need to read the spaces in Loy's lineation. One could make a parallel argument concerning Loy's use of the body, which involves a Cixous-like celebration of the grounding of women's experience in the body but also a Christian sense of the body as husk and an ironic / feminist sense of it as trap.

'Anglo-Mongrels' has certain features of the bildungsroman or, more specifically, the *Künstlerroman*, in itself a highly teleological and self-confirming form, in that it explains its own existence, as the product of the artistic mind the development of which it charts. The equivalent work by Loy's fellow Parisian expatriate, Joyce's *A Portrait of the Artist as a Young Man*, ends in archetypal fashion with the moment of impending escape, a moment which is also a return, since Joyce's persona is about to escape from Dublin, but perhaps, like Joyce himself, in order to spend the rest of his life writing about it. 'Anglo-Mongrels', as Susan Gilmore notes, doesn't reach the *Künstlerroman* conclusion, being 'constituted, instead, by Ova's repeated attempts to run away from home'. 'Though her efforts to escape are continually foiled', notes Gilmore, 'the circular shape of her wanderings and the poem's overall non-linear structure enacts Ova's resistance to narrative in general [. . .] [especially her parents'] narratives of cultural and domestic assimilation'.[23] Circular wanderings and a wish to escape are features that Loy's protagonist shares with Joyce's, but Loy's poem gestures towards departures without returns. Loy emphatically did not spend the rest of her life writing about London, England, or her parents, and if her poem does not show her escape, that escape seems ultimately to have been a more complete one than Joyce's. As Leigh Gilmore writes:

> The traditional development of the male autobiographical self begins in relationship (to a person, a family, a place) but develops into an understanding of his separateness from others, the nonidentical correspondence of relationship, the self-identical foundation of the proper name. Thus the autobiographical self closes the hermeneutic circle on others and rests on the mimesis of the self as self-naming and self-named, where identity has its meaning in the identical relationship between self and name.[24]

Gilmore contrasts this with *Zami*, the autobiographical work of Audre Lorde (who, like Loy, begins by changing the spelling of her name). *Zami*, Gilmore argues:

> pulls at the coherence of autobiography, refuses the identity of its name, constructs and claims a subject position that renders genre and gender codes unintelligible by looking to other textual forms for self-representation and other geographies for identity [. . .] the ontological status of the autobiographical self is everywhere questioned and, ultimately, nowhere bound for too long.[25]

Like *A Portrait*, 'Anglo-Mongrels' begins with the infant self, but whereas Joyce attempts a certain imitation of an infant language, or of parents addressing an infant ('He was baby tuckoo. The moocow came down the road'), Loy goes to the opposite stylistic extreme with her mannered, pseudo-technical diction:[26]

> (The incontinent
> exudes into involuntary
> retention
> Uncouth conception of the incalculable) (*LLB I* 131)

Joyce's trajectory of style points towards his ultimate escape from the narrated instance (the child self, which is the 'I' observed and analysed by the text) into the narrating instance (the self-observing artist, which is the 'I' that organises the narrative), but for Loy the two are, from the outset, held far apart by the irony of her style. Loy's style holds her past self at a distance and does not imply a teleological link, a reunification of narrating and narrated selves. We might see this as Loy protecting herself from her past; if the *Künstlerroman* is a form of conversion narrative (the conversion of the traumas of childhood into the material of art), then it is subject to the risk described by Laura Marcus 'that in the process of confession, the present "reformed" self will be overwhelmed by the past it ostensibly seeks to put behind itself'.[27] In refusing developmental narrative, as well as by the irony of style, 'Anglo-Mongrels' perhaps holds this risk at bay. Loy protects herself from her past, because Ova, her past childhood self, is not her. In 'Illumination', Ova, alone in the garden, experiences an epiphany in which her consciousness escapes from the body. This is a rare moment in Loy's writing (which in general persistently embodies the self):

Ova is standing
alone in the garden

The high skies
have come gently upon her
and all their
steadfast light is shining out of her

She is conscious
not through her body but through space

This saint's prize
this indissoluble bliss
to be carried like a forgetfulness
into the long nightmare (*LLB I* 163–4)

As Susan Gilmore observes, Loy here approaches the very different sensibility of T.S. Eliot: '"Illumination" [. . .] may be Loy's equivalent of an Eliotic "still point" [. . .] the motif of the child in the garden functions, here, as an augur of rejuvenation'.[28] In Loy's paradoxical formulation, the child is endowed with a prized faculty of escape, to help her through the 'nightmare' (her childhood or her life?). This faculty is based on the memory of a moment of forgetfulness (can one remember forgetfulness?); or, more precisely, it is a memory which is 'carried *like* a forgetfulness' (how does one carry a forgetfulness — not in the memory, presumably, but where then?). The escape might be thought of, either as an escape from the self, or an escape into the self, since the light of the 'high skies' is shining, not into Ova, like a religious transfiguration, but out of her, and since her consciousness seems to escape her body but remains consciousness. The passage seems to suspend the category of self, yet its play of absence and presence, remembering and forgetting, might also suggest Eliot's grand aphorism: 'time is no healer: the patient is no longer here'.[29] In the first fragment of 'Notes on Existence' (Roger Conover's title for what one might read as an autobiography without a subject), we find another evocation of an escape from or to the self:

> It matters not that in our own location we may have travelled a million miles in that desolate dimension—inwards. Our apparent person, which marks the confines of the ego, though seemingly what we must *be*, is actually where we leave off. Our apparent person remains a changeless mannequin, arranged by accident. (*LLB I*, 312)

In this geography of the self, huge spaces open up invisibly, under the cover of a 'mannequin', just as Loy's lineation, her generic multiplicity (not only within literature, but across other forms and activities, such as art and fashion), even her biographical travels, open up spaces across which self-representations are dispersed. In *Nomadic Subjects*, Rosi Braidotti proposes a nomadic form of subjectivity, for which 'identity is a retrospective notion':

> The nomad's identity is a map of where s/he has already been [. . .] there is no triumphant *cogito* supervising the contingency of the self [. . .] the nomad's identity is an inventory of traces.[30]

This might usefully be distinguished from the Poundian periplus, the unfolding horizon of constant movement.[31] The periplus has elements in common with the nomadic, since the former may suggest 'a process of discovery which is not governed by a predetermined plan, and instead finds and marks out geographical terrain on the trace of its own progress'.[32] However, as Alan Durant has argued, 'the "periplum" dwells in an ambiguity between a voyage of continuous discovery, and one of conquest and annexation', and the movement of the *Cantos* gives priority to 'the sense of "periplum" which is drawn towards unity and stasis'.[33] Loy's affiliation to various versions of the avant-garde (most notably Italian Futurism) introduces into her prose writings the rhetoric of the relentless conquest of the new.[34] Yet a characteristic mode of her poetry involves a more oblique tracking of her own elusive development through and across such avant-garde positionings. Whereas Pound moves towards the unity of recovered origins, the self represented in Loy's poetry often seems a nomadic one, always moving on into the non-identical.

However, Loy's small number of (surviving) critical and prose works, representing varying stages in the development of her ideas, tend to imply that she valued the expression of the self. The most interesting is perhaps 'Modern Poetry' (1925), where she presents poetic structure and rhythm as expressions of the individuality of the poet:

> The structure of all poetry is the movement that an active individuality makes in expressing itself. Poetic rhythm [. . .] is the chart of a temperament. (*LLB II* 157)

Loy stressed the signature of the poet's mind: 'one can recognise each of the modern poets' work by the gait of their mentality' (LLB II 157), a phrase which Peter Nicholls has intriguingly suggested revised Pound's definition of logopoeia, 'dance of the intelligence among words' (later revised to 'dance of the intellect'). For Nicholls, this reworking of Pound's famous phrase shows Loy reconnecting logopoeia with the body and the mundane:

> Loy substitut[es] for the stylish symbolic dance the more deliberately mundane figure of walking (a 'gait' is also something a horse has). It is not necessary to retrace here the historical progress of the partially disembodied dancer, from Mallarmé through Yeats, to Stevens, to signal the emphatic embodiment conveyed in this one word when read against its Poundian precursor.[35]

Nicholls seems to me absolutely right about Loy's reconnecting of the intellect with the body here, but rather than moving away from dance, the phrase may point to a different form of dance, more fully embodied than that of the symbolic dancer of Mallarmé or Yeats. The next sentence after 'gait of their mentality' modifies that formulation: 'Or rather that the formation of their verses is determined by the spontaneous tempo of their response to life' (LLB II 157–8). 'Tempo' reintroduces the idea of music, and if we are in doubt about what sort of music, that is surely resolved by a later sentence: 'on the baser avenues of Manhattan every voice swings to the triple rhythm of its race, its citizenship and its personality' (LLB II, 159). The swing of the voice, the swing of jazz, and of jazz dance and the swing of a walk, are used here to invoke a relationship between self, body and expressive medium (poetry or music) which provides a much more subtle model than the 'self-expression' which the essay might at first seem to endorse. While reworking a dominant modernist trope that links poetry and music, the jazz context takes that trope away from ideas of the purity or transcendence of music.[36] This 'response to life' is linked to individuality, personality or temperament, but also to collective allegiances and influences ('race' and 'citizenship'), and especially to the collective mood, rhythm and voices of the most hybrid of urban metropolises. Loy begins the essay by linking American poetry and American jazz, both of which Loy claims are 'the reflection' of 'the collective spirit of the modern world' (LLB II 157) and suggests that 'it was inevitable that the renaissance of poetry should proceed out of America' because of the development there of 'a thousand languages', each one

> English enriched and variegated with the grammatical structure and voice-inflection of many races, in novel alloy with the fundamental time-is-money idiom of the United States, discovered by the newspaper cartoonists. (*LLB II* 158)

The second half of this 'alloy', as well as evoking another non 'high' art form (though one which played its part in the American avant-garde of Loy's time), introduces a different measure of time from the 'spontaneous tempo' of the artist's temperament, but as part of a cultural continuity rather than as a contrast.[37]

Here, then, we might find a modernist formulation of the relationship of self to poem, rather different from the masks, personae or impersonality of the canonical figures of Yeats, Pound and Eliot. The poem is intimately connected with the self through rhythm and structure, but that self is articulated in time with cultural and linguistic rhythms. A number of Loy's poems allude to jazz, most notably 'The Widow's Jazz' (*LLB II* 95–7), performed by Loy at Natalie Barney's salon in May 1927.[38] This poem emerges out of the 'negrophilia' of avant-garde Paris in the 1920s and, superficially at least, its evocation of jazz music in association with ideas of the primitive and of unrestrained sexuality, places it squarely within that ambivalent set of attitudes.[39] Michael Borshuk, while noting that Loy's jazz poems 'charge ahead into a sensual, irreverent modern consciousness', comments that

> this progression is founded on a questionable representational scheme that demeans black subjectivity as uncivilized, primitive [. . .] Loy's efforts to become modern too easily regress into a tendency that Sander Gilman has noted among nineteenth-century whites: to view 'the sexuality of the black [. . .] as an icon for deviant sexuality in general'.[40]

Certainly, 'The Widow's Jazz' deploys the discourse of modernist primitivism, in its stereotypical allusion to 'the negro soul', its allusions to 'ecstasy' and the 'primeval'. This is confirmed by some lines from an unpublished Loy poem which are quoted by Marisa Januzzi:

> If we are to preserve our civilisation we must avoid climax
> Keep em jumpin—

> And jazz is such a stimulus to memory—
> right back to when you were nothing but steam in a coal
> forest—
> We can recapitulate our reproductive history—
> through the saxophone—[41]

But Loy, surely already thoroughly modern in 1927 when she first performed 'The Widow's Jazz', differs from the nineteenth-century tendency that Gilman describes in the positive value that she attaches to so-called 'deviant' sexuality, just as the above lines, while buying into the primitivist (and ultimately racist) idea of African-American jazz as historical-evolutionary regression, sees that regression, as Januzzi comments, as necessary to a progressive art.[42] Rather than the nineteenth-century colonialist ideology which demeans black culture as regressive and 'primitive', Loy's attitude is symptomatic of 1920s avant-garde ideas, and in particular the French sensibility of the time which made the 'exotic black other' fashionable.[43] This sensibility was, of course, ambivalent. As Brett A. Berliner comments:

> Negrophobia was a cultural corollary to negrophilism, and exoticism, both the affinity for and repulsion of the black other, would come to serve many cultural needs in France in the 1920s.[44]

The intense, enigmatic, but overpowering sexuality with which Loy's poem, problematically indeed, associates black jazz, is tinged by revulsion and the *frisson* of the transgressive, notably in the opening line ('The white flesh quakes to the negro soul') and in the allusion to the band members as 'The black brute-angels / in their human gloves'. Such imagined sexuality is seen as liberating, if overwhelming, and as transcending the binary of mind or soul and body ('seraph' and 'ass') to touch a universal language of desire; the 'unerring esperanto / of the earth' (*LLB II* 96). Berliner comments that

> [t]he imagined primitive, unleashed on the dance floor, enabled one to transcend the bourgeois world and enter a fantastic Edenic paradise of primal enjoyments and sexual delights. But the primitive also corrupted, ruining the bourgeoisie, even those who had already tasted sin.[45]

Loy, one feels, would not object to the ruination of the bourgeoisie, but she is certainly partly in thrall to its eroticizing imaginings of the black Other as sexualised escape. This must add a profound ambivalence to the ways in which Loy is here representing or imagining her self. In such primitivist fantasies, the process is generally regarded as one in which the 'white' metropolitan subject appropriates a fantasy of the black 'other', in a dynamic driven by desire but tinged by fear or revulsion. A liberation for the white self is imagined in part through a projection of transgressive desires onto the other, where they can be simultaneously (or alternately) idealized and repudiated as primitive. The social world of inter-war Paris, especially in avant-garde circles, could be welcoming to, and appreciative of, African-American and Caribbean musicians and performers. But critics and historians have generally concluded that such positive cultural exchange was very limited.[46] Furthermore, the terms in which it was imagined remained influenced by ideologies of racial hierarchy and fantasies of primitive sexuality. In Loy's poem the imagined transgressive sexuality associated with jazz is a stimulus to, and reminder of, her frustrated desire for her lost husband. The black musicians (and perhaps dancers) prompt her desire, but are not its object. That desire is already thwarted and displaced by the disappearance of its ideal object, Arthur Cravan.

Tim Hancock suggests the value of 'historical particulars' in reading Loy's poems. 'The Widow's Jazz' certainly suggests an experience, on Loy's part, of being in a Paris club or dance hall, responding to a band of (probably) African-American musicians while thinking of Cravan, who had disappeared nearly ten years before the likely composition date of this poem. Maria Januzzi, in her important discussion of the poem, refers to the setting as an 'American nightclub', perhaps because of the second line 'Chicago! Chicago!' (which might, however, refer to the music's source rather than its location). But when Loy read the poem in 1927 she had probably recently composed it, and had been living in Paris since 1923, while the contemporaneous 'Lady Laura in Bohemia' has an explicit setting in Paris Bohemian night-life.[47] There is a recognisable continuity between the tone of 'The Widow's Jazz' and contemporary descriptions of the famous Bal nègre at 33 rue Blomet in the 15th arrondissement:

On finira la nuit au bal de la rue Blomet où, au milieu d'une âcre fumée secouée par les pulsations de la grosse caisse et la grêle du tabour, dans un atmosphère chargée de senteur sauvage, s'ébat en liberté une gaieté tout animale, innocence de paradis terreste nègre que gâtent nos costumes de civilisés et l'intrusion d'Eves trop blanches et de pécheresses trop averties.[48]

We will end the night at the dance hall on the rue Blomet where, in the midst of acrid smoke buffeted by the throbbing of the bass drum and the hailstorm of the snares, in an atmosphere charged with savage scent, a completely animal gaiety freely cavorts, an innocence of black earthly paradise which is spoiled by our civilized dress and the intrusion of Eves too white and of sinners too experienced.[49]

The Bal nègre, 'discovered' for the avant-garde by Robert Desnos in 1926, and subsequently a favourite haunt for artists and writers as well as the rich and famous, seems a likely place for Loy to have visited in the late 20s.[50] It does not, however, seem to be the setting for 'The Widow's Jazz': the music at the Bal nègre was the Martinique biguine, rather than African-American jazz, the dominant instrument being the clarinet, with the four-piece house band at the Bal nègre being completed by piano, banjo and drum.[51] This offers no basis either for the (rather surprising) 'oboes' or the 'monstrous growth of metal trunks' of Loy's poem, the latter suggesting brass, probably trombone (or saxophone). The reference to 'shampooed gigolos' might point to Zelli's (or Zelly's), mentioned in the near-contemporaneous Loy poem 'Lady Laura in Bohemia', a bar which Conover notes was 'frequented by ML and her fellow expatriates in the 1920s'.[52] There is some confusion about the precise location implied by a reference to 'Zelli's', since Joe Zelli, an Italian American jazz impresario owned and managed various Paris clubs at various points.[53] Zelli's is often mentioned in tandem with The Tempo Club (which was above it, or 'upstairs next door', in rue de Caumartin).[54] However, Lynn Haney's biography of Josephine Baker places Zelli's 'high up on rue Florentine, catty-corner to Bricktop's' (another favourite Bohemian haunt). Her description, attributed (at least in part) but without a reference to 'jazz musician Jack O'Brien, who worked there', a makes it sound an odd but disturbingly appropriate place for Loy to be mourning her lost husband:

> Zelli's was a big, raffish, cavernous room lined with tables decorated with B-girls, whose business it was to 'mount the check' [. . .] Zelli's was also populated by sleek-haired, wasp-waisted men who guided women of 'a certain age' up and down the dance floor.

An American hangout, attracting a wide range of regional and social types, Zelli's catered to aging satyrs, Texas ranch hands and peppery Rotarians anxious to embrace the vices they denounced at home.[55]

It is not hard to see why Zelli's should represent a personal 'hell' for 'Lady Laura', the aristocratic but no longer respectable subject of 'Lady Laura in Bohemia'. It was at Zelli's that Josephine Baker met 'Count Pepito de Abatino' (Guisseppi Abatino), working as a gigolo or 'professional dance instructor', who was to become her companion for nine years.[56] Loy's allusion to 'oboes' makes a further possible link to Zelli's. The oboe is certainly rare in jazz and the *All Music Guide to Jazz* notes only one pre-war use: Don Redmon occasionally played the oboe in the Fletcher Henderson Orchestra in the early 20s (but only one oboe; and not in Paris).[57] However, there is historical evidence to support Loy's plural oboes. The memoirs of the clarinettist, Garvin Bushell, describe his travels 'On the Road with *Chocolate Kiddies*'.[58] Bushell, on his own account, was 'one of the only black musicians around who played all the horns — English horn, bassoon, oboe, clarinet, and all that'.[59] *Chocolate Kiddies* was a revue, with Sam Wooding's orchestra of eleven players, accompanying 'more than thirty chorus girls, dancers and comedians', and in 1925 they embarked on a wide-ranging European tour, which lasted until 1927 and in 1926 included spells at the Olympia Theater in Paris, and, later in the year, at the Apollo Theater in Paris. Bushell recalls that 'we'd change horns a lot [. . .] We even did a thing with three oboes (although Gene Sedric and Willie Lewis couldn't do very much on the instrument)'.[60] And, of their spell at the Apollo, he recalls that '[t]hey had a big floorshow, and we were part of it. By 11:30 every night we were back up in the Montmartre. Then we went to Bricktop's, Zelly's, and the Flea Pit— that's where all the black musicians used to hang out with the Arabs, Algerians, and Africans'.[61] One only has to imagine the horn section taking their oboes with them to Zelli's, and indulging in an informal session, to create the combination of gigolos and oboes that marks Loy's poem. That such a scenario is not implausible is apparent from the memories of Leo Arnaud-Vauchant, an early European convert to black American jazz: 'I'd go somewhere to jam. I'd go to the Abbaye Thélème or Zelli's — anywhere. I knew all the musicians so I could go where I wanted'[. . .] I'd go to the little clubs and sometimes there'd be black Americans and we'd play until about five o'clock in the morning'.[62]

For its first twenty-eight lines, then, 'The Widow's Jazz' evokes the scene in a Paris nightclub, with black musicians, gigolos and a clientele, probably of many nationalities, drinking and dancing. Given the fashionability of such places, it is not hard to find visual analogues for Loy's evocation, though the differences are as instructive as the similarities. For example, Georges Goursat Sem's drawing 'Le Bal de la rue Blomet' (drawn to accompany his description, already quoted), shows elegant young white women in short dresses dancing in the embraces of unpleasantly caricatured black men in suits; the racist stereotyping here goes far beyond Loy's allusion to 'brute-angels'.[63] In Paul Colin's Art Deco style lithograph of a jazz band, a black band swings across the bottom of the page with piano, brass and drums while images of modernity (an ocean liner, skyscrapers, the Eiffel Tower, cranes and rooftops, are scattered across the top half of the picture).[64] The message here is primarily the connection of jazz and modernity, but it was also Colin who produced the most famous images of black jazz dance of the era, in his portfolio of lithographs, 'Le Tumulte noir', with its iconic, but highly racially-inflected, images of Josephine Baker.[65] Most prejudicially of all, perhaps, John Souter's painting, 'Breakdown' (1926), 'which depicts a naked blond dancer enraptured by the music of a black saxophone player seated on top of an overturned and broken classical statue' expressed a fear, prevalent in some quarters, of 'the downfall of Western cultural tradition, the undermining of Europe's social fabric, and the ascendancy of Africa to political dominance'.[66] Jody Blake, who describes the picture thus, comments that 'all these cultural, social and political threats were, in the popular imagination, subsumed into the compact but explosive words *jazz* and *l'art nègre*', a remark which enriches our sense of the import of Loy's title, 'The Jazz Widow'.[67] Though Loy's poem draws on such rhetoric, its own rhetoric is not one of cultural decline or racist hostility. An instructive contrast to these ideologically loaded images is the photograph, by Brassaï, *The Bal Nègre, rue Blomet*, 1932, which shows 'a fashionable Parisienne dancing with a Caribbean partner'.[68] The elegant, turbaned white woman (with a profile not unlike Loy's) has her eyes closed, and smiles slightly, suggestive of a slightly dreamy pleasure rather than some regressive ecstasy, while her black partner, smartly dressed in dark suit with a handkerchief projecting from the breast pocket, stylish tie and what looks like a good-quality watch, smiles with what seems unfeigned and innocent enjoyment. It would be naïve to suggest that the photo is ideology-free, or the expressions simply 'natural'; indeed, one might detect in the woman's air of sophisticated abandon and the man's seemingly inno-cent smile, a hint of the classic primitivist binary, and specifically of the image of the 'smiling grand enfant' that Berliner identifies as a dominant representation of the 'nègre'.[69] Yet the superficial impres-sion created by the photograph, which is that of two attractive people enjoying themselves, seems a breath of fresh air after the obsessive racial coding of so much art of the period representing comparable scenes.

In Loy's poem her characteristic ironic detachment is in evidence, generated by mannered and abstract diction, minimal punctuation, ambiguous syntax and fragmenting lineation:

> the pruned contours
> dissolve
> in the brazen shallows of dissonance
> revolving mimes
>
> of the encroaching Eros
> in adolescence (*LLB II* 95)

But such detachment is modified here by the attraction and repul-sion, present in the first line: 'The white flesh quakes to the negro soul', and by the combination of lyric beauty with horrified fascina-tion:

> Haunted by wind instruments
> in groves of grace
>
> the maiden saplings
> slant to the oboes
>
> [. . .]
> The black brute-angels
> in their human gloves
> bellow through a monstrous growth of metal trunks (*LLB II*
>   95–6)

Near the start of the poem, the imagery with which the dancers in the club are described invokes the primitivism so explicit in 'Lady Asterisk':

An uninterpretable wail
stirs in a tangle of pale snakes

to the lethargic ecstasy of steps
backing into primeval goal (*LLB II* 95)

This is followed by two lines which Michael Borshuk describes as 'an exaggerated version of plantation dialect', used 'to assert a binary opposition between the cerebral white and the passionate black'[70]:

White man quit his actin' wise
colored folk hab de moon in dere eyes (*LLB II* 95)

Borshuk associates this use of language with Loy's celebration of American English as 'enriched and variegated with [. . .] the voice-inflection of many races', but sees it as creating 'a communicative bridge between the animal and the celestial in "The Widow's Jazz"', a configuration which contributes to 'an uneasy slippage between jazz and depravity' (*LLB II* 158). Loy's two lines of 'plantation dialect' sound like a quotation, parody or echo, though the source is not apparent. Relevant here, though, is Alfred Appel Jnr's comment on Louis Armstrong's 'greatness as a man and an artist [. . .] predicated on the way he slipped the yoke or prison of show-business negritude and the cult of the primitive, which are often discussed loosely as one and the same thing when in truth they are quite distinctive'.[71] Appel offers many examples of how Armstrong and Fats Waller used but resisted or subverted the language of 'show-business negritude'. It is to that discourse that Loy's lines seem to me to belong and, while there is no evidence that the discourse is being subverted here, nor is it clear that it is being endorsed.

Only in line 29 does the poem become evidently autobiographical, with the mention of Loy's dead husband, Arthur Cravan, as a 'colossal absentee' of the scene. 'Husband', ten lines later, identifies Loy herself as the 'widow' of the title, and the following line marks the first appearance of the first-person pronoun in the poem ('you cuckold me'), the only such pronoun until line 51, five lines from the end of the poem:

as my desire
receded
to the distance of the dead (*LLB II* 97)

This sends us back to the somewhat enigmatic title. What is the relationship between the poem's evocation of jazz and its theme of bereavement and loss? Bearing in mind that, in the twenties, 'jazz' could as easily mean sexual intercourse or orgasm as a type of music, the title provocatively revises the familiar song title, 'The Widow's Lament'.[72] The poem *is* a lament, but one which refuses to see loss, or the situation of a widow, in terms of a respectably sublimated sentimental longing. Both Cravan's embrace of death and Loy's jazz-stimulated longing, are overtly sexualised:

> Husband
> how secretly you cuckold me with death
>
> while this cajoling jazz
> blows with its tropic breath
>
> among the echoes of the flesh (*LLB II* 96)

Yet Loy's desire is as much alienated by the music as expressed by it, since her desire is focused on an absence:

> as my desire
> receded
> to the distance of the dead
>
> searches
> the opaque silence
> of unpeopled space. (*LLB II* 97)

What the 'widow' possesses, and is possessed by, is finally silence and emptiness, the antithesis of the jazz club setting; we are back with 'that desolate dimension—inwards'.

Petrine Archer-Shaw comments that, in the 1920s, jazz in Paris 'attracted a young, urban, bohemian audience that identified the music's syncopated rhythms with its own feelings of anxiety and anarchy', and that jazz:

> [r]epresented the pulse beat of modernity, in particular its speed and urban sense of everything happening at the same time. Jazz thus mirrored modern life's simultaneity, which obliterated a linear sense of time and space.[73]

Loy seems both to identify the rhythms of jazz with her own feel-ings, and to register the estrangement of those feelings: the 'widow's jazz' is both the sensual jazz that evokes her desire and the unheard music of desire that inhabits an empty space, a subjectivity defined in relation to an other who is colossally absent. The poem stages a non-linear subjectivity, a self at once present and absent, a desire at once articulated and inarticulate. Natalie Barney, in the passage in her memoirs where she records Loy's performance of this poem, empha-sises both the physicality of Loy's approach and her 'ethereal [. . .] detachment':

> Mina Loy, with a trainer such as boxers have, exercised and hardened in the solitude of my second floor. This ethereal being, forevermore withdrawn from humanity because of her own evolution, because of shocks she has undergone, needed to get back in touch, if only during the five minutes required to explain to us her detachment and her almost hermetic work.[74]

When Loy came to read 'The Widow's Jazz', it was 'spoken in a dream-like voice, with the air of a somnambulist whom life will no longer succeed in rousing'.[75] The vision of an ethereal, somnambu-list boxer is an arresting one, parallel to the poem's vision of the widow carried away by the jazz into a space far beyond it. Loy's train-ing, like a boxer, for a performance, in itself seems a tribute to Cravan, himself both a boxer and performance artist, who regarded boxing as a performance.[76]

Time, autobiography and subjectivity are, of course, intimately connected. Autobiography constructs (or fails to construct) a coherent sense of a self through a linear narrative that unifies the subject either through teleology — the destination — or retrospect; often a combination of the two. The avant-garde, committed to looking forward, must also look back even if in irony and negation: it must attack what comes before to provide the fuel for its own momentum forward into the future that it hopes to bring about. Loy's nomadism was both literal and psychic: leaving England at the age of 20, she did not become an exile or migrant but, at least for the next 20 years, a nomad, between countries and artistic movements. She evolved, but not in such a way as to offer a teleological pattern: her evolution seemed to withdraw her from humanity, according to Barney. Loy often seems to operate somewhere between Braidotti's idea of nomadic identity ('a map of where s/he has already been') and Pound's periplus, a projection of unfolding horizons. The latter offers the dark as optimistic avant-garde invitation, as in Loy's 'Aphorisms on Futurism':

> BUT the Future is only dark from outside.
> *Leap* into it—and it EXPLODES with *Light* (LLB II 149)

The former records the bleaker, but more human, vision of 'the opaque silence / of unpeopled space', 'the substitute dark' in which the trace of desire 'rolls to the incandescent memory' ('The Widow's Jazz', *LLB II* 97, 96).

What might it mean to use jazz or, more specifically, jazz rhythms, as a way of modelling the self? Such a way of thinking, responding and writing would involve body, movement and expressivity, linking the rhythms of language and the rhythms of physical movement. Loy's poetry and thought consistently work in bodily terms.[77] This is apparent in her address to subjects such as sexual experience and childbirth, in her use of 'unpoetic' terms such as 'mucous membrane' and 'saliva' ('Songs to Joannes', *LLB II* 53), in physicality of metaphor—'Your cities lie digesting in our stomachs' ('The Dead', *LLB II* 72)—, in the hints of eugenics and biological determinism in some of her prose declarations (see Frost), and, strikingly, in Barney's description of her warming up to perform 'The Widow's Jazz'. A number of aspects of Loy's poetry, such as her use of space within lines, lines displaced from the left-hard margin and (in poetry and prose), the use of dashes, while they work in one way as visual effects on the page, can also be taken in indications of how to 'perform' her words. Her sustained irony of tone and diction might also invite an oral delivery. The visual and the aural might seem opposing ways of understanding. But Loy's spaces on the page (visual gaps which can't be heard in performance, or clues to oral delivery which can only be hinted at on the page?) enhance the physicality of the poem, whether through material space on the page or the presence of the breathing body of the poet / performer. Loy does seem to think of self and experience in intensely physical terms and, when she evokes the dualism of body and mind / soul, as in 'The Effectual Marriage', it is with heavy irony:

> Gina and Miovanni   who they were God knows
> They knew   it was important to them
> This being of who they were

They were themselves
Corporeally   transcendentally   consecutively
conjunctively   and they were quite   complete (*LLB II* 36)

If Loy rarely represents the self as estranged from the body, this is perhaps because she represents the self as rhythmically dispersed and articulated across time, language and sequential experience. The modernist cliché of the 'fragmented self' does not seem appropriate here, resting as it does on an underlying idea of a self which ideally exists outside time, but has fallen into time, or a self which ideally moves through time as a coherent agent, but is threatened with disintegration by internal or external forces. Nor do the classic modernist strategies of mask or persona (still less Eliot's grand 'impersonality') suit Loy's self-representation. With reference to the separation of gender from the 'personal mental attitude' in 'Three Moments in Paris' (*LLB II* 15), Peter Nicholls comments that:

> This is quite different from the more conventional 'impersonality' of Moore's work or, indeed, from the *personae* favoured by other modernists, for Loy seems to reject any coherent model of the self as something both imaginary and conventional.[78]

The strategies of mask, persona and impersonality imply a self 'elsewhere'. This self may reside in a transcendent system, as in Yeats (a conception based on the soul), or in a deep structure (a conception linked most obviously to Freud), multiple but coherent by virtue of its structural principles, and hence potentially analysable as a complex whole existing at any given moment. Loy does indeed seem to reject 'any coherent model of the self' if coherence means unified in such a manner. But her sense of the self is rather a sense of process, the movement through time of a subject, existing as a node of experiences, both physical and psychic. The dynamic nature of this 'self process' can present itself as dispersal and disintegration (entropy) or as articulation and formation (energy). But the disintegration is not that of a whole which did, or will exist; nor does the articulation create something permanent; both are different modes of movement through space and time. In Loy's work the space of the page and the time of performance are energized by the rhythms of a jazz self, always in motion.

Notes

[1] Leigh Gilmore, *Autobiographics: A Feminist Theory of Women's Self-Representation* (Ithaca, NY; London: Cornell University Press, 1994), 18.

[2] Ibid., 18.

[3] Maeera Shreiber and Keith Tuma, 'Introduction', in Shreiber and Tuma, eds., 12.

[4] 'Loy's Self-Representation', paper delivered at a symposium on Mina Loy, University of London, Institute of English Studies, March 2000.

[5] Tim Hancock, '"You Couldn't Make it Up": The Love of "Bare Facts" in Mina Loy's Italian Poems', *English: The Journal of the English Association* 54 (Autumn 2004), 192. Hancock quotes from Jerome McGann who states that 'Part of what it means to be human is to have a body, to occupy physical space, and to move in real time. In the same way the products of literature [. . .] are not disembodied processes [. . .] we must pay attention to a variety of historical particulars'. See Jerome McGann, *The Beauty of Inflections: Literary Investigations in Historical Methods and Theory* (Oxford: Clarendon Press, 1985), 95–6.

[6] Andrew Michael Roberts, '"How to Be Happy in Paris": Mina Loy and the Transvaluation of the Body', *Cambridge Quarterly* 27 no. 2 (1998), 129–47.

[7] I am aware of the objection that this is simply to add another critical approach — that of New Historicism — to the theoretical stances of deconstruction and feminist biography already evoked. This leads me back to my initial sense of the inevitability of some sort of underlying theoretical disposition in the discussion of works of the past. I am not seeking to evade that inevitability; rather it is a question of the degree of responsiveness and self-awareness with which we deploy ways of reading and understanding texts of the past.

[8] Laura Marcus, *Auto/biographical Discourses: Theory, Criticism, Practice* (Manchester: Manchester University Press, 1994), 183.

[9] Carolyn Burke, 'Supposed Persons: Modernist Poetry and the Female Subject (a Review Essay)', *Feminist Studies* 11 no.1 (1985), 136.

[10] Eric Murphy Selinger, 'Love in the Time of Melancholia', in Shreiber and Tuma, eds., 29, 32, 33.

[11] See especially Susan Gilmore, 'Imna, Ova, Mongrel, Spy: Anagram and Imposture in the Work of Mina Loy', in Shreiber and Tuma, eds., 271–317; Carolyn Burke, 'What's in a Name? Or, Mina/Myrna/Muna', *PN Review* 135, 27 no. 1 (September– October 2000), 30–2.

[12] Susan Gilmore suggests that 'The Effectual Marriage' 'can be read as a prototype for Loy's portrait of her parents' marriage in *Anglo-Mongrels*. See Susan Gilmore, 284.

[13] Marjorie Perloff, 'English as a "Second" Language: Mina Loy's *Anglo-Mongrels and the Rose*', in Shreiber and Tuma, eds., 136.

[14] Susan Gilmore, 299.

15 Ibid., 302.

16 Marcus, 192.

17 Leigh Gilmore, 16–17.

18 I am indebted to Tim Armstrong for pointing out this pattern and for other helpful comments on a draft of this article.

19 Perloff, 139.

20 Compare Winnicott's description of a new-born baby as an 'armful of anatomy and physiology', with a 'potential for development into a human personality'. See 'Communication Between Infant and Mother, Mother and Infant, Compared and Contrasted' (1968), quoted in Madeleine Davis and David Wallbridge, *Boundary and Space: An Introduction to the Work of D.W. Winnicott* (Harmondsworth: Penguin, 1983), 47.

21 Keith Tuma, 'Mina Loy's "Anglo-Mongrels and the Rose"', in Shreiber and Tuma, eds., *Mina Loy*, 183.

22 Elisabeth Frost, 'Mina Loy's "Mongrel" Poetics', in Shreiber and Tuma, eds., 149, 173.

23 Susan Gilmore, 292.

24 Leigh Gilmore, 29.

25 Ibid., 29.

26 James Joyce, *A Portrait of the Artist as a Young Man* ed. Seamus Deane (London: Penguin, 1992), 3.

27 Marcus, 195.

28 Susan Gilmore, 294.

29 T. S. Eliot, 'The Dry Salvages' III, 'Four Quartets', in *The Complete Poems and Plays of T. S. Eliot* (London: Faber, 1969), 187.

30 Rosi Braidotti, *Nomadic Subjects: Embodiment and Sexual Difference in Contemporary Feminist Theory* (New York: Columbia University Press, 1994), 14.

31 Derived from Hanno's *Periplus*, though Pound often used the word periplum, as in Canto 59: 'periplum, not as land looks on a map / but as sea bord seen by men sailing'. *The Cantos of Ezra Pound*, 4th Collected Edition (London: Faber & Faber, 1987), 324.

32 Alan Durant, *Ezra Pound: Identity in Crisis* (Sussex: Harvester Press, 1981), 47.

33 Ibid., 49.

34 See 'Aphorisms on Futurism', *LLB II*, 149–52.

35 Peter Nicholls, '"Arid Clarity": Ezra Pound, Mina Loy, and Jules Laforgue', in Rachel Potter and Suzanne Hobson, eds, *The Salt Companion to Mina Loy*, 140.

36 See Sally Kilmister, '"Listen in to the Past": Myth, Music and the Unsayable', *Poetry Wales* 32 no. 2 (October 1996), 12–16.

37 For examples of the caricatures of Marius de Zayas, exhibited at Alfred Stieglitz's 291 Gallery in New York in the period 1909–1913, see Steven Watson, *Strange Bedfellows: The First American Avant-Garde* (New York, London and Paris: Abbeville Press, 1991), 76–7.

38 See Conover's notes to 'The Widow's Jazz', *LLB II*, 204.

39 See Petrine Archer-Straw, *Negrophilia: Avant-Garde Paris and Black Culture in the 1920s* (London: Thames and Hudson, 2000); Jody Blake, *Le Tumulte Noir: Modernist Art and Popular Entertainment in Jazz-Age Paris, 1900–1930* (University Park, PA: Pennsylvania University Press, 1999); Brett A. Berliner, *Ambivalent Desire; The Exotic Black Other in Jazz-Age France* (Amherst and Boston: University of Massachusetts Press, 2002).

40 Michael Borshuk, '"A Synthesis of Racial Caress": Hybrid Modernism in the Jazz Poems of William Carlos Williams and Mina Loy', in *William Carlos Williams: A Commemoration*, ed. Ian A. Copestake, (Bern, Switzerland: Peter Lang AG, 2003). Quoted from typescript, 17–18; I am grateful to Michael Borshuk for sending me a copy of this article.

41 Mina Loy, 'Lady Asterisk', Mina Loy Papers, YCAL MSS 6, fol. 163; quoted by Marisa Januzzi in 'Mongrel Rose: the "Unerring Esperanto" of Loy's Poetry', in Shreiber and Tuma, eds., 433.

42 Januzzi, 443. Alex Goody argues that 'rather than a typical modernist exploitative and /or Eurocentric notion of the "primitive" as an unmarked, originary culture [. . .] Loy's work expresses a continuity with, not an appropriation of, African-American Jazz culture'. See 'Gender, Authority and the Speaking Subject, or: Who is Mina Loy?', *How2* 1 no. 5 (March 2001), 40. I suspect it is both a continuity *and* an appropriation. Loy's view of such African-American culture is partly admiring, but she still understands it as 'primitive' rather than just different: indeed, she admires it for that reason.

43 Berliner, 235.

44 Ibid., 235.

45 Ibid., 212.

46 See Berliner, 237–8; Blake, 156–8.

47 Januzzi's own invaluable bibliography describes 'The Widow's Jazz' as a poem which Loy 'had just completed' when she read it in 1927. See Shreiber and Tuma, eds., 524.

48 Sem [Georges Marie Goursat], 'Bars et cabarets de Paris' *Illustration* (7 December 1929), n.p.

49 Whereas Berliner describes a fantasy in which the white bourgeoisie ('even those who had already tasted sin') are corrupted by the primitive, Sem imagines them as corrupting the primitive because they are 'too experienced' as sinners already.

50 Berliner, 206.

51 Ibid.

[52] Roger L. Conover, 'Introduction', *LLB II*, 205. Conover does not give a source for this information.

[53] Joe Zelli seems to have started with 'a clandestine club in rue de Caumartin [. . .] crowded every night, raided several times by the police, and eventually closed'. See William A. Shack, *Harlem in Montmartre: A Paris Jazz Story Between the Great Wars* (Berkeley and London: University of California Press, 2001), 30, 53. Shack notes that '[i]n time Chez Florence was sold to Joe Zelli [. . .] [who] owned and managed several other Parisian clubs, including the Royal Box at 16 Rue Fontaine and the Tempo Club above Zelli's in rue de Caumartin' (30). But Shack also notes that different sources place Chez Florence in different places: either 'in the Théâtre Caumartin at 17 rue de Caumartin, or in rue Pigalle in Montmartre' (30); Shack attributes this information to P.J. Carisella and James W. Ryan, *The Black Swallow of Death* (Boston: Marlbourgh House, 1972), 202.

[54] Chris Goddard, *Jazz Away from Home* (New York and London: Paddington Press Ltd, 1979), 17.

[55] Lynn Haney, *Naked at the Feast: the Biography of Josephine Baker* (1995; London: Robson, 2002), 116.

[56] Haney, 117–18, 120.

[57] *All Music Guide to Jazz*, ed. Vladimir Bogdanov, Chris Woodstra and Stephen Thomas Erlewine, 4th edn (San Francisco: Backbeat Books, 2002), 957.

[58] Garvin Bushell (as told to Mark Tucker), *Jazz From the Beginning* (New York: Da Capo Press, 1998), 54–71.

[59] Bushell, 128.

[60] Ibid., 54, 57.

[61] Ibid., 68.

[62] Goddard, 274.

[63] Drawing by Sem [Georges Marie Goursat], 'Bars et cabarets de Paris'. Berliner argues that this caricature 'playfully subverted metropolitans' Prospero Complex' because 'the negrès were so caricatured that they could not be imagined to have much power or sexual prowess' (213–4), but I find this argument rather unconvincing.

[64] See http://www.npg.si.edu/img2/noir/TN2.jpg [accessed 8 June 2005], from *Le Tumulte Noir: Paul Colin's Jazz Age Portfolio*, an exhibition held at the Smithsonian National Portrait Gallery, 31 January – 14 September 1997. The on-line catalogue notes that '[t]hese lithographs were never given individual titles by the artist. Descriptive titles have been created for the purposes of this exhibition'.

[65] See Paul Colin, *Josephine Baker and la Revue nègre: Paul Colin's Lithographs of Le Tumulte noir in Paris*, 1927 (New York: Harry A. Abrams, 1998).

66 Jody Blake, *Le Tumulte Noir: Modernist Art and Popular Entertainment in Jazz-Age Paris, 1900–1930* (University Park, Pennsylvania: Pennsylvania State University Press, 1999), 89.

67 Ibid., 91.

68 Ibid., 115.

69 Berliner, 236.

70 Borshuk, 8.

71 Alfred Appel Jnr, *Jazz Modernism: From Ellington and Armstrong to Matisse and Joyce* (New York: Alfred A. Knopf, 2002), 37.

72 On the term 'jazz', see Mervyn Cooke and David Horn, eds., *The Cambridge Companion to Jazz* (Cambridge: Cambridge University Press, 2002), 2–3.

73 Archer-Straw, 107, 109.

74 Natalie Clifford Barney, *Adventures of the Mind*, trans. John Spalding Gatton (New York and London: New York University Press, 1992), 158.

75 Barney, 160.

76 Archer-Straw, 49.

77 I have argued elsewhere that Loy 'resisted a masculinist repression or denial of the body'. Roberts, 139. Carolyn Burke suggests that Loy's early poetry 'shows her trying to think through the body'. See 'Becoming Mina Loy', *Women's Studies* 7 (1980), 149.

78 Peter Nicholls, *Modernisms*, 222.

'Arid clarity': Ezra Pound and Mina Loy

Peter Nicholls

To review the connections between Mina Loy and Ezra Pound should be a relatively straightforward matter. There is, after all, no shortage of biographical material on Pound, and we now have Carolyn Burke's *Becoming Modern*, as well as the essays brought together in *Mina Loy: Woman and Poet*.[1] Yet, while Pound's reading of Loy and his support for her work have received a fair amount of comment, the available biographical studies of the two poets tell us suprisingly little about their meetings and intellectual exchanges. Of course, Loy hardly seemed a significant player when Charles Norman and Noel Stock wrote their early books on Pound, but it is slightly surprising to find no mention of her in Humphrey Carpenter's more recent work (and Carpenter certainly has a developed interest in Pound's relations with women, particularly in the early stages of the poet's career).[2] What is even more striking is the absence of any hard information about their meetings in Paris in the early twenties in Carolyn Burke's *Becoming Modern*, especially as she reproduces two photographs of them together (Burke is equally unforthcoming about Loy's encounters with Wyndham Lewis in Paris and London — tantalizing indeed).[3] One can actually glean very little: we know, for example, from Virgil Thomson's autobiography (but not from Burke) that Loy attended the Parisian première of Pound's opera, *The Testament of Villon* in 1926, and she must have heard other arrangements by him because she notes in the recently recovered essay of 1925, 'Modern Poetry', that 'his music was played in Paris',[4] but of the conversations they must have had only one intriguing trace seems to remain: in a 1943 interview, Loy recalled that 'Pound was like a child, and an old professor at the same time. His craze then was endocrine glands. He would talk about it a great deal — very learned discussion. Glands. . . were the latest thing at the time.' Just how illuminating Loy found this it's impossible to know, but it's likely that Pound's often hectoring manner did not appeal. Loy went on: 'He was a sensitive man who didn't think other people were sensitive. One of his friends said he had brought from America the faults of America, and none of the virtues.'[5] (Williams Carlos Williams is the likely source of that last remark.)

There is surprisingly little to go on, then, apart from Pound's isolated comments on Loy which are, with the exception of the 1918 *Little Review* piece on the *Others* anthology, usually brief, but insistent that Loy be considered part of the American vanguard. The 1918 account of Loy and Moore is well-known, for it was there that Pound first produced his account of 'logopoeia', 'a dance of the intelligence among words and ideas and modification of ideas and characters' (in the 1929 'How to Read' the formulation would be slightly modified to 'the dance of the intellect', now the most familiar version).[6] Pound famously aligned the 'arid clarity' he discerned in Loy and Moore with a specifically American modernism. Several months later, in a review section for the magazine *Future*, he wrote of the *Others* anthology again, this time quoting passages from Loy's 'Effectual Marriage' (misremembering — perhaps deliberately?— its title as 'Ineffectual Marriage') and observing that 'Laforgue's influence or some kindred tendency is present in the whimsicalities of Marianne Moore, and of Mina Loy'.[7] Beyond this, we have sporadic comments in letters to the editor of the *Little Review*, Margaret Anderson, which tell us little more than that Pound wanted to retain Loy as a regular contributor, and several remarks in letters to Williams and Moore which argue more forcefully for her prominence in the American literary scene ('is there anyone in America,' he writes to Moore, 'except you, Bill and Mina Loy who can write anything of interest in verse?')[8] Pound, of course, spent parts of 1924 in Italy and settled permanently in Rapallo the following year, thus removing himself from the round of dinners and parties which Loy attended and which Williams enjoyed during his visit to Paris during Pound's absence in 1924.[9] With his attention shifting increasingly to political and economic matters, it is thus surprising to find Pound suddenly returning to Loy's work as late as 1933. The occasion was an open letter from Marinetti to Pound, published in *Il Mare*, the Rapallo paper to which Pound was a frequent contributor during the early thirties. While addressing Pound in a friendly spirit, Marinetti drew a distinction between what he called masculine/heroic and feminine/pessimistic types of writing, noting that some of the writers Pound had been publishing in *Il Mare* unfortunately represented the second tendency. The criticism was enough to prompt Pound to write a long piece in which he paid tribute to the women writers of his generation. Noting first that 'the most valuable part of Anglo-American literature in my half-century has been nursed, nourished, and supported in reviews edited by WOMEN', he went on to affirm the importance of three writers: Mary Butts, Kay Boyle, and Mina Loy. His comment on Loy is as follows: 'MINA LOY holds her position in Anglo-American poetry of my decade, perhaps the most spontaneous, perhaps the most original, a bit absent-minded, who sometimes succeeded and sometimes didn't. It would take an entire article for an adequate discussion.'[10] Whether or not Pound was trying to needle Marinetti by praising the futurist's ex-lover, his comment at this remove in time suggests that Loy's work had made a deep and lasting impression on him. Indeed, he had recently returned to the poem he called 'Ineffectual Marriage', including it in his 1932 anthology *Profile*, a work he described as 'a collection of poems which have stuck in my memory and which may possibly define their epoch'.[11]

These fragmentary comments raise the interesting possibility that, the paternalistic tone of the *Little Review* piece notwithstanding, Pound's discovery of Loy was actually in some way pivotal to the development of his own work. Most critics, of course, have tended to read the influence the other way, drawing comparisons between 'Anglo-Mongels and the Rose' (1923) and the earlier *Hugh Selwyn Mauberley* (1920),[12] but Carolyn Burke for one has suggested that the example of 'logopoeia' in Loy's work allowed him to develop 'a critical theory that could justify and explain' his recently published *Homage to Sextus Propertius*.[13] As far as I know, though, only Reno Odlin in a brief aside in his review of *The Last Lunar Baedeker* has gone so far as to propose that the *style* of *Mauberley* was somehow directly affected by Pound's reading of Loy: 'it must now be plain to everyone where he got the cadences which come off so beautifully toward the end of *Mauberley*' says Odlin.[14] The observation is not developed, but it has confirmed my growing sense of a kind of reciprocal influence at work across these texts of Pound and Loy. Certainly, Pound had been following *Others* magazine before his *Little Review* piece on Loy and Moore (he was an active contributor) and he would have read *Songs to Joannes* there.[15] And while it remains difficult to specify the extent to which Loy and the poets of *Others* impelled him in a new direction, the publication of 'Moeurs Contemporaines' in 1918 made it clear that

Pound was trying to supplement the often coy refinements of his imagist verse with a lighter, more ironic *vers de société*.[16] But the anecdotal observations of 'Moeurs Contemporaines' rarely approached the complex and impacted verbal forms of Loy's *Songs*, and it was not until *Hugh Selwyn Mauberley* that Pound was really able to approximate the 'logopoeic' handling of abstract vocabulary that already made Loy's satirical style so distinctive. Part of the section from 'Effectual Marriage' that Pound reproduced in his review for *Future* seems, in fact, to ghost the cadence and verbal play of *Mauberley*:

> But she was more than that
> Being an incipience   a correlative
> an instigation of the reaction of man
> From the palpable to the transcendent
> Mollescent irritant of his fantasy
> Gina has her use   Being useful
> contentedly conscious
> She flowered in Empyrean
> From which no well-mated woman ever returns (LLB II 36–7)

Loy's use of abstract words like 'incipience', 'correlative' and the soon-to-be-Poundian 'instigation' mimes the shift from 'palpable' to 'transcendent' which for Miovanni/Papini is the ultimate test of Gina/Mina's usefulness. The 'fantasy' is Papini's, though it is ironically undercut as an expression of male privilege by the fact that this is Mina's vocabulary not his. He may like her softness and pliability, but the pseudo-scientific word 'mollescent' reserves to itself the force of ultimately superior judgement, its analytic clarity providing the necessary 'irritant' to this lamely conventional male fantasy. Pound has been criticised for his view that Loy's work displays 'no emotion whatever' and that it demonstrates an 'arid clarity', but in one sense this might seem a valid response to a language which gains its power from its sheer externality or from what Lewis would term the 'external method' of satire.[17] Compare Pound's epitaph for Mauberley:

> A consciousness disjunct,
> Being but this overblotted
> Series
> Of intermittences[18]

The cadence and phrasing definitely recall Loy's 'Being an incipience . . .', and Pound's latinate vocabulary ('disjunct', 'intermittences') simi- larly catches the lazy fantasizing of Mauberley even as it coldly holds the persona at arm's length. If Loy's 'Effectual Marriage' was particu- larly important to Pound (and it was the one poem of hers that he cited repeatedly) it was partly because, as he put it in the *Little Review* piece, 'It has none of the stupidity beloved of the "lyric" enthusiast and the writer and reader who take refuge in scenery description of nature, because they are unable to cope with the human'.[19] The idea of 'cop[ing] with the human' already expresses a Lewisian contempt for the purely 'natural'. 'Art', says Lewis memorably, 'consists . . . in a *mechanizing* of the natural',[20] and the cadence and idiom that Pound develops from Loy offer a way of subordinating psychology to aesthetic form, with this vocabulary, ostensibly so inappropriate to lyric, conducting its own implicit critique of romantic fantasy.

For it is precisely that fantasy that apparently destroys the 'artist's urge' in the second part of Pound's poem and accounts for the hedo- nistic 'drifting' memorialised in Mauberley's epitaph. Hence the coldly 'aesthetic' presentation of the soprano in the final poem, 'Medallion', a part of the sequence which has caused much disagree- ment, with critics still tending to read it as an evocation of artistic impoverishment.[21] Yet there is a crucial intertext for this poem, a review by Pound of a performance given by the soprano Raymonde Collignon on whom the singer in 'Medallion' is generally thought to be modelled. Part of the review is as follows:

> No one has a more keen perception than she has of the difference between art and life; of the necessary scale and proportion required in the presentation of a thing which is not the photograph and wax- cast, but *a re-creation in different and proportional medium*. As long as this diseuse was on stage she was non-human; she was, if you like, a china image. . . .[22]

This argument against mimesis affirms a fundamental principle of Pound's aesthetics, announced as early as the 1911/12 series of arti- cles titled 'I Gather the Limbs of Osiris', where he argues the point in strikingly similar terms:

> There are few fallacies more common than the opinion that poetry should mimic the daily speech. Works of art attract by *a resembling unlikeness*. Colloquial poetry is to the real art as the barber's wax

dummy is to sculpture. In every art I can think of we are damned and clogged by the mimetic. . . .[23]

So whether we like it or not (and most critics have not), Pound does seem to have intended the sequence to end on a high note, with the confusing immediacy of the passion which sets Mauberley drifting temporarily overcome by making the experience of desire one which is thoroughly *mediated* by previous cultural contexts — a move which interestingly inverts Loy's concluding snub to Love as 'the preeminent littérateur' in *Songs to Joannes*. In 'Medallion', the woman becomes an object of desire only in so far as she is cast in a 'different medium' and thereby rendered 'non-human' and thoroughly aesthetic. In repudiating any confusion of what Pound elsewhere calls the 'caressable' with artistic values,[24] he here deviates quite deliberately from the usual idiom of passionate celebration — it is, for example, *the,* not her, 'sleek head' which emerges from the frock, and in the typescript Pound had originally used the very un-erotic 'pate' instead of 'head', the eventual deletion showing, perhaps, that he was unwilling to go as far as Loy in demystifying the romantic body.[25]

If there is, then, some kind of buried dialogue between 'Effectual Marriage' and *Mauberley*, the relation between *Mauberley* and *Anglo-Mongrels* is more obviously suggestive. Thematic connections between the two poems have often been noted, especially the relevance of the Brennbaum section and the similarity between Esau and Mauberley.[26] But beyond these parallels or allusions, there are also numerous half-echoes of Poundian phrases — 'The isolate consciousness / projected from back of time and space' (131), and 'devoid / of invitation to vitality' (156), and again 'it passes beyond the ken / of men' (128), and so on.[27] There are even passages where Loy seems deliberately to invoke *Mauberley* (note her Poundian use of rhyme in the following):

> His passionate-anticipation
> of warming in his arms
> his rose   to a maturer coloration
> which was all of aspiration
> the grating upon civilisation
> of his sensitive organism
> had left him
>
> splinters upon an adamsite
> opposition
> of nerves like stalactites (*LLB I* 127)

The rhymes seem calculatedly to echo Pound's 'Incapable of the least utterance or composition, / Emendation, conservation of the "better tradition"', while Loy's overly delicate reference to the 'sensitive organism' cannot help but recall the 'new found orchid' that Mauberley so gauchely attempts to 'designate'. Elsewhere in 'Anglo-Mongrels', Loy also seems to allude to Mauberley's drifting isolation:

> A wave
> 'out of tide'   with the surrounding
> ocean   he breaks
> insensitized   non-participance   upon himself (*LLB I* 117)

a passage that draws us back to Mauberley's solipsistic fascination with 'the imaginary / Audition of the phantasmal sea-surge'. Such lines do seem to stage an oblique encounter with Pound's poem, and the sense of an acknowledged relation between the two is strengthened when we hear that Pound apparently admired *Anglo-Mongrels* as an example of the 'free verse novel', a description which cannot but bring to mind his own account of *Mauberley* as 'an attempt to condense the James novel'.[28]

The partial and momentary intersection of these works by two essentially very different poets may tell us something useful about divergent strands within this period of Anglo-American modernism. For Pound's review of Loy's work occurred at a particularly rich moment in the evolution of his poetics, a moment (1918) in which he was also exploring 'the prose tradition in verse' through the writings of Flaubert, James, Lewis and Joyce, and coordinating these with an intensive reading of Laforgue initially inspired by Eliot's enthusiasm for the French poet.[29] It is Laforgue, of course, about whose irony Pound had written an important essay the year before, who provides the context in which he reads Loy and Moore. In that essay of 1917, 'Irony, Laforgue, and Some Satire', Pound had praised Laforgue for his command of what he called a 'good verbalism' ('Bad verbalism', he says, 'is rhetoric, or the use of *cliché* unconsciously, or a mere playing with phrases').[30] Pound emphasises that this is not 'the popular language of any country but an international tongue common to the excessively cultivated', and it is that internationalism which Pound specifies in the idioms of Loy and Moore as a 'distinctly *national* product', the paradox affirming the exorbitantly polyglot nature of the American language. All these concerns centring on satire and 'verbal-

ism' are focused in what Pound sees as Laforgue's *modernisation* of
poetic style, and I want to look at this in more detail since it provides
the key to Pound's interest in Loy and also explains why, after
Mauberley, his own work would move in a very different direction
from hers. Certainly, the 'modern' qualities of Laforgue's poetry are
clear enough: there is his exploration of free verse and his fascination
with types of 'social' subject matter; there is the daringly hybrid and
neologistic vocabulary, and the often risqué management of familiar
romantic themes (Laforgue is said to be the first French poet to use
the word 'clitoris' in verse). Above all, there is, as Pound notes in his
1917 essay, the 'delicate irony' and the intellectual cast of the writing: 'The ironist', observes Pound, 'is one who suggests that the
reader should think' (281). Yet with its appeal to the 'excessively cultivated', Laforgue's work is also very much of its time, the time of deca-
dence. Pound notes in passing that Beardsley's *Under the Hill* was 'until
recently the only successful attempt to produce "anything like
Laforgue" in our tongue' (283), but he doesn't pursue the question far,
moving instead to a discussion of satire. The more we look at Pound's
account, though, the more we may be struck by its partiality. It is,
above all, Laforgue as 'purge and critic' that Pound wants to stress,
and accordingly one hears very little about the poet's darker side,
about his 'Buddhistic sense of fatality',[31] his preoccupation with solitude and with moments of psychic fragility, his Schopenhaurian view
of the will, and his quite un-Poundian pursuit of self-mortification.
Laforgue's 'nonchalance of manner', as Pound terms it, actually represents only one aspect of his work, certainly masking the mordant and
macabre features of his irony to which Eliot was predictably drawn.

To this we can add that the decadent and the modern are, in fact,
more closely interwoven than Pound would have us believe,[32] though
Laforgue, he does admit, is 'exquisite', another indication that the
'hardness' for which he is to be admired is not quite yet the 'hardness' of modernist style. Indeed, the dazzling coinages which feature
so prominently in Laforgue's work are closely allied to the decadent
cult of the 'rare' word, which, drawing on Mallarmé, sought to create
the effect of a language partially dead and not in any practical sense
for use (we can find more obviously decadent forms of it in, say, the
work of Stefan George and Walter Pater). In fact, the 'verbalism' for
which Pound praised Laforgue might suggest something not so very
different from the allegedly 'false' autonomy of the decadent style

which always threatens to substitute a purely artificial language for a social one (the *OED* defines 'verbalism' as 'the predominance of what is merely verbal over reality or real significance'). What is of particular interest about this question is that it points up a major ambivalence within Anglo-American modernism, an ambivalence which turns on the relation of the modern to the decadent, and which is focused on exactly this issue of linguistic self-sufficiency and verbal 'materiality'. This strand of modernism derives much of its power from such ambivalence: on the one hand there is the turn to a 'writerly' language (in Roland Barthes's sense of the term), while on the other there is an insistence on the need for modes of objectification, for the 'welding of word and thing' of which Pound spoke so forcefully.[33]

If it's not always easy, then, to see precisely what Pound took from Laforgue it's partly because he seems to have seized on the poet's irony as a sort of mediating term between these two ways of writing. Irony offers the necessary escape from sentimentality and romantic expressivism, providing a strategic means by which to affirm the self as strong and authoritative — 'modern' as opposed to 'decadent' in Pound's scheme of things. Of course Pound himself would never actually be much of an ironist, lacking both the delicate touch of Laforguian humour and the poet's related fascination with the minutiae of social behaviour. Instead, Pound came to associate the satirical aspect of Laforgue's verse with the key terms of his own modernism — 'image', 'form', 'energy', 'objectivity' — all terms whose technical application also implies the agonistic relation the avant-garde would assume toward its subject matter and audience. 'Form' must be seen to be won through what Pound, in a discussion of Lewis's painting, calls the 'combat of arrangement',[34] a combat only marginally less dramatic than his description elsewhere of the artist as 'the phallus or spermatozoide charging, head-on, the female chaos'.[35] The connection exceeds simple analogy, reminding us that this privileging of intellect above emotion, along with its related activities of 'seeing' and 'knowing', leads not to forms of rigorous *self*-scrutiny but rather to an often aggressive objectification of the other. To which we can add that the 'inorganic' style of decadent writing is not so much jettisoned as reworked so as to produce an ideal of psychic authority and coherence where the fin-de-siècle writers had discerned the instability and, sometimes, the very extinction of the self.

What is especially interesting about Pound's construction of a Laforguian modernism and his way of using this as a lens through which to read Loy's work is precisely its programmatic partiality. Yet while the values of surface and 'hardness' so crucial to his avant-garde polemics of 1918 would certainly shape the ostensible technical protocols of *The Cantos*, Pound would actually never lose his parallel attraction to the 'softer' Swinburnian poetics which were to characterize many of the visionary sequences of the poem, early and late. Indeed, Laforgue makes an appearance in the very last 'full' Canto Pound ever wrote, Canto 116, where we read:

> And I have learned more from Jules
>   (Jules Laforgue) since then
>   deeps in him
>   and Linnaeus[36]

This late revisiting of Laforgue suggests another dimension of the French poet's work, reminding us again that a strand of decadent style runs through *The Cantos*, with the specially heightened lyric mode drawing attention to verbal and phonic values in a way which the ideologically clearer parts of the poem would dismiss as fetishistic. These richly ornamental passages exploit linguistic density and sound-patterning to produce effects quite removed from Laforguian logopoeia as Pound had defined it in 1918. On the other hand, though, these highly stylized, Pre-Raphaelite tableaux, with their frozen gestures and inorganic landscapes, *are* reminiscent of some of Laforgue's prose writings — and notably of the celebrated prose passage about the Berlin Aquarium which, significantly, Pound had cut from his 1918 translation of *Salomé* but to which the Laforguian 'deeps' at the very end of *The Cantos* undoubtedly refer:

> As far as the eye can see, meadows enameled with white sea anemones, fat ripe onions, bulbs with violet membranes, bits of tripe straying here and there and seeming to make a new life for itself, stumps with antennae winking at the neighbouring coral, a thousand aimless warts; a whole fetal, claustral, vibrating flora, trembling with the eternal dream of one day being able in whispers to congratulate itself on this state of things. . . .[37]

Eva Hesse and Donald Davie have both observed that the 'deeps' which Laforgue discovered in the Berlin aquarium offered Pound 'the motif of nature in reverse, an immutable anti-world' which figured the transformation wrought by art upon the real.[38] Yet Laforgue's version of Nirvana is, I think, more ambiguous than this reading suggests. For in these 'deeps', he tells us, there is

> no day, no night. . . no winter, no spring, no summer, no autumn, no other chopping and changing of weather. Loving, dreaming without moving, in the cool of imperturbable blindness. O satisfied world, you dwell in a blind and silent blessedness, while we dry up with our supert-errestrial pangs of hunger. Why aren't the antennae of our own senses bounded by Blindness, Opacity and Silence? Why must they seek out what is beyond their proper domain? Why can't we curl up, encrusted in our little corners, to sleep off the drunken deaths of our own little Egos? (96)

The narcotic life of these aquarium 'deeps' is as much a product of Laforgue's desire for a state of will-less 'Nirvana', with its fixity, calm and silence, as it is of an intense feeling for language, whose items it enumerates with an almost sensual pleasure.[39] Phrases like 'fetal, claustral, vibrating flora' exemplify less the 'dance of the intelligence', as Pound had originally defined logopoeia, than an almost fetishistic delight in language for its own sake, in the rich 'opacity' of words, to use Laforgue's own term. In becoming 'opaque' in this way, language provides the poet with a luxurious freedom, a freedom from the obsessive self-consciousness which characterized Laforgue's genius but which he also felt as a constant affliction. So 'the ideal things', he observed in another account of the Berlin aquarium, 'are these sponges, these star-fish, these plasmas, in the opaque, cool, daydreaming water.'[40]

At first sight, such mindless drifting might see anathema to Pound, who had, of course, satirised it as a weakness of the aesthete in *Mauberley*, but by the time he reappraised Laforgue a lot of water had flowed under the bridge. The experience of profound mental and physical debility which Pound underwent during his years at St Elizabeths arguably made him more responsive to several new things in Laforgue's writing. In the closed regions of the Aquarium's dream-like, subaquatic world, words no longer had to cleave to things but could be relished for themselves; and furthermore, Pound might have been led to notice that Laforguian word-play wasn't just a matter of active social satire — it was also intensely reflexive and internalised, a matter of intricate cross-reference and echo, stylistic qualities which would come very much to the fore in late Cantos such as 110.[41]

I have sketched these two Laforguian moments in Pound's thinking in a very abbreviated way, but I hope it is clear that neither of them fully defines Loy's particular brand of logopoeia. While her 'verbalism' seems closer in kind to the materiality of the second type, with an emphasis on internal play rather than on Poundian 'objectification', it also departs from the quasi-symbolist reflexivity we might discern in some of the late Cantos. We can best understand this difference by looking more closely at Loy's recently recovered essay on 'Modern Poetry',[42] where, as some critics have noted, the American language is characterized as a 'composite language', a 'welter of unclassifiable speech', 'English enriched and variegated with the grammatical structure and voice-inflection of many races'(*LLB II* 159, 158).[43] In view of this 'novel alloy' (the word-play seems deliberate), 'It was inevitable', says Loy, 'that the renaissance of poetry should proceed out of America, where latterly a thousand languages have been born' (*LLB II* 158). What has not so far been noted about this essay is that it seems deliberately to allude to the terms of Pound's 1918 review of her work. Not only does Loy celebrate at the outset Pound's 'magnificent Cantos' and his role as 'the masterly impressario of modern poets' (*LLB II* 158), but she also follows him in elaborating the paradox of a national language as a polyglot one and in arguing that this is the true idiom of modernity. The Laforguian idea of verbal coinage is prominent, too, for, as she puts it, 'Every moment [the true American] ingeniously coins new words for old ideas' (*LLB II* 159). Even more intriguing, though, is the following passage: 'The variety and felicity of these structural movements in modern verse has more than vindicated the rebellion against tradition. It will be found that one can recognise each of the modern poets' work by the gait of their mentality' (*LLB II* 157). It is hard not to feel that this last phrase — 'the gait of their mentality' — is a calculated reformulation of Pound's 'dance of the intelligence'. If it is, it's a telling one, with Loy substituting for the stylish symbolist dance the more deliberately mundane figure of walking. It is not necessary to retrace here the historical progress of the partially disembodied dancer, from Mallarmé through Yeats, to Stevens, to signal the emphatic embodiment conveyed in this one word when read against its Poundian precursor. This 'mentality' takes pleasure in its pedestrian encounter with words whose ungainliness and imperfection incite new rhythms and cadences which root them in a human world with all *its* acknowledged grubbiness and rough edges. We are already far from the 'non-human' soprano figured in Pound's 'Medallion', and we can also note that where Pound's 'logopoeic' words are rooted in a traditional if abstract lexicon, Loy's move between, on the one hand, the recondite and archaic ('changeant', 'eclosion', 'insuccess', 'stoppled') and, on the other, deliberate if recognisable coinages, such as 'inideate'. This, then, is the 'foreign language' she told Julien Levy she was trying to make (*BM* 361),[44] and 'foreign' not just in its repudiation of the normative and familiar, but also because it is the alienating language of satire, a medium which Lewis was currently reconstituting as one in which the intellect derives its power from a head-on confrontation with the grotesqueries of the 'wild body'. This is something very different from the epigrammatic wit of *Mauberley* and its concluding celebration of the 'non-human', reminding us that Loy's 'Pig Cupid' also finds his home in the messy materiality of the garbage heap. In that sense her vision is finally closer to Lewis's world of big babies and overheated German frauleins than it is to Pound's celebration of 'Luini in porcelain'. Satire, in this sense, renews its connection to the tradition of the grotesque as Bakhtin describes it in his study of Rabelais:

> . . . the artistic logic of the grotesque image ignores the closed, smooth, and impenetrable surface of the body and retains only its excrescences (sprouts, buds) and orifices, only that which leads beyond the body's limited space or into the body's depths. . . . If we consider the grotesque image in its extreme aspect, it never presents an individual body; the image consists of orifices and convexities that present another, newly conceived body. It is a point of transition in a life eternally renewed, the inexhaustible vessel of death and conception.[45]

The contemporary scandal of Loy's work was due, I think, as much to its outrageous invocation of this tradition as it was to her outspoken feminism and her public role as a 'new woman' (the two were in fact, of course, closely linked). As a result, Loy's logopoeia was a notably hybrid one, turning Pound's elegant symbolist conception upside down and showing the 'logos' of 'logopoeia' to be embedded in the very body it was supposed to rise above. The 'verbalism' of phrases like the 'sub-umbilical mystery / of his husbandry' and the 'impenetrable pink curtain' (*LLB I* 126, 128) here made partial obscurity a means at once of evading censorship *and* of being almost gratuitously specific, with linguistic density being simultaneously the measure of the unseen *and*, obliquely, the embodiment of what convention seeks to hide. There was a humour here to which Pound, with his rather Pre-Raphaelite notion of sexual passion, was not particularly well-attuned and which can be missed even by contemporary commentators like Carolyn Burke who seem keen to emphasise depressive tendencies at work in Loy's writing. As the connection with Pound shows, however, it was precisely Loy's achievement to push 'logopoeia' to a boisterous extreme, where even the ironist's pretensions to aloof superiority would ultimately fall victim to the 'humid carnage' of the bodily life (*LLB I* 57).

Notes

[1] Maeera Shreiber and Keith Tuma, eds., Mina *Loy Woman and Poet* (Orono, ME: National Poetry Foundation, 1998).

[2] Noel Stock, *The Life of Ezra Pound* (London: Routledge & Kegan Paul, 1970); Charles Norman, *Ezra Pound: A Biography* (1960; rev. ed. London: Macdonald, 1969); Humphrey Carpenter, *A Serious Character: the Life of Ezra Pound* (London and Boston: Faber and Faber, 1988).

[3] Loy wrote one poem in praise of Lewis — '"The Starry Sky" of Wyndham Lewis', in *LLB II*, 91–2 — and Burke quotes an unpublished letter from Loy to Mabel Dodge Luhan in which she describes Lewis as 'a marvellous draftsman of the Picasso school — in method — but himself alone in vision' (140).

[4] Virgil Thomson, *Virgil Thomson* (New York: Knopf, 1966), 83; Mina Loy, 'Modern Poetry', in *LLB II*, 158. See also R. Murray Schafer, *Ezra Pound and Music: The Complete Criticism* (London: Faber & Faber, 1978), 312: Loy attended the première along with Joyce, Hemingway, Eliot, Djuna Barnes, and Cocteau.

[5] George H. Tichenor, 'This Man is a Traitor: A Story of the Life and Works of Ezra Pound, Who Scorned the People', PM 4 no. 50 (New York, 15 August 1943), quoted in Charles Norman, *Ezra Pound: A Biography* (London: Macdonald, 1969), 273. See also Marisa Januzzi, 'Mongrel Rose', in Shreiber and Tuma, eds., 416–17, n22.

[6] Ezra Pound, 'A List of Books', *Little Review* IV no. 11 (March 1918), 54–8. Part of the section on Moore and Loy is reprinted in William Cookson, ed., *Ezra Pound: Selected Prose* 1909–1965 (London: Faber and Faber, 1973), 394–5. Pound, 'How to Read' (1929), rpt. in T.S. Eliot, ed., *Literary Essays of Ezra Pound* (London: Faber and Faber, 1968), 25.

[7] Ezra Pound, 'Books Current, Reviewed by Ezra Pound: The New Poetry', *Future* II (June 1918), 188. The section quoted by Pound and omitting lines from Loy's original is reprinted in Ellen Keck Stauder, 'Beyond the Synopsis of Vision:

the Conception of Art in Ezra Pound and Mina Loy', *Paideuma* 24 no. 2/3 (Fall and Winter 1995), 224.

8 For the comments to Anderson, see *Pound/The Little Review: the Letters of Ezra Pound to Margaret Anderson*, ed. Thomas L. Scott and Melvin J. Friedman (London: Faber and Faber, 1988), 207, 268, 297. Pound's opinion of Loy sometimes seems uncertain here: 'We must have some American contributions. ???? Mina Loy ?? (On re-reading I find parts of her better than Marianne Moore, though perhaps she sinks further and worser [sic] in others).' For the letter to Moore, see D. D. Paige, ed., *The Selected Letters of Ezra Pound 1907–1941* (London: Faber and Faber, 1950), 168. See also ibid., 135, 158.

9 See Norman, *Ezra Pound: A Biography*, 266–67.

10 Translated as 'Crawfish?' by Tim Redman, in *Helix* 13/14 (1983), 117–20. For the original and for Marinetti's letter see Roberto Bagnasco, ed., *Il Mare Supplemento Letterario* 1932–1933 (Commune di Rapallo, 1999), 321–4, 316.

11 Pound, ed., *Profile: An Anthology Collected in MCMXXXI* (Milan: John Scheiwiller, 1932), quoted in Marisa Januzzi, 'Bibliography', in Shreiber and Tuma, eds., 524.

12 See, for example, Jim Powell, 'Basil Bunting and Mina Loy', *Chicago Review* 37 no. 1 (1990), 13; Elizabeth A. Frost, 'Mina Loy's "Mongrel" Poetics', in Shreiber and Tuma, eds., 164, 172

13 Carolyn Burke, 'Getting Spliced: Modernism and Sexual Difference', *American Quarterly* 39 (1987), 99.

14 Reno Odlin, 'Her Eclipse Endur'd', *Antigonish Review* 59 (1984), 58–9.

15 The first four sections of *Songs* appeared as 'Love Songs' in *Others* 1 no. 1 (July 1915) and the full sequence occupied the entire issue of *Others* 3 no. 6 (April 1917).

16 'Moeurs Contemporaines', in Pound, *Collected Shorter Poems* (London: Faber and Faber, 1952), 196–201.

17 See Wyndham Lewis, *Men Without Art*, ed. Seamus Cooney (1934; Santa Rosa, CA: Black Sparrow Press, 1987), 98–9. After a critique of the 'internal method', which Lewis associates with 'the subterranean stream of the "dark" Unconscious', he concludes that 'Satire is *cold*, and that is good! It is easier to achieve those polished and resistant surfaces of a great *externalist* art in Satire' (Lewis's emphases).

18 Pound, *Collected Shorter Poems*, 221.

19 Pound, 'A List of Books', *Selected Prose*, 394.

20 Lewis, *Men Without Art*, 129 (his emphasis).

21 See, for example, Ronald Bush, 'It Draws One to Consider Time Wasted: *Hugh Selwyn Mauberley*', *American Literary History* 2 no. 2 (Summer 1990), 56–78. I have offered a critique of this view in '"A Consciousness Disjunct": Sex and the

Writer in Ezra Pound's *Hugh Selwyn Mauberley'*, *Journal of American Studies* 28 no. 1 (April 1994), 61–76, and draw on that essay in the following account.

[22] Pound, 'Music' (1920), rpt. in *Ezra Pound and Music*, 225 (emphases in original).

[23] Pound, 'I Gather the Limbs of Osiris, XI' (1912), rpt. in *Selected Prose*, 41–2 (emphases added). Note especially the prefiguring here of the contrast later drawn in *Mauberley* between the 'mould in plaster' and 'the sculpture of rhyme'.

[24] See Pound, *Gaudier-Brzeska: A Memoir* (1916; Hessle: Marvell Press, 1960), 97.

[25] See the typescript reproduced in Jo Brantley Berryman, *Circe's Craft: Ezra Pound's Hugh Selwyn Mauberley* (Ann Arbor, MI: UMI Research Press, 1983), 238.

[26] See above, note 12.

[27] See, respectively, in *Hugh Selwyn Mauberley*, 'a consciousness disjunct', 'Invitation, mere invitation to perceptivity', 'He passed from men's memory'.

[28] J. J. Wilhelm, *Ezra Pound in London and Paris* 1908–1925 (University Park and London: Penn State University Press, 1990), 326; Pound, *Selected Letters*, 180.

[29] A helpful account of Pound's dealings with Laforgue is Jane Hoogestraat, '"Akin to Nothing but Language": Pound, Laforgue, and Logopoeia', *ELH* 55 no. 1 (Spring 1988), 259–85. In the following I draw also upon my own '"Deeps in him": Ezra Pound and the persistent attraction of Laforgue', *Revue Francaise d'Etudes Americaines* 84 (March 2000), 9–20.

[30] Pound, 'Irony, Laforgue, and Some Satire' (1917), in T. S. Eliot, ed., *Literary Essays* (London: Faber and Faber, 1960), 283. Further references will be given in the text.

[31] Warren Ramsey, *Jules Laforgue: the Ironic Inheritance* (New York: OUP, 1953), 66. In a 1957 letter Pound does ask 'Anyone yet noted the hindoo depth in LaForgue [sic]', but he does not pursue the matter (see Ezra Pound, *Letters to John Thoebald*, ed. Donald Pearce and Herbert Schneidau (Redding Ridge, CT: Black Swan Books, 1984), 27.

[32] See my *Modernisms: A Literary Guide* (London: Macmillan, 1995).

[33] Pound, *Selected Letters*, 158.

[34] Pound, *Gaudier-Brzeska*, 121.

[35] Pound, 'Translator's Postscript', in Remy de Gourmont, *The Natural Philosophy of Love*, trans. Ezra Pound (1922; New York: Liverlight, 1972), 150.

[36] Pound, *The Cantos* (London: Faber and Faber, 1986), 810.

[37] Jules Laforgue, *Moral Tales*, trans. William Jay Smith (London: Pan, 1985), 95. Further references will be given in the text. For Pound's translation, see *Pavannes and Divagations* (London: Peter Owen, 1960), 189–200.

[38] Eva Hesse, ed., *New Approaches to Ezra Pound* (London: Faber and Faber, 1969), 29.

[39] See also Scott Hamilton, *Ezra Pound and the Symbolist Inheritance* (Princeton, NJ: Princeton UP, 1992) for a discussion of the late 'reversal of Pound's earlier poetics of assertion and . . . his new willingness to entertain previously treatneing and unexplored states of mind' (184). Hamilton notes that 'Pound's regard for Laforgue's Buddhist passivity [is] gradually modified' (183) and that a certain reflexivity in some of the late Cantos reconnects Pound to the Symbolist (Mallarméan) tradition.

[40] Quoted in Francois Ruchon, *Jules Laforgue: sa vie, son oeuvre* (Geneva: Editions Albert Ciana, 1924), 137 (my translation).

[41] For a more detailed discussion of this development, see my '"To Unscrew the Inscrutable": Myth as Fiction and Belief in Ezra Pound's *Cantos*', in Michael Bell and Peter Poellner, eds., *Myth and the Making of Modernity: The Problem of Grounding in Early Twentieth-Century Literature* (Amsterdam: Rodopi,1998), 139–52.

[42] First published in the fashion magazine *Charm* in 1925, the essay has been reprinted in *LLB II*, 157–61. Subsequent references to this essay are given in the text.

[43] See Marjorie Perloff, 'English as a "Second" Language: Mina Loy's *Anglo-Mongrels and the Rose*', in Shreiber and Tuma, eds., 146.

[44] '"I was trying to make a foreign language", she wrote, 'because English had already been used."'

[45] Mikhail Bakhtin, *Rabelais and His World,* trans. Helen Iswolsky (Indiana University Press, 1984), 317–18.

Stumbling, Balking, Tacking: Robert Creeley's For Love and Mina Loy's 'Love Songs to Joannes'

John Wilkinson

To stumble and to stammer are cognate, and each such mis-articulation predicts its own righting, an almost-falling resolved into the step forward, the words stabilizing as the speaker gets his mouth into gear. In neither case does stumbler or stammerer ordinarily resolve the disturbance through a change of mind, as a stutterer might by substituting a more readily pronounced phrase, or the balker stock-still who decides to adopt a different path; the stutterer and the balker might through steadfast purpose risk failing completely, as the stumbler will not, for he is destined to walk his way out of trouble—since as Laurie Anderson has noted, in a tone of such equanimity that her stammering or stuttering are alike unthinkable, falling is itself a component of the complex articulation of walking.[1] Fear of falling might prevent walking, but not so actual falling through stumbling (leave aside such special risk factors as osteoporosis), for even if you stumble-and-fall you will likely pick yourself up, dust yourself down and continue to walk. You might even make a dance out of such righting, like Fred Astaire, falling with panache and the confidence that the earth will be soft or arms stretch out to catch you.

Should you wish to stumble with panache in poetry, you might study Robert Creeley's lyric poetry, for this is the special thing it does. Following this example, you might discover real advantages in your adept stumbling, for every mistake you made would be rescued by a self-righting mechanism, while your righteousness would be found tolerable because of your openly-acknowledged mistakes. This might be true especially if you were male and your stumbling and stammering occurred in the purview of a woman whose definitive womanliness incorporated that maternal care exercised over a toddler. At once you could be a precocious and loved toddler, and an adorably clumsy, fallible man — and the universe would conform to your arms-out terror and trust, to your longings, being organised about you in a way you could feel more or less responsible for, perhaps even prompting you to reproach or thank a woman.

At first acquaintance the poetry of Robert Creeley between 1950 and 1960 collected in *For Love* looks engagingly modest, where the early poetry of Mina Loy in her 'Love Songs to Joannes' (published 1915—1917) looks enjoyably brazen, even exhibitionist. This is especially marked when the two poets write of physical sex, something they both do with a rare and exact descriptiveness. What I wish to argue in this paper is that Creeley's poetry exhibits a sustained poise in both presented self and in prosody through its hesitancy, tending towards self-regard even when self-doubting, through a circuit requiring the presence of a woman. By contrast, Loy's categorical-sounding starts and stops are driven by internal contradictions at the level of argument or *position*, producing abrupt changes of direction marked prosodically; which in turn encounter new oppositions and tensions, these also subsequently reconsidered although not necessitating any revision or suppression of the prior record. Loy's poems know nothing of time passing; instead they gather their positions and stages in an uneasy coexistence.

On this account it might be tempting to call Loy's poetry dialectical (and it has already been termed 'analytical' by Rachel Blau DuPlessis and Michael Palmer, and as exemplary of 'logopoeia' by Ezra Pound as long ago as 1918[2]), even if this is a curious term to apply to 'love songs,' but then, these are love songs of a very particular time, when relations between the sexes were under the most intense debate and personal negotiation among people associated with progressive politics in the United States and Great Britain. Since this historical context has been treated extensively by Carolyn Burke in her biography of Loy and by other writers, it will not be a major consideration here (*BM* 195–208).[3] Rather, the concern will be with the particularities of internal movement through the configurations of Loy's poems, which are, in Donna Haraway's usage, *situated* as to gender but where situatedness is a continually renewed process rather than a settled fact. The originality of 'Love Songs to Joannes' lies in their phrasal and prosodic sensitivity to a changing situated-

ness, demanding a linear and relational reorientation. Their lines are
as it were incised definitely but run into objections, they refuse and
are refused by each acknowledged new configuration, but will not
allow of being transfixed; rather, they transgress each other in the
argument in which they participate, but do not erase or disfigure.
Creeley's poetry of the late 1950s and early 1960s may seem hesitant,
but its hesitations occur within a situation never understood as situated in its fundamental configuration — relations between woman
and a man being taken as archetypal — and the hesitations, the stumbles, always redound to the advantage of the stumbler even if he may
dream betimes of a perfect masculine ease.

   To stumble or stammer implies a directedness interrupted, which
on resumption will spur consciousness of bodily motivation and
impediment both; it is expressive of individual will and of personal
embodiment with its attendant fallibility — for while one may stumble over a chance hazard, maybe a broken paving-slab, the obstruction causing one to stumble is not social, and even a stammer is social
only by way of a looped self-consciousness, feedback induced by a
break in the intersubjectivity of speech. Its correction brings mastery,
rather than restoring the *status quo ante*. It is in such terms that
Charles Altieri expatiates on three poems by Robert Creeley through
a fine-grained reading in his book *The Art of Twentieth-Century American
Poetry*, associating Creeley's procedures with a Spinozan view of individuation founded in conativity:

> The goal of expression is not self-knowledge as a concept or image;
> expressing the self consists simply in an awareness of how "the body's
> power of activity is increased or diminished, assisted or checked,
> together with the ideas of these affections." Conativity is the felt power
> to find reflexive satisfaction within one's capacity to control the phys-
> ical and imaginative space a being occupies.[4]

Since Altieri is at this point interested in establishing an affiliation
between Creeley and Robert Lowell and Adrienne Rich, and in down-
playing Creeley's conventional assignation to 'Black Mountain,' he
neglects to note — a lapse surely tendentious — the kinship between
Creeley's conativity and Charles Olson's proprioception, proprioception being the phenomenological expression of conativity. Will and
desire (conativity) expressed through the body's reaching and being
reached, lead to an ontological position whereby 'the extent of long-

ing and desire is both our own extent and the extent of the world around us, and we are at the centre of the world around us by a supreme prerogative'.[5] This position is stated stumblingly but assuredly by Creeley at the close of his poem 'The Awakening' dedicated to Charles Olson:

> God is no bone of whitened contention.
> God is not air, nor hair, is not
> a conclusive concluding
> to remote yearnings. He moves
>
> only as I move, you also move to
> the awakening, across long rows, of beds,
> stumble breathlessly, on leg pins and crutch,
> moving at all as all men, because you must.[6]

The final line's 'at all' is extremely carefully poised, 'at all' implying 'towards all beings and all things' as well as 'in the least'. God then is not an entity to be subject to scholastic argument, nor ubiquitous and general as air, nor arbitrary as 'hair' (such slippage carrying over from a flurry in the previous stanza, 'err to concur', 'the seen, the green green'), nor to be distanced from 'yearnings' which can only be located in the body, here both creature and instrument of male will. Male will, because 'all men' attains its gender specificity from the poem's earlier allusion to 'a woman's impression,' whereby a woman not merely is the recipient of impressions rather than a mover by intention, but present only in her absence — the impression perhaps of the woman departed from the bed; perhaps also the woman who answers the door bell earlier in the poem and the telephone later, both sounding off-stage. If 'we are at the centre of the world,' that 'we' is figured not in the first person's relationship with 'a woman's impression' but in 'all men' following the instance of Charles Olson and Robert Creeley, whose sense of a shared *project* for all the difference in scale, is conveyed amply through the ten volumes of their published correspondence.

While the problem of how a viable and ethical 'we' is constituted on its specific terrain drives the drama of *The Maximus Poems*, Creeley's poetry of the period 1950–60 is so sparing of that pronoun as to draw attention to its absence and to the mechanisms which substitute for it. One is the generic 'he' as in 'A Song,' 'Which one sings, if he sings it, with care.' Another is 'a man' as in the Preface to *For Love*: 'a sudden instance of love, and the being loved, wherewith a man also contrives a world (of his own mind)'.[7] 'A man' and 'the man' occur more frequently than 'men,' and 'man' as an abstraction does not seem to appear at all whereas 'woman' often does; to read Robert Creeley's poems in any number is to notice that the world is actuated by 'a man,' his perception of the world and his acts upon it, that world having grown to include 'woman' even if structured by her originally. But specifically, the effective substitutes for 'we' are line-breaks and commas, as evident in the demonstrative stumbles of the final stanza of 'The Awakening,' where they admit the self-consciousness which first identifies 'you' as an aspect of the split self, and then enjoins 'you' the reader into a union with the exemplary (male) self. The pause enforced rhythmically and by enjambement prior to 'the awakening,' a phrase prefigured in the poem's title and therefore a realised portentousness, creates a space for the awakening of an immanence of the other in the self, a recognition evoking the world in a quasi-divine way. The world then is the precipitate of self-recognition. It is on this ground that 'you' come into being, through the exemplary acts of a stumbling poet, whose purposeful breaks give you utterance: Creeley gives you a break.

Just so with the beautiful lyric 'The Rain' where Altieri claims 'we find poetry pursuing a form of resolution quite distinct from the imaginary satisfactions sought by confessional poetry' while bracketing off the final words of the poem with the curiously evasive phrase (for a critic not notably reluctant to moralise) 'whatever "decent happiness" can be'.[8] The poem's final two stanzas read:

> Love, if you love me,
>   lie next to me.
> Be for me, like rain
>   the getting out
>
> of the tiredness, the fatuousness, the semi-
>   lust of intentional indifference.
> Be wet,
>   With a decent happiness.[9]

Altieri is right on the button in identifying the frank sexuality of 'Be wet,' and it is an instance of Creeley's rigorous attention to his own moral state that he can ask help in overcoming 'the semi- / lust of intentional indifference' — one might indeed feel that a 'we' appears on the horizon here, yearned-for and almost conceived, were it not for the phrase which stumps Altieri. But not this only, for multiple devices of objectification and subservience come into play: the injunction (Be wet), the line-break, the comma, and most strikingly, the initial capital letter after the comma. 'With a decent happiness' operates then as a form of dismissal, 'decent happiness' being a happiness fitting to the speaker's needs, only the speaker being present to judge her decency in the instance of such unselfconsciousness. Hence the poem enacts for the speaker his moment of potentially unselfconscious union in orgasm followed by a turning away. With this break and comma and capital letter to follow, the wetness appears less the evidence of female sexual arousal than the residue of male sexual arousal, since the poem earlier has referred to 'the ease, / even the hardness, / of rain falling' as representing the suspension of self-consciousness to which the too-persistently self-scrutinizing poet aspires, the achieved Lawrencian phallicism.

In an interview published in 1971 Robert Duncan talked of Creeley's 'practised stumbling' as symptomatic of castration and impotency, the halting of self-consciousness being his privilege and his shame — yet Creeley surely expecting to be forgiven in the understanding that he must go his own way, bound henceforward to survey the earth for its adventitiousness. How could prosody be more exacting, more controlled than by such footfall? Nathaniel Mackey mentions Duncan's phrase when citing lines from Creeley's slightly earlier poem dedicated to his Black Mountain colleague, 'The Door': 'The Lady has has always moved to the next town / and you stumble on after her'.[10] The Lady here comports herself as a particular case of generic 'woman' because she is unmistakably The Muse, and following Duncan's lead Mackey identifies this poem's indebtedness to a poem of the same name by Robert Graves. The late romantic manner also constitutes a homage to Duncan, albeit Duncan's muse-worship showed no propensity to subordinate the muse whereas Creeley interrupts this rhetoric with self-conscious commas and line-breaks calculated precisely to reclaim creative agency from Lady to poet. The most salient lines of Creeley's poem read:

> So I screamed to You,
> who hears as the wind, and changes
> multiply, invariably,
> changes in the mind.

Running to the door, I ran down
as a clock runs down. Walked backwards,
stumbled, sat down
hard on the floor near the wall.

Where were You.
How absurd, how vicious.
There is nothing to do but get up.[11]

Although there is nothing to do but pursue The Lady, the Lady's task amounts merely to setting the direction of travel; whilst what engenders poetry of value is exactly that stumbling whereby world, body and the perceiving of their relatedness, a perceiving out of which world, body and poetry are born — proprioception —, here fall into place. For Olson the work of place may be social, economic, mythic and geological, and collectively proprioceptive, but for Creeley the adamant place of 'the floor near the wall' is conjured through his stumble. Writing of Creeley's prose, Mackey observes that 'a certain "sure-footedness" characterizes women as portrayed by Creeley, as opposed to insistent awkwardness, a tendency to stumble, on the part of the men' and acknowledges 'a binarism that is not innocent of sexual equations (man = mind, woman = matter)'.[12] The surefootedness is doubtless related both to the singularity of 'woman' as entity in the poems, and, ironically enough, to the lack of selfconsciousness to which the poet aspires in 'The Rain' and more so in another poem admired by Altieri, 'Something.' Here watching a woman piss in a sink after having sex, Creeley reflects (and what can a man do but reflect) 'What / love might learn from such a sight.' Singularity then, makes women 'woman' as well as making woman whole, as distinct from the special role of men in the plural, especially Black Mountain poets, even one as habitually cool and unstumbling as Edward Dorn: 'Well, I think there's only one Woman, anyway. It seems to me that men are multiple and women are singular.'[13]

While Creeley's enterprise may be conative, as Altieri characterizes it, Mina Loy's might be held to be wilful more in the sense of obstinacy and unwillingness to accept convention or authority, to the extent that decisively adopted positions of challenge and refusal in turn become the objects of denial, even of revulsion. This characteristic has confounded attempts to read Loy as feminist according to its late twentieth-century formations, much as it restrained her from throwing in her lot with any particular group in the contemporary women's movement, despite being recognised as an embodiment of 'new woman' in the popular press as well as by literary contemporaries like William Carlos Williams (with admiration) and Amy Lowell (with horror).

Such restiveness requires its proper form of expression. It is more than irksome that the eighth edition of *The Norton Anthology of English Literature* canonises Loy's 'Feminist Manifesto' (probably 1914), which went unpublished at its time with good reason, while passing over her poems. Discussing the Futurist manifestos which were Loy's model for the 'Feminist Manifesto,' Marjorie Perloff celebrates Marinetti's innovative embedding of statements and directives in a narrative context so compelling that the banalities and contradictions of his 'cult of energy, aggressiveness, violence and heroism' go unnoticed.[14] Wholehearted buffoonery can wow the most unlikely audience (as well understood by Hugo Chávez, the present-day master of the mode); a manifesto should elicit, at least imaginatively, a commentary of roars and gasps rather than critical analysis. Although Loy's manifesto starts with Futurist brio, it makes the fundamental error of confusing a manifesto with a wish-list. Rhetorically this produces bathos; after the great line which brings the second paragraph to a head, 'Are you prepared for the WRENCH?,' the text descends to the flaccid prose of 'Another great illusion that woman must use all her introspection, innate clear-sightedness, and unbiased bravery to destroy is the impurity of sex — for the sake of her self-respect,' so adding afterthought to afterthought in a discouraging sequence (*LLB I* 269–71).[15] As for content, Loy's inability to stay single-minded leads her to temper her assault on men by acknowledging the mutual deformation of men and women in the master-slave dialectic, and scornfully to admit 'the advantages of marriage' for women. This is much too reasonable, and buffers the shock-value of the demand for 'the *unconditional* surgical *destruction of virginity* throughout the female population at puberty.' For a manifesto, equivocation is far more damaging than contradiction.

The weakly-linked exposition into which the 'Feminist Manifesto' declines, contrasts to its great disadvantage with the abrupt expostulations comprising 'Love Songs to Joannes.' Since the shocking opening of the sequence has attracted much analysis, this example is taken from close to the end and is relatively decorous.

31.
Crucifixion
Of a busybody
Longing to interfere so
With the intimacies
Of your insolent isolation

Crucifixion
Of an illegal ego's
Éclosion
On your equilibrium
Caryatid   of an idea

Crucifixion
Wracked arms
Index extremities
In vacuum
To the unbroken fall[16] (*LLB I* 106)

The 'longing' here bears no resemblance to the conative 'longing' of
Olson and Creeley, extending phallically from where 'a man' stands;
and the difference in longingness is felt at once through Loy's distinctive prosody. Even in this poem, among the most densely-woven and
linguistically consistent of the sequence, every line starts with an
effort of resumption from which rhythmically it falls rapidly away.
This is yet more marked owing to Loy's propensity for offending
against the most basic precepts of verse writing by starting a line with
a customarily forceless conjunction such as 'of' or 'with.' The act of
conjunction is thereby asserted as the central performative task of
verse, reinforced by the formal decision to retain the initial capital
of traditional verse lineation while suppressing the punctuation
which would bring a line to a close, or at least to a lengthened pause
(for the stanza here conforms to a sentence or a colon-divided period).
'Nor does she enjamb lines to modify semantic or syntactic significance,' as Maeera Shreiber observes; enjambement recruits the force
necessary for resumption.[17] The pauses in this poem occur at the start
of its lines, not at their ending. While the third stanza cannot be read
except with a powerful emphasis on each line's first syllable, the first
stanza's greater grammatical fluency is disturbed by the weakly
dactyllic line-endings: indeed, the poem's every line could be read as
an extended dactyl. Short lines, the emphasis on conjunction, and
extreme intricacy of internal rhyme as a kind of syllable-shuttling,

distinguish Loy's verse which, as Perloff notes in a brilliantly anachro-nistic association, is so far removed from anything that might be called 'free verse' that it recalls the 'skeltonics' of the Tudor poet John Skelton.[18]

Loy's syllabic intricacy is such that her lines risk falling over their own feet, as in the phrases 'Of an illegal ego's' and 'Index extremi-ties.' Their resumptions then sound like continual new starts pitched against a syntax approaching discursive regularity, borrowing strength from such regularity and the prominence of conjunction so as to prevent the lines from either trailing away or fragmenting into discrete entanglements. They would be left-hand jabs but cannot connect with the man shrugging them off. Rather than a conative pressure, 'longing' denotes a kind of battering at the fixity of the loved object's 'insolent isolation,' epitomized in his 'streetcorner smile' of poem 24 — a phrase capturing perfectly the male narcissism of 'hanging out' with a smile both self-satisfied and appraising (*LLB I* 102).[19] No wonder these lines so nearly balk.

To fall over your own feet is not the same as to stumble. Stumbling induces self-consciousness whereas falling over your own feet is a product of self-consciousness; it is the fault of a 'busybody' rather than of a man going about his business and surprised by stumbling, that sudden unmeshing of the unconscious accord between body and environment. The crucifixion of this poem reduces (or multiplies) the body to limbs, whereas the narcissistic male lover's projection of the speaker is as the 'Caryatid of an idea', a draped and therefore limbless female statue. While it might seem perverse to disregard Christian iconography by departing from others who read Loy here as claim-ing a Christ-like suffering, I believe such a reading mistakes the nature of Loy's appropriations. These tend to be arbitrary as to cultural and symbolic association; that is, the poet arbitrates by immediate context. 'Crucifixion' for Loy's present purpose is more like being pinned by an entomologist than self-sacrifice in pursuit of human redemption; it involves being ascribed within a taxonomy according to the configuration of limbs or lines: 'Crucifixion / Wracked arms / Index extremities.' In such tightly-wound verse, cultural resonance is far less powerful than local intensities of abut-ment and exchange — and it therefore departs much further from symbolism than Pound's.

This poem's prosody grants resonance only to the final phrase, to 'unbroken fall,' which dangles unbound from the intricate sound-texture. Such a terminal irresolution plays back across the preceding poem, and introduces (if not suspected previously) the possibility of a deep ambivalence. As against Rachel Blau DuPlessis, whose essay "'Seismic Orgasm'" is far the most precise and intelligent published account of 'Love Songs to Joannes,' I disagree that this poem treats 'specifically her "crucifixion" as the bearer of a new and controversial idea (she is the "Caryatid of an idea"): that women should freely bear the children of their lovers, and that superior women will bear superior children in a eugenicist sense.'[20] This construction rests on too linear a reading of the sequence, and takes Loy's eugenicism as internally uncontested, whereas poem 29 appears to challenge eugenics in a negative version as 'own-self distortion,' contrasting it with genetic diversity and mutation and their wider potential. Furthermore, DuPlessis tends to make this poem monolingual and resolute, contrary to its prosodic cues. Instead, 'Unbroken fall' can be read as suggesting that Christ's crucifixion failed to fix anything, that mankind's fall continues unimpeded since expulsion from the Garden of Eden; and more radically as celebrating what that continuing fall implies and portends: that human beings have responsibility for their own future (which may indeed entail eugenicist policies in Loy's view at the time).

But if Christ was crucified to no good purpose except negatively in a busted eschatology, that may not apply to Loy's crucifixion. It is at least an allowable question, whether crucifixion in the nailed lines of this poem is not a fate more exemplary, more potent, than either that of the memorialised 'caryatid,' a smooth-surfaced and sexless representation of female sensibility, or the 'insolent isolation' of the phallic master. If that is the case, the phallic master has a value in ordaining the 'equilibrium' provoking the 'illegal ego's' development (its 'éclosion,' that is, its nesting), rather like the justification for Judas in his act's outcome but contrariwise, in that here it is the fall that matters. 'A busybody,' 'an illegal ego,' wracked arms' and 'index extremities' engage in an immense tension forced by the poem's conjunctions and a sentence structure overcoming a continual risk of falling mute, or halting and shying in the face of 'your equilibrium.' This compages of force makes the parataxis of the contemporary imagist poem look slack, and too prissily aestheticized in its suspension and invitation to commentary in the circumtextual space.

What of 'Longing to interfere so / with the intimacies / Of your insolent isolation'? Loy's longing does not organise the world from a phallic vantage but rather, in a present-day phrase, mixes it with the world. 'The intimacies / Of your insolent isolation' seems linked to the sequence's use of slang terms for masturbation, apparently unremarked hitherto. To 'pull a weed' (poem 1) is to masturbate, to 'pull the wire' also (poem 6) — and although the later is recorded as current in the late sixties, it was already considered quaint (fathers' era) when I was at boarding school at the close of the fifties and therefore probably had a long history. The 'one eye' in poem 6 is reminiscent of the Australian sexual slang 'one-eyed trouser snake.' In writing about Loy of all poets, it must be permissible to state that she frequently regards Joannes as a wanker, and that his 'intimacies' amount to little more than self-gratification — hence the 'clockwork mechanism' of poem 2, associated with Italian Futurism and Loy's recent sexual relationship with Marinetti, and contrasted with female sexual insatiability and tenderness ('My fingertips are numb / From fretting your hair').[21] It is contrasted too with the timeless instantaneity of wholly joined sexuality, neither masturbatory nor distracted: 'You could look straight at me / And Time would be set back'. That said, Loy can be brisk in response to sentimentality about sexual activity, celebrated and reduced as 'Only the impact of lighted bodies' (poem 14), and associating tenderness with a vulnerability perhaps post-coital or impotent — 'I had to be caught in the weak eddy / Of your drivelling humanity / To love you most' (poem 15). 'Drivelling' seems to belong to a word-cluster connected with Loy's reflex of disgust against non-reproductive sex, often after descriptions of unselfconsciously 'good sex' have tended by negation towards the inhuman and mechanical, and staged again through poems 25–27: her poems are driven by such unresolvable contradictions and flex about their skeleton.

Longing figures in Loy not as a narrative project strong enough to brush aside opponents and persist through setbacks, but as a polyvalent force sustaining at its tensest (as in the crucifixion poem) an improvised and somewhat ramshackle structure, much as might be said of cubist collage, and at its strangest a three-dimensional and timeless figure where events coexist in an occult but proclaimed intimacy — more, perhaps, like a harder-edged variety of the Surrealist painting of Yves Tanguy. Nodal words in 'Love Poems to Joannes' undergo radical reorientation, donning and shrugging off historical associations at will; in this way (for example) 'white' and 'coloured' become as critically contested as the pronouns 'you' and 'me'. The relationship between their contradictory usages is pressured, but reconciliation is neither attempted nor even seen as called-for. The comparison with painting or collage holds; this is a poetry of space, perhaps of an inner space within which entities coexist, and one single entity may split into positive and negative part-objects, turning round to bite after leading on.

The first dab of white appears in poem 7, where 'the scum of the white street' is transmuted through lungs and nostrils into 'Exhilarated birds / Prolonging flight into the night'. Here the negative connotations of 'scum' and its echo of 'sperm' link the phrase 'the scum of the white street' to the masturbator of the previous poem, and the wind performs fellatio. At that instant 'the white street' with an upward cadence unusual in these poems, breaks into radiance and prepares to release its soaring birds. 'Prolonging flight into the night' converts the scum, the day's residues, into dream-work; or maybe this is the expression of female sexuality, of repeated orgasm, of 'Never reaching,' that is, never being spent. Or again, it may speak of the delirium of fully shared sexual expression. Whiteness may be male, female, positive, negative, vacant or entire, cold or hot, perfect or diseased, and it recurs in poem 9,

> And spermatozoa
> At the core of Nothing
> In the milk of the Moon

in poem 23,

> Rot
> To the recurrent moon
> Bleach
> To the pure white
> Wickedness of pain

and particularly in poem 28, here given in full:

> The steps go up for ever
> And they are white
> And the first step   is the last white
> Forever
> Coloured   conclusions
> Smelt   to synthetic

Whiteness
Of my
Emergence
And I am burnt quite white
In the climacteric
Withdrawal of your sun
And wills and words all white
Suffuse
Illimitable monotone

White   where there is nothing to see
But a white towel
Wipes the cymophanous sweat
—Mist rise of living—
From your
Etiolate body
And the white dawn
Of your   New Day
Shuts down on me

Unthinkable   that white over there—
Is smoke from your house[22] (*LLB I* 103–4)

'Illimitable monotone' maybe, but it would be difficult, apart from the stagey oxymorons of the baroque, to imagine a monotone more comprehensive of contradiction and variety. To begin with, white can be 'the core of Nothing' or the final incorporation of all colour. In poem 28, whiteness confronts the reader in marble or in Busby Berkeley icing-sugar at the foot of a sweep of stairs, divides into the colours of the rainbow and recombines into 'synthetic / whiteness,' a whiteness which is the nuptial or heavenly restoration of virginity, the flower of a synthetic new 'emergence.' The lineation proceeds by steps, adding dab to dab until it reaches beyond synthesis with the astonishing lines 'And I am burnt quite white / In the climacteric / Withdrawal of your sun'. To be 'burnt quite white' is to be subject to a radical negation, to the extinction of personal qualities and personality within a consuming solar dazzle. These lines unite total loss with total ecstasy, fulfilment with abasement. 'Climacteric' is a brilliantly polyvalent usage; critical, ripened to fulfilment, and condemned to infertility, all radiate from the pivot of this one word, and all are subsumed in a universal climax, an orgasm. What follows is nothing less than white-out, where white overlays white as in a painting by Robert Ryman. With 'words all white,' writing as well as its referents should be indiscernible, but the whiteness of script and of will 'suffuses' the whiteness of dazzle, and breaks down 'Illimitable monotone' into textures — actually into a textile at first, a white towel. Absorbent white wipes the laden white of mist, and the encounter of white with white, the full varietal range of whites, concentrates in 'cymophanous mist,' 'cymophanous' meaning 'opalescent' — from the Greek signifying 'shining billows' but with 'billows' pertinently evolved from a root-word for 'pregnant.'

White now has condensed from dazzle and burning heat into mist, sweat and discriminable textures. Whiteness also tracks an incarnation, whereby 'your sun' returns 'where there is nothing to see' as an 'etiolate body,' 'etiolate' here indicating loss of colour as much as gauntness, white towel wiping white sweat off a white body in white mist. What then does a 'white dawn' display? What else but what this poem unfolds and spills, mops up and abruptly breaks from — what André Green has termed a 'psychose blanche,' as here summarised on the website of the *Association lacanienne internationale*:

> sa notion de "psychose blanche" : "Hypocondrie négative du corps et plus particulièrement de la tête, impression de tête vide, de trou dans l'activité mentale . . . également ruminations, pensées compulsives, divagations subdélirantes".
>
> Mais on en reviendra finalement, avec cet auteur également, aux notions de fusion primaire et d'indistinction entre sujet et objet. Il insistera sur l'importance de la limite pour tout sujet, en évoquant différentes formes de limites plus ou moins perméables tels que la peur, le tissus cutané ou tout ce qui peut faire surface, enveloppe psychique pour un sujet et organiser son rapport à l'objet.[23]

Primary fusion with its effacement of all entities and distinctions, swirls mistily as the terrifying threat this poem faces, succumbing repeatedly and as often pulling back to re-identify objects and re-identify the psychic boundaries of both 'me' and 'you' as distinct from each other and as distinct from amniotic illimitability and sepulchral mephitis. Never has a 'New Day' sounded more like a groaning slab drawn over the mouth of a funeral vault; the marble step which opened the poem now recycled in a bid to solidify indistinctness itself into death's seal. 'Me' at this ground zero is no more than a hole in mental activity. Once again Loy has recourse to a vicious parody of the Christ myth: the tomb is empty because it contains the nothing

which is *me*, while *you*, having obliterated me and all the world, casu-
ally climb down from your cross and walk home. Consequently this
departure, by another irony, delivers my salvation owing to the
distance it introduces, for my renewed ability to point to 'that white
over there —' heralds the first step back towards the prismatic
decomposition enacted in the poem's first lines. 'White smoke'
signifies the ex-lover's disinterest and domestic comfort, as well as a
last onanistic ejaculation, a sign of departure as mournful as a puff
from a steam-engine.

The 'New Day' shutting down may read as one more contemptuous
dismissal of the promise of religious salvation, reaffirming the grace
of the quotidian in the almost Wordsworthian cottage where 'you'
are now relegated; but it surely carries a bitter overtone of the 'New
Woman' which Loy discovered herself to represent. Loy's compulsion
to shed doubt is once again in evidence, and her passionately-driven
contrariness. The force of Loy's feminism derives from the force of
her desire for submission; and the force of her desire for a perfectible
futurity from the force of her disappointment with the temporizing
of practical politics and with her body's longings. In every direction,
blockage or oblivion, or a false identification would shut her trap.

Yet such twists and turns make this poetry considerable; its 'wills
and words' are concentrated with rare vehemence. What has to be
learnt in reading 'Love Songs for Joannes' is first the necessity to
follow the writing with the kind of alertness one would bring to
Celan, a poet who furrows where Loy tacks; then to take account of
the 'dance of intelligence among words and ideas' Pound saw in Loy's
writing, entailing a restless back-tracking and side-glancing, and
recognition of a kind of skittish scepticism not to be found elsewhere
— until the poetry of Marjorie Welish, at any rate.[24] To play with this
logopoeically, Loy's cognitions are always subject to further recognition. But this skittishness is serious and actuated by an extraordinary
truthfulness, the recognition of each position as provisional, potentially self-serving, potentially serving others' interests, potentially a
way-station towards a more provocative mark of position. And Loy is
provocative in the best sense, of calling-forth, of challenging, then
dancing beyond reach, wry and exacting.

To use the word 'truthfulness' in talking of a poet whom it is hard
to imagine knowing where any of her poems might end up, is of
course to presume a particular test of truth, and one which is highly
contingent; nothing could be further from Laura Riding's brand of

truthfulness, for instance. But the comparison with Robert Creeley is a fair one since Creeley's poems attend so intently to their own manoeuvres, and claim a truth to the minutest fluctuations of perception. After reading Loy, the continuity of perceptual movement in Creeley becomes problematic; the test of truth becomes exactly self-interested, subordinate to the continuity which is never put seriously in jeopardy. Loy's self-consciousness forever makes her tongue-tied, but does not lead her to privilege self-consciousness as a basis for self-esteem through the reflexive estimation of a projected other. Because she balks before she utters, and fails at the thought of a course ahead, Loy cannot rest satisfied with any position, or the promise of salvation or extinction — she cannot adopt a line; even the 'terrific Nirvana' of poem 13, 'terrific' in both of its obvious and powerful senses, leads to the formula 'Me you—you—me' which makes at least three persons out of the instant of depersonalisation and possibly six. 'Myself' is but a 'nascent virginity' (*LLB II* 58), and virginity was not a state Loy admired or aspired to mimic.

Twentieth-century taste in lyric poetry tended to favour either a mystical dilation of significance around the sphinx-like object, or the felt authenticity of nearly-tangible and embodied voice. Robert Creeley's poetry does not belong entirely to either of these traditions, although Altieri's revisionism in associating him with the latter is illuminating, and sheds an interestingly reflective light upon Adrienne Rich's poetry. Creeley's invention is to make of his errors a finely responsive linguistic and emotional environment, an *envelope* as Green would have it, within which sexual clumsiness and stumbling words can be safe and yield for him, in the psychological cliché, an enormous secondary gain. Mina Loy's poetry has more in common with the poem as object than first appears, since its forthrightness makes the initial impact, but the status of the poem as an achieved thing is never allowed to rest; in this regard, the 'Love Songs to Joannes' point towards the serial poems of Jack Spicer, a logopoeic poet if ever there was one.

When Loy halts it is because the ground is uncertain, it is because the 'she' who would occupy the ground is unreliable, and it is because the very idea of occupation is questionable. The 'Love Songs to Joannes' are opinionated, but they are poems, and their opinions are applied, donned and foisted at will and at necessity. Constructive strategies such as reading the sequence as the history of an abortion, or foregrounding Christian and Classical mythical derivations as

Shreiber does in her essay, work only to a point, for throughout its course the sequence wages war with all its preoccupations.

> We might have given birth to a butterfly
> With the daily news
> Printed in blood on its wings (*LLB II* 54)

Wit and precision are indefatigably deployed against introspection, and nowhere more movingly than in this stanza. The second the conventional image of the soul of the new-born is given birth, its ephemerality is asserted, and the image becomes material. Simultaneously the lines present a horrifying picture of a back-street abortion, and a vividly specific description of a butterfly's wings, with its fractal markings the announcement of its short life. Each line end-stops and resumes effortlessly as a reconsideration of the place arrived at, a new utterance and a new birth into unforeseen conjunctions. Each line goes as far as it goes, but another tack follows. This is what Mina Loy does, and her writing remains news at every turn, at every stress-point — news that a new generation of poets and readers might be among the first to read, and to take up in their writing.

Notes

[1] Laurie Anderson, 'Walking and Falling,' *Big Science* (CD), Warner Brothers 1982. But as Stephen Fredman reminds me, Anderson has stuttered unwittingly through imitation: in *Home of the Brave* she tells a story about memorising her lyrics in Japanese for a concert in Japan. Afterwards someone comes up and says, 'Sorry, excuse me, sorry, but you speak English flawlessly; I can't understand why you speak Japanese with a stutter.' The Japanese translator she copied impeccably had a stutter. I am grateful to Stephen Fredman and Christine Froula for reading this essay in draft, and for their very helpful comments.

[2] See Rachel Blau DuPlessis, 'A Letter on Loy', in Shreiber and Tuma, eds., 501. Also, Ezra Pound, 'Marianne Moore and Mina Loy', in *Selected Prose 1909–1965* (New York: New Directions 1973), 424.

[3] See also Eric Murphy Selinger, 'Love in the Time of Melancholia' in Shreiber and Tuma, eds., 19–43.

[4] Charles Altieri, *The Art of Twentieth-Century Poetry: Modernism and After* (Oxford: Blackwell 2006), 182.

[5] The gloss is borrowed from Keston Sutherland, 'Ethica Nullius' (on J.H. Prynne's late poetry) in *Avant-Post: The Avant-Garde Under 'post-' Conditions* (Prague:

Literaria Pragensia, 2006); republished in *Foreign Literature Studies* (Wuhan, China) 30 no. 3 (June 2008), 14–23.

[6] Robert Creeley, *The Collected Poems of Robert Creeley 1945–1975* (Berkeley: University of California Press, 1982), 205.

[7] Creeley, 105. It is remarkable that Creeley chose to reprint this preface in his *Collected Poems*.

[8] Altieri, 189.

[9] Creeley, 207.

[10] Nathaniel Mackey, *Discrepant Engagement: Dissonance, Cross-culturality, and Experimental Writing* (Cambridge: Cambridge University Press, 1993), 108–9. What Duncan says is: 'Yes, but the figure of Creeley stumbling after the muse, it's a fool stumbling after the White Goddess; the White Goddess is not the figure of a man with no wife at all. It's the wife that undoes you and that leaves you stumbling and actually crippled, isn't it, finally? There is a subdued castration in which your heel is injured, so you're a stumbler, and Creeley's practised stumbling is an embodiment of a castration and impotency which is the experience we have in his poems.' Robert Duncan, *An Interview by George Bowering and Robert Hogg*, 19 April 1969, published as A Beaver Kosmos Folio (without date or pagination).

[11] Creeley, 200.

[12] Mackey, 109.

[13] Stephen Fredman, *Roadtesting the Language: An Interview with Edward Dorn*, Documents for New Poetry I, Archive for New Poetry (San Diego: University of California, 1978), 11.

[14] Marjorie Perloff, *The Futurist Moment: Avant-garde, Avant Guerre, and the Language of Rupture* (Chicago: Chicago University Press, 2003), 89.

[15] For the 'Feminist Manifesto' *LLB II* deploys a typographical resourceful characteristic of the Futurist manifesto and removes the uniform paragraphing of *LLB I*. No explanation is given for this editorial decision. The relevant passages read '— are you prepared for the <u>Wrench</u>—?' where 'Wrench' is in outsize type; 'Another great illusion that woman must use all her introspective clear-sightedness and unbiassed bravery to destroy—for the sake of her self respect is the impurity of sex'; and 'the <u>unconditional</u> surgical <u>destruction</u> of <u>virginity</u> through-out the female population at puberty—.'

[16] *LLB II* uses roman numerals to identify the poems and Poem XXXI has 'busybody' and 'Eclosion' (no acute accent). For *LLB II* Conover seems to adopt an undiscussed compromise between new manuscript or first-appearance evidence and the exigencies of conventional publishing — so, for instance, while punctuation is no longer regularised, he refrains from isolating Poem XVII in the centre of the sequence as Loy wished.

[17] Maeera Shreiber, 'Love is a Lyric/Of Bodies', in Shreiber and Tuma, eds., 90.

18 Marjorie Perloff, 'English as a Second Language', in Shreiber and Tuma, eds., 136–7.

19 *LLB II* has 'street-corner'.

20 Rachel Blau DuPlessis, 'Seismic Orgasm', in Shreiber and Tuma, eds., 63.

21 See Burke, 164, citing Loy's description of her absconding with Marinetti from her first marriage: 'She felt herself slipping into his world, she recalled, "where everything seemed to be worked by a piston." Hiding away from the past in his jacket, she continued (speaking of herself in the third person), "she was caught in the machinery of his urgent identification with motor-frenzy."' See also Linda A. Kinnahan, *Poetics of the Feminine* (Cambridge: Cambridge University Press, 1994), 56, for this clockwork as 'the male's libidinal experience from a woman's perspective.'

22 LLB II has 'Unthinkable that white over there / — Is smoke from your house'. The previous two quotations are unchanged in LLB II.

23 Jean-Jacques Tyszler, 'Objet clinique non identifié', Association Lacanienne Internationale, entry posted 4 April 2005, www.freud-lacan.com/articles/article.php?url_article=jtyszler040405 [accessed 11 July 2008].

24 See my article 'Faktura: The Work of Marjorie Welish', *Chicago Review* 51 no. 3 (Autumn 2005), 115–127.

The Ecstasy of Mina Loy

Alan Marshall

1.

My intention in what follows is to examine the place of ecstasy in the poetry of Mina Loy, and at the same time to illuminate what I would call the ecstatic character of her work, for ecstasy, I will suggest, describes Loy's purview, her attitude, as well as a considerable part of her subject matter. In order to do this I will be looking at her poetry in the light of the experience of ecstasy as it is described in the writings of some exemplary nineteenth-century ecstatics, including Emily Dickinson ('I find ecstasy in living—the mere sense of living is joy enough'),[1] Ralph Waldo Emerson, Henry David Thoreau, and above all Friedrich Nietzsche. My approach is not ideological but phenomenological. Nietzsche's ideological influence on modernism is well established and can be traced through existentialism, psychoanalysis and specific art movements such as Vorticism and Futurism. It is here, in relation to Futurism specifically, that we might be expected to look if we were simply trying to measure how far Loy might be said to move in Nietzsche's intellectual and ideological orbit.[2] That is not my purpose. Instead I shall assume that Nietzsche's account of ecstasy has its own phenomenological validity and usefulness, something which can be corroborated by referring to those other brilliant connoisseurs and exponents of this exceptional state of mind whom I have already mentioned. I do not mean to suggest that ideology is unimportant, but there is a tendency these days always to put it first, whereas I think that we shall better understand the ideological convergence of Nietzsche and Loy, perhaps above all for example in relation to Darwinism, by first recognising how both authors set about articulating what might be called an ecstatics and dynamics—or more accurately, perhaps, a dynamic ecstatics—of the self. It is quite clear that they were both haunted by the theory of evolution, as being one of the nightmare guises in which the democratic age would manifest itself, that is to say, in the biological identity of each with each. For both of them writing was a way of resisting the raving madness, as Loy expressed it, of evolving from protoplasm—and never transcending it. They turn from evolution to the histrionics of writing, where the self stages itself, finds a new word for itself, or as Nietzsche would say, a new value, and one thereby delights, contra Darwin, in becoming who or what one is ('how one becomes what one is'—*Wie man wird, was man ist*—is the subtitle of *Ecce Homo*). Ecstasy is a matter of survival (of the individual) in the face of survival (of the species): a matter of life and death.

There is something about Loy's life that seems to incarnate the myth of Ariadne: left alone on the shore by the disappearance at sea of her second husband Arthur Cravan, it could be said that as an artist she always had Dionysus to fall back on (*BM* 264).[3] It was a myth that resonated profoundly with Nietzsche, who in some moods almost seemed to cast himself as the bride of Dionysus: 'Who besides me', he wrote, 'knows what Ariadne is!'[4]

I have drawn mainly on what could be seen as Nietzsche's most ecstatic book, his autobiography *Ecce Homo*, the book in which he is inspired by his own example:

Does anyone at the end of the nineteenth century have a clear idea of what poets in strong ages called *inspiration*? If not, I will describe it. — If you have even the slightest residue of superstition, you will hardly reject the idea of someone being just an incarnation, mouthpiece, or medium of overpowering forces. The idea of revelation in the sense of something suddenly becoming *visible* and audible with unspeakable assurance and subtlety, something that throws you down and leaves you deeply shaken—this simply describes the facts of the case. You listen, you do not look for anything, you take, you do not ask who is there; a thought lights up in a flash, with necessity, without hesitation as to its form, —I never had any choice. A delight whose incredible tension sometimes triggers a burst of tears, sometimes automatically hurries your pace and sometimes slows it down; a perfect state of being outside yourself, with the most distinct consciousness of a host of subtle shudders and shiverings down to the tips of your toes; a profound joy where the bleakest and most painful things do not have the character of opposites, but instead act as its conditions, as welcome components, as *necessary* shades within this sort of excess of light; an instinct for rhythmic relations that spans wide expanses of forms—the length, the need for a rhythm that *spans wide distances* is almost the measure of the force of inspiration, something to balance out its pressure and tension . . . All this is involuntary

to the highest degree, but takes place as if in a storm of feelings of freedom, of unrestricted activity, of power, of divinity . . . The most remarkable thing is the involuntary nature of the image, the metaphor; you
do not know what an image, a metaphor, is any more, everything offers
itself up as the closest, simplest, most fitting expression. It really seems
[. . .] as if things approached on their own and offered themselves up as
metaphors [. . .] This is *my* experience of inspiration; I do not doubt that
you would need to go back thousands of years to find anyone who
would say: 'it is mine as well.'[5]

In this typically vivid passage Nietzsche describes some of the characteristics not only of what he calls inspiration but also of ecstatic
consciousness and he indicates the close relationship between the
two conditions. Both of them, for a start, are *excessive*: exceeding the
profoundest joy and the bleakest pain. Ecstasy may be understood
as, in Nietzsche's words, 'a perfect state of being outside yourself' ('*ein
vollkommnes Ausser-sich-sein*').[6] As Stanley Cavell remarks, in his study of
Thoreau's *Walden*: 'Being beside oneself is the dictionary definition
of ecstasy.'[7] As Cavell understands it, to stand apart from oneself
(beside or outside) is both to exist and to be perfectly conscious that
one exists: to exist, and then, *with what feels like another part of oneself*, to
be conscious of oneself as existing; in Thoreau's words, to 'stand as
remote from myself as from another.'[8]

In the state of inspiration, according to Nietzsche, the ecstatic
consciousness of self now takes the form of ecstatic consciousness of
involuntary thought or expression. Thoreau concurs: one becomes 'the
scene, so to speak, of thoughts and affections', a spectator before the
autonomous creative torrent of the self ('a mouthpiece or a medium
of overpowering forces . . . [A]s if things approached on their own
and offered themselves up as metaphors'). The artist, like the ecstatic,
is 'sensible of a certain doubleness.'[9] Or as Emerson puts it, 'The man
is only half himself, the other half is his expression.'[10] The ecstatic
or inspired person feels at the moment of ecstasy or inspiration that
he doesn't hear himself speak so much as he hears language speak;
thought think; expression express itself—not fitfully but fittingly,
leaving no room for doubt.

For Nietzsche and Thoreau alike the distance that seems to obtain
now within the living space of the self expresses itself in an art that
partakes of distance and radiates it: for the poet it is 'the need for a
rhythm that *spans wide distances*.' Accordingly, the artist is someone
who *distances* himself—'The name of the nearest friend sounds then

foreign and accidental', as Emerson puts it.[11] Thoreau observes in *Walden* that, 'One inconvenience I sometimes experienced in so small a house, the difficulty of getting to a sufficient distance from my guest when we began to utter the big thoughts in big words.'[12] As Nietzsche confirms in *Ecce Homo*: 'it seems that nothing is more insulting than suddenly letting a distance be felt, — *noble* natures who do not know how to live without admiring [*verehren*] are few and far between': i.e., *admiration* requires *distance*; one must always find out whether someone has 'a feeling for distance'.[13] If not, as Thoreau says, 'we thus lose some respect for one another'.[14] In Emerson also, ecstasy ('I am glad to the brink of fear') expresses itself in spatial terms: 'Standing on the bare ground,—my head bathed by the blithe air, and uplifted into infinite space,—all mean egotism vanishes . . . In the tranquil landscape, and especially in the distant line of the horizon, man beholds somewhat as beautiful as his own nature.'[15] The self here is the bare ground beneath one's feet and the landscape stretched out in the distance, it is where one stands and where one looks.

2.

> The *fundamental fact* of the Hellenic instinct—its 'will to life'—expresses itself only in the Dionysian mysteries, in the psychology of the Dionysian state [. . .] That is why the *sexual* symbol was inherently venerable for the Greeks, the truly profound element in the whole of ancient piety. All the details about the acts of procreation, pregnancy, and birth inspired the highest and most solemn feelings. In the doctrines of the mysteries, *pain* is pronounced holy: the 'woes of a woman in labour' sanctify pain in general,—all becoming and growth, everything that guarantees the future involves pain.[16]

Loy's 'Parturition' is a poem haunted by ecstatic data. It begins with a finite declaration of 'the infinite I AM'—with what Coleridge called 'a repetition in the finite mind of the eternal act of creation in the infinite I AM'.[17] The Kantian self-conscious ego announces itself, whose subjectivity helps to constitute a universe: 'I am the centre' (*LLB II* 4). In other words: I am, for myself, my own most central fact. And a cosmic fact too: 'the centre / Of a circle' (*LLB II* 4). Here is another common intuition of the egocentric self: that the world revolves around each one of us. But Loy has something in store that will give us pause. It turns out that this particular consciousness is,

pre-eminently, ringed round with pain (Lear's 'wheel of fire' almost
comes to mind). Pain concentrates the mind, puts us right at the
centre of our lives whether we wish to be there or not. As Emily
Dickinson wrote:

> Pain—expands the time—
> Ages coil within
> The minute Circumference
> Of a single Brain—
>
> Pain contracts—the Time—[18]

For Loy as for Dickinson this solitude, the unremitting solitude of
pain, feels round. 'When a thing becomes isolated, it becomes round',
writes Gaston Bachelard.[19] Dickinson seems to emphasise this not just
through the words 'coil' and 'circumference' but through the prominence of the letters *c* and *o*. For both poets the experience of pain may
also be described as a dynamic cross-rhythm of contractions and
expansion, simultaneously taking you out of yourself and bringing
you back to yourself. It is a doubleness within a singleness ('single
Brain'), a splitting of the I that paradoxically consolidates or *centres*
the I. '*I am bound* / Upon a wheel of fire', as Lear says (my emphasis).[20]

Instead of obliterating consciousness, pain raises it to the pitch of
ecstasy: 'Exceeding its boundaries in every direction.' Besides sounding uncannily like Dickinson ('You left me Boundaries of Pain'),[21] this
third line is ambiguous. It seems to be saying that pain, or the circle of
pain, exceeds its own boundaries (pain, as Dickinson also wrote, is
'Infinite contain');[22] but the speaker might also be saying that *she*, who
is at the centre, exceeds the boundaries of the circle of pain—and in
every direction. She is like Guy Fawkes being quartered, torn between
the four corners of the universe. As the prefix *ex* indicates, the infinite
I AM is thrust out of and beyond the body by way of the body. 'I like
a look of Agony, / Because I know it's true.'[23] Agony—with its suggestion that one is the centre of a contest—is a path to truth, at any rate
to deeper insight.

If the poem begins by sounding like one exponent of the ecstatic
life, Emily Dickinson, then it starts in the fourth line to sound like
another—John Donne. 'The business of the bland sun', recalls
Donne's 'Busy old fool, unruly sun', and the pun on 'affair' is a minor
instance of Loy's sharp sardonic Donne-like wit.[24] But whereas in
Donne's poem, the sun seems to fancy, Oedipus-style, a nice ménage

à trois, in Loy's he is simply bland and a businessman to boot. Besides, he is too late, the woman is pregnant.

The lines, 'In my congested cosmos of agony / From which there is no escape', recall us once again to the kind of oxymoronic images of cosmic claustrophobia in which Dickinson is so adept (*LLB II* 4). For both poets, pain, naturally, attacks the nerves, or attacks us via the nerves: 'After great pain, a formal feeling comes— / The Nerves sit ceremonious, like Tombs', wrote Dickinson;[25] Loy writes of 'infinitely prolonged nerve-vibrations', which contract, in much the same paradoxical style as things do in Dickinson, 'To the pin-point nucleus of being' (*LLB II* 4). Loy's imagery of nerves and pins has an unnerving finesse.

Then comes what Bachelard might have called an episode in the 'dialectics of outside and inside'—except that Bachelard was thinking of a different kind of 'intimate space', the home rather than the body. Loy brings the dialectic home to the body, the most intimate space of all (about which Bachelard is curiously reticent), and she ramps up the dialectical turnover:

> Locate an irritation   without
> It is   within
>   Within
>
> It is without
> The sensitized area
> Is identical   with the extensity
> Of intension
>
> I am the false quantity
> In the harmony of physiological potentiality
> To which
> Gaining self-control
> I should be consonant
> In time
>
> Pain is no stronger than the resisting force
> Pain calls up in me
> The struggle is equal (*LLB II* 4)

Bachelard's is a pretty tame kind of ecstasy as compared to this— where consciousness can neither stay in the body nor escape from it. Pain *extends* and *intends*; it is 'identical'—another pun, which is to say that it partakes of identity; it becomes one's identity. And while the rhythm is altogether different, the theme, tone and imagery once again recall Dickinson:

> For each ecstatic instant
> We must an anguish pay
> In keen and quivering ratio
> To the ecstasy.[26]

Despite beginning the poem by invoking consciousness, Loy has so far not used the word. It doesn't make an appearance until the second half of the poem, in the passage beginning 'Relaxation'. Nevertheless I think that when we read the first four syllables of line 6, 'In my congested cosmos of agony', we can almost hear the speaker say *In my conscious . . .* (the unstressed final *e* of *congested* also corresponds to the unstressed final *e* of *consciousness*). But more significantly, by leaving out the word consciousness, by thus immersing the concept in the body—and then observing it as it is violently repelled to the surface—Loy makes it even more explicit that as Nietzsche expressed it, 'consciousness *is* a surface.'[27] Consciousness is epidermal. It is 'an irritation' on either side of the skin ('Within / It is without').

Loy also tells us that pain is always temporal ('In time') no matter how a-temporal it temporarily feels. 'I should be consonant / In time', she writes: but the pain of giving birth or creation makes such consonance, of the self with itself, of the self with its pain, impossible. Here Loy's emphasis is quite different from what we find in Dickinson, where the illusion of a-temporality—pain's timelessness—becomes a highly ironical metaphor for the elastic moment of the lyric poem, in its 'Infinite contain' (the pain/poem spread across the 'Blank' page):

> Pain—has an Element of Blank—
> It cannot recollect
> When it begun—or if there were
> A time when it was not—[28]

In Loy's poem, pain propels one through time, one piece at a time, it divides one across it. The propulsive forward and downward movement of the poem, which seems at other moments to launch itself upward ('I am climbing a distorted mountain of agony'), embodies this idea. 'Parturition' exemplifies Loy's style at its most headlong and dithyrambic—dizzy rambling!—Nietzsche's preferred term for the

Dionysian period of *Thus Spoke Zarathustra*. 'The art of the *great* rhythm', he writes, in Walter Kaufmann's slightly more stylish translation, 'the *great* style of long periods to express a tremendous up and down of sublime, of superhuman passion, was discovered only by me; with a dithyramb like the last one in the third part of *Zarathustra* [. . .] I soared a thousand miles beyond what was called poetry hitherto.'[29] In 'Parturition' poetry is a process of overcoming, of trying, most obviously, to overcome pain, which is to say, a process of overcoming in time. The speaker overcomes the pain if only by enduring it, outlasting it, at any rate the latest spasm of it:

> I am climbing a distorted mountain of agony
> Incidentally with the exhaustion of control
> I reach the summit
> And gradually subside into anticipation of
> Repose
> Which never comes
> For another mountain is growing up
> Which   goaded by the unavoidable
> I must traverse
> Traversing myself (*LLB II* 5)

She overcomes it 'Incidentally' (as who should say: 'By the way, I am climbing a distorted mountain of agony here, if anybody's listening'). Pain, like ecstasy, is *alpine*. Up here, on these pinnacles, even one's 'Inferiority' is 'superior' ('the male / Leaves woman her superior Inferiority'). This sense of being *above it all*, alone on the peaks of a mountain range, is one of the phenomenological characteristics of ecstatic overcoming: there is an acute sense of isolation, of being alone up there, on these jagged lines.

> Anyone who knows how to breathe the air of my writings will know that it is the air of high places, a *strong* air. You need to be made for it or you will catch a cold. The ice is close by, the solitude is tremendous—but how peacefully everything lies in the light! How freely you can breathe! How many things you feel to be *beneath* you! —Philosophy as I have understood it and lived it so far is a life lived freely in ice and high mountains.[30]

For Loy as for Nietzsche, life is agonistic, one is borne upwards by a relentless conflict, which is first and foremost a conflict between one's weakest self (vulnerable to pain) and one's strongest self (which meets pain head on and 'traverses' it). The speaker is 'goaded by the unavoidable / I': 'goaded' here incidentally suggests to my ear not just torment, provocation, but also those sure-footed mountain animals, goats. But the central point is that the 'I' is 'unavoidable': that is, conflict with the 'I' is unavoidable: 'I must traverse / traversing myself': meaning, I must overcome myself, I must pass across myself (as one might cross a ravine); and I must also 'traverse / traversing'—overcome overcoming; and I must do it in verse—*traverse*.

Now we get an exceptionally vivid description of the ecstatic state: 'a climax in sensibility' beyond joy and pain, when the self becomes exotic even to itself. In ecstasy, as we know, the self is beside itself:

> Something in the delirium of night-hours
> Confuses while intensifying sensibility
> Blurring spatial contours
> So aiding elusion of the circumscribed
> That the gurgling of a crucified wild beast
> Comes from so far away
> And the foam on the stretched muscles of a mouth
> Is no part of myself
> There is a climax in sensibility
> When pain surpassing itself
> Becomes Exotic (*LLB II* 5)

One of the things that is remarkable about this is the way the self's relation to itself blurs and escapes normal 'spatial contours' and even pain seems to come 'from so far away', as if it were an animal in the distance somewhere. The image of distance, space, emerging within the self, and of a scene unfolding like a diorama within that emergent space, testify to the accuracy of Thoreau's famous diagram of ecstatic consciousness:

> I only know myself as a human entity; the scene, so to speak, of thoughts and affections; and am sensible of a certain doubleness by which I can stand as remote from myself as from another. However intense my experience, I am conscious of the presence and criticism of a part of me, which, as it were, is not a part of me, but spectator, sharing no experience, but taking note of it.[31]

But whereas Thoreau's experience of being beside himself is the direct result of thinking as what he calls 'a conscious effort of the mind', Loy is describing being brought to this pass by the action of her body—by something more spontaneous and involuntary.[32] For Loy, as for Nietzsche, as for later phenomenologists like Maurice Merleau-Ponty, the ecstatic mind does not stand outside itself, it floats upon—or say more accurately that it is *floated by*—the body, enjoys or enjoins, spontaneously, *for no apparent reason*, the power of the body. As against Thoreau's *conscious effort of the mind*, 'The great activity', as Nietzsche wrote, 'is unconscious'.[33] This unconscious activity also corresponds to the poetry's startling investment in irrational, dream-like imagery—bodies or body parts, whether of humans or animals, stretched, gurgling, foaming or pulsating beyond conscious control. Later on in the poem Loy reveals her affinity for images of insects, those most uncannily primitive of animals, which she unambiguously relishes for their look of life-in-death: 'A dead white feathered moth / Laying eggs'; 'small animal carcass / Covered with blue-bottles' (*LLB II* 6, 7). The main point once again is the way the speaker observes or monitors this unfolding in inner space of irrational imagery; the way she monitors it ecstatically.

3.

In 'Parturition' Loy deliberately sets the ecstasy of being pregnant and giving birth against the ecstasy of impregnating—the expansiveness that radiates outwards into the world, and issues forth into it, bears a child out into it, against that narrower action so to speak which turns its back on the world and addresses itself narrowly to, or into, one woman (or one woman at a time). As the psychoanalyst Karen Horney wrote:

Man's attitude toward motherhood is a large and complicated chapter [. . .] Even the misogynist is obviously willing to respect woman as a mother and to venerate her motherliness under certain conditions [. . .] It was this life-creating power of woman, an elemental force, that filled man with admiration. And this is exactly the point where problems arise. For it is contrary to human nature to sustain appreciation without resentment toward capabilities that one does not possess. Thus, a man's minute share in creating new life became, for him, an immense incitement to create something new on his part. He has created values of which he might well be proud. State, religion, art, and science are essentially his creations, and our entire culture bears the masculine imprint.

However, as happens elsewhere, so it does here; even the greatest satisfactions or achievements, if born out of sublimation, cannot fully
make up for something for which we are not endowed by nature. Thus
there has remained an obvious residue of general resentment of men
against women.[34]

Loy's poem is an ironical examination of the 'life-creating power of
woman' in the context of a culture that 'bears the masculine
imprint'—a culture that is written by men. The poem is thus ambiguously poised: it is a rip-roaring evocation of the agonies of childbirth,
which also invites us to find within it a metaphor for the creative
labours of the artist, the process of creating cultural monuments—
objects of which one 'might well be proud.' Thus the wonder of motherhood is described not only from inside, where it is revealed as
incorporating an ability to endure pain that implicitly unmans all
those (*men*) who haven't felt the like of it; it is also simultaneously
seen from outside, from the point of view of a masculine culture that
rivals and resents it—beginning with the biggest Maker of them all: 'I
once heard in a church / —Man and woman God made them— /
Thank God' (*LLB II* 8).

The poem is also, as I have discussed, a study in ecstasy—in childbirth as an ecstatic experience—that also functions ecstatically, exalt-
ing experience at its most extreme, and imposing a gulf of
misunderstanding between self and others.

We can see something of what Horney is getting if we look at John
Donne's poem, 'The Ecstasy', where the artfulness of Donne's metaphysical invention might well be interpreted as an attempt ultimately
to match the pregnancy it begins by contemplating, or indeed—with
God-like omniscience—by anticipating:

> Where, like a pillow on a bed,
>   A pregnant bank swelled up, to rest
> The violet's reclining head,
>   Sat we two, one another's best;
>
> Our hands were firmly cemented
>   With a fast balm, which thence did spring,
> Our eye-beams twisted, and did thread
>   Our eyes, upon one double string.[35]

There is an implicit suggestion that for the woman this has all been much too effortless ('a pillow on a bed'; 'The violet's reclining head'), whereas for the man 'the body is his book' (line 72) and he must work the pages.

As the poem continues Donne ingeniously lays out the architecture of ecstasy: doubleness within singleness; body and soul; elevation and stasis, and so on. And he deftly interweaves in his usual fashion sexual and metaphysical notions of ecstasy: an out-of-the-body experience ('Our souls', he writes, 'were gone out' and 'hung' in the air), for which we nevertheless owe the body thanks:

> We owe them thanks, because they thus,
>   Did us, to us, at first convey,
> Yielded their forces, sense, to us,
>   Nor are dross to us, but allay.[36]

Yet in the end 'The Ecstasy' perfectly exemplifies the fact that Donne is doomed to do no more than impregnate, and that much as he tries he cannot 'get with child'[37]—and it would be an interesting exercise to examine, from Horney's point of view and across the range of his oeuvre, the poet's envy of the woman's body, and his attempts to smother it or rival it with the 'body [of] his book.' By contrast, Loy's approach to ecstasy—including the ecstasies of inspiration and creation—comes from the perspective of someone for whom the out-of-the-body nature of ecstasy is felt from the inside out rather than from the outside in.

There is a handful of remarkable allusions to pregnancy in *Ecce Homo*. Nietzsche writes of the 'profound tension of the spirit', to which his 'whole organism is condemned' by pregnancy. 'You need to steer clear of chance, of external stimuli as much as possible. In spiritual pregnancy a certain cleverness of instincts directs you to wall yourself in.'[38] But it is the passage concerning the birth of *Zarathustra*, his favourite child and most exalted book, that is especially impressive:

> If I count forwards from that day up to the sudden birth that took place in February 1883 under the most improbable of circumstances [. . .] this gives eighteen months for the pregnancy. The figure of exactly eighteen months might suggest, at least among Buddhists, that I am really a female elephant.[39]

Stanley Cavell has written about what he calls the 'remarkable state-ment of pregnancy' in the middle of Emerson's essay 'Experience', taking up the fantasy of 'Emerson's imagining his giving birth some-how as a man rather than as somehow a woman.'[40] The subject's experience of pregnancy includes, we could say, a fantasy of binary fission which is also evident in Loy's poem: 'Negation of myself as a unit', she writes: the person is on the contrary divided by nature, by 'cosmic reproductivity' (*LLB II* 6, 7). The fantasy of binary fission also becomes a fantasy of a truly immaculate conception ('unpredicted Maternity'), which repudiates God's role in it, hence the ironical reference to the church in the final lines ('I once heard in a church . . . ') (*LLB II* 6, 8). Like the ecstatic condition it describes, 'Parturition' contains, as in Donne's poem, an apprehension of double life, life within and alongside life: 'I should have been emptied of life / Giving life.' 'The *body* is inspired', Nietzsche wrote, 'let us leave the "soul" out of it.'[41] Nevertheless, pregnancy, as Horney observed, is one area in which a woman has traditionally enjoyed a very clear advantage as regards bodily inspiration, and a man has had little choice but to turn to his soul.

4.

As close as Nietzsche and Emerson are in their sense of ecstasy as visionary exaltation, bearing one upwards 'into infinite space', there is an important difference between them which is most powerfully conveyed in the final sentence of the long passage from *Ecce Homo* I quoted at the beginning of this essay. It comes from Nietzsche's alto-gether more jealous conviction of his exaltation over others, which is at once more troubled, menaced and vertiginous than anything we find in Emerson. 'This is *my* experience of inspiration', he writes; 'I do not doubt that you would need to go back thousands of years to find anyone who would say: "it is mine as well."'

Since it emerges out of his confrontation with nihilism, Nietzsche's capacity for affirmation, the ethos of amor fati, the sanguine acceptance of eternal return, always feels more than a little hard-won. The challenge for Nietzsche is to rise above all feelings of *ressentiment* or vengeance vis-à-vis the nihilism he critiques and tran-scends. He has to remain both cynical (about nihilism) and innocent (of it).[42] And some of the euphoria that informs his writings seems to come from the daily conviction—which he is bound to renew from one morning to the next—of having remained untouched himself by what he was obliged to touch. It is a feeling of relief, of having escaped—to live another day ('The time for me hasn't come yet: some are born posthumously').[43] 'My humanity', as he says, 'is a constant self-overcoming'.[44] His 'solitude', then, unlike Emerson's, is always ranged, excitably, against the shiftless gregariousness of others. It is always having to prove itself. Emerson is altogether more phlegmatic:

> The great man is not convulsive or tormentable; events pass over him without much impression. People say sometimes, 'See what I have overcome; see how cheerful I am; see how completely I have triumphed over these black events.' Not if they still remind me of the black event. True conquest is the causing the calamity to fade and disappear, as an early cloud of insignificant result in a history so large and advancing.[45]

Nietzsche's, then, is a polemical ecstasy, an ecstasy born out of polemic, whereas Emerson's, despite the polemics, is a thing apart. And where Nietzsche's ecstasy feels compulsive or propulsive—something he throws himself into—Emerson's feels whimsical; it still surprises him.

Ecstasy in Loy, as we shall see, has more in common with the condition as we encounter it in Nietzsche: seeking to overcome not only what it overcomes, but its own reactiveness to everything it overcomes, it is a reaction that eschews reaction ('Another clever idea and principle of self-defence is to *react as infrequently as possible* and avoid situations and conditions where you would be condemned to unhook your "freedom", as it were, from your initiative, and turn into a simple reagent').[46] Nevertheless, while there remains something of the hermaphrodite about Nietzsche, despite (or in keeping with?) his Whitman-like championing of sexuality,[47] Loy is willing, for the sake of ecstasy, or should we say at the risk of it, to engage, or do battle with, to practice and to agonize over, sexual coupling itself—of which 'parturition' is in a sense the proof.

Ecstasy is central to 'Songs to Joannes', where it seems to take three forms: sexual, verbal and psychological—in the broad sense in which Nietzsche uses that term, where it cuts through to the heart of philosophy. Most startling is Loy's unprecedented willingness to evoke sexual ecstasy—not by directly describing the act or by mystifying it, but by having the courage to evoke the sheer bloody excessiveness of it, its unreasonableness, its involuntariness (with the disarming sense of biological autonomy: 'the procreative truth of Me / Petered out'), its humiliations and its sensationalism, as if it is all too much for the poor human brain (*LLB II* 62). In the face of sex Loy's imagery takes off. As if the sexual act itself generated images and words—as if it made one speak in tongues, in ecstatic babble. There are constant images of flight. Sex projects things into the air: birds, butterflies, shuttle-cocks, feathers, sparks, breath, *words* . . . Babies are bird-like; the body's fluids fall feather-like ('A little pink-love / And feathers are strewn') (*LLB II* 56). Language talks itself out of intelligible meaning—or it's as if tongues talked to each other rather than human beings:

> We might have lived together
> In the lights of the Arno
> [. . . . .]
>
> And   talked till there were no more tongues
> To talk with   (*LLB II* 59)

In Loy's 'Songs', language's ability to break out in a kind of automatism, which is the special gift of poetry, and which discloses once again the animism or animation of the world ('I don't care / Where the legs of the legs of the furniture are walking to'), corresponds to and evokes the automatism of sex:

> Licking the Arno
> The little rosy
> Tongue of Dawn
> Interferes with our eyelashes
> ———————
> We twiddle to it
> Round and round
> Faster
> And turn into machines (*LLB II* 63)

Love is close to infantilism ('We twiddle to it'): sex not only begets babies, it turns grown adults into them.

So much for sexual and verbal ecstasies, then. Loy has great fun with them. The psychological dimension of ecstasy is more equivocal, as it raises the question of whether one can, as Thoreau thought, 'stand as remote from [oneself] as from another': or more precisely, in

Loy's case—since unlike Thoreau, Nietzsche or even Emerson, she is willing to risk an ecstatic relation to the other—the question of *whether one can stand as remote from another as from oneself*. In other words, we could say that the artist-individualist is almost Nietzschean by definition: he or she will know all about ecstasy as described by Thoreau or Nietzsche or any of the great nineteenth-century ecstatics. But what about ecstasy together with another human being? For Nietzsche, on the endless carousel of self-overcoming, this appears to have been an impossibility: it was bound to lapse into a struggle for superiority—that is to say, into a quest for that obliviousness as regards the other which is the sign of perfect independence. But for Loy, the very idea of love songs, or dithyrambs, whether they are addressed to a Joannes or a Dionysus, raises the question of whether ecstasy can be shared, or to put it another way: whether one can share and at the same time feel ecstatic.

In the fifteenth 'Song', Loy even raises the matter in explicitly Nietzschean terms:

> Seldom   Trying for Love
> Fantasy dealt them out as gods
> Two or three men   looked only human
>
> But you alone
> Superhuman   apparently
> I had to be caught in the weak eddy
> Of your drivelling humanity
>   To love you most (*LLB II* 59)

The lover is, in Nietzsche's phrase, *human, all too human*, with a 'disheartening odour / About [his] nervy hands' (*LLB II* 57). The word 'Superhuman' is brilliantly and equivocally poised: it seems at first to be saying that only that person whom the speaker loves looked 'Superhuman.' But the word is so pivoted at the start of the line that it can also be read as saying 'Superhuman apparently / I . . .': the speaker herself was 'apparently' superhuman. Thus speaker and lover are permitted to merge for a moment in that unlikeliest of words— i.e. in a concept which as far as Nietzsche was concerned left no room for another person. But Loy pushes it even further: the speaker's superhumanity, so to speak, is made to depend, quite possibly, upon a recognition of its opposite: 'drivelling humanity'—on abasing itself to what is abased.

This could of course be taken to prove Nietzsche's point (or Emerson's or Thoreau's) that the sole provenance of ecstasy is the self-reliant, or as Wordsworth would say 'self-sufficing' self. One must give birth to oneself—be father of the man and of the child.

Loy won't be seduced by the short-lived 'terrific Nirvana' of sexual ecstasy into taking it for something more long-lived (*LLB II* 58). She won't make that fantastic mistake. But again and again in the sequence the speaker is aroused to an ecstatic consciousness, which is nether wholly *with* nor wholly *without* the other. 'It is true', she says, 'That I have set you apart' (*LLB II* 57). The notion of the lover's being 'apart' is crucial. In this state she seems capable of monitoring her fructuous and 'infructuous impulses' without trying to fuse her identity with that of her lover:

> The skin-sack
> In which a wanton duality
> Packed
> All the completion of my infructuous impulses
> Something the shape of a man
> To the casual vulgarity of the merely observant
> More of a clock-work mechanism
> Running down against time
> To which I am not paced
> My finger-tips are numb from fretting your hair
> A God's door-mat
> On the threshold of your mind (*LLB II* 53–4)

Equivocally suspended between irony and pathos, some of the brilliance of this second 'Song' also derives from what Nietzsche calls *distance* and *admiration*.[48] The beloved is 'Something the shape of a man / To the casual vulgarity of the merely observant': but to the lover he transcends the merely human: let him be a god or an animal or a machine ('a clock-work mechanism'), anything but 'drivelling humanity.' She prefers to remain 'on the threshold of [his] mind', not to get inside it. There is a relish of the hard outside, the external, the human being in his or her transcendent shape and outline. To see the human being without engaging the mess of his or her subjectivity is to see him for a moment like a Greek god. As I noted earlier, in Nietzsche's view, 'it seems that nothing is more insulting than suddenly letting a distance be felt,—*noble* natures who do not know how to live without admiring are few and far between.' Here Loy imposes a distance precisely so as to feel it and, presumably, to let the other feel it; to give him space to feel it. But we may judge that nobility is only his by first being hers; that it is her capacity for admiration that facilitates everything else—and the passage is fully alive to the irony of that.

Loy's poetry is habited by the shades of 'Goddesses and Young Gods' ('O Hell'). All through its groves, 'Apollo haunts Apollo' ('Marble'). Part of the attraction of the gods, for Nietzsche as for Loy, and probably for the whole fin-de-siècle mindset, has to do with the fact that they are not tormented by their inner lives, by Arnoldian or Kierkegaardian crises of subjectivity or faith. They exist in their actions, their embodiments—they are what they are. Loy's peculiar gift for hardness is something that has been remarked both by those critics who have misunderstood it (Ezra Pound) and those who have appreciated it (Thom Gunn). Once again Nietzsche's words are apposite: the 'certainty that *all creators are hard* is the true sign of a Dionysian nature.'[49] The hardness of Loy's stare is a reflection, I'm suggesting, of her ecstatic disposition, of something Dionysian in the posture of her muse. We can see it at work in poems like 'Sketch of a Man on a Platform' or 'Der Blinde Junge.' In the first of these, while Roger Conover is quite right to say that Loy mocks what he calls this 'Marinetti as marionette', all Futurist brawn, she also, I think, celebrates the power of her gaze (*LLB II* 181) —enjoys her capacity to see this man as a body, a machine, a prodigious automaton:

> Your genius
> So much less in your brain
>
> Than in your body (*LLB II* 19)

He stands on a platform—we might even say a pedestal—as the poet makes a kind of sculpture out of him, like the Greek marbles in another poem, 'Marble':

> A flock of stone
> Gods
> perched upon pedestals (*LLB II* 93)

Here the very blindness of the statues ('Greece has thrown   white shadows / sown / their eyeballs with oblivion') communicates their existence as surface, marble, free of all corrosive interiority. At the same time the interiority of the poet is thereby turned outwards, articulated in the space between where she stands and what she looks at.

In 'Der Blinde Junge' the youth begins, so to speak, as a struggling artist (blowing out 'damnation and concussive dark / Upon a mouth-organ') (*LLB II* 84), and by the time Loy is finished with him he is a work of art—as finished as art is, as 'Brancusi's golden bird' is, in the poem of that title. The light is outside, not inside:

> This gong
> of polished hyperaesthesia
> shrills with brass
> as the aggressive light
> strikes
> its significance (*LLB II* 79–80)

> this slow blind face
> pushing
> its virginal nonentity
> against the light (*LLB II* 83)

Both objects are flightless birds: Brancusi's sculpture is 'unwinged unplumed'; the blind youth 'strains . . . in static flight upslanting.' They are 'static' and *ek-static*—i.e. ecstatic for those who can look at them unsentimentally, and who by looking at them get outside them-selves.

Notes

[1] Emily Dickinson, letter 342a, in Thomas H. Johnson, ed., *Selected Letters* (Cambridge and London: Harvard University Press, 1971), 211.

[2] For a comparison of Loy and Nietzsche on ideological grounds see Rachel Potter, *Modernism and Democracy: Literary Culture 1900–1930* (Oxford: Oxford University Press, 2006).

[3] Burke puts it like this: 'She waited for him on the beach, wrapped up in his coat. But Cravan did not return. She never saw him again', *BM*, 264.

[4] Friedrich Nietzsche, *The Anti-Christ, Ecce Homo, Twilight of the Idols and Other Writings*, ed. Aaron Ridley and Judith Norman, trans. Judith Norman (Cambridge: Cambridge University Press, 2005), 133. Hereafter cited as *Ecce Homo*.

[5] Ibid., 126–7.

6 Friedrich Nietzsche, *Der Fall Wagner, Götzen-Dämmerung, Der Antichrist, Ecce Homo, Dionysus-Dithyramben, Nietzsche contra Wagner*, kritische Studienausgabe herausgegeben von Giorgio Colli und Mazzino Montinari (München: Deutsche Taschenbuch Verlag, 1999), 339.

7 Stanley Cavell, *The Senses of Walden*, an expanded edition (Chicago and London: University of Chicago Press, 1992), 104.

8 Henry David Thoreau, *Walden and Civil Disobedience*, ed. Owen Thomas (New York and London: W. W. Norton & Company, 1966), 91.

9 Ibid.

10 Ralph Waldo Emerson, 'The Poet', *Essays and Lectures*, ed. Joel Porte (New York: Library of America, 1983), 448.

11 Emerson, 'Nature', 10.

12 Thoreau, 94.

13 *Ecce Homo*, 129, 142.

14 Thoreau, 91–2.

15 Emerson, 'Nature', 10.

16 Nietzsche, *Twilight of the Idols*, 227–8.

17 Samuel Taylor Coleridge, *Biographia Literaria*, ch.13, 'On the imagination, or esemplastic power'.

18 Emily Dickinson, 967, *The Complete Poems of Emily Dickinson*, ed. Thomas H. Johnson (London: Faber and Faber Limited, 1970).

19 Gaston Bachelard, *The Poetics of Space*, trans. Maria Jolas (Boston: Beacon Press, 1994), 239.

20 *King Lear*, 4.7.46–7.

21 Dickinson, 644.

22 Ibid., 650.

23 Ibid., 241.

24 John Donne, 'The Sun Rising', *The Complete English Poems*, ed. A.J. Smith (Harmondsworth: Penguin, 1971), 80.

25 Dickinson, 341.

26 Ibid., 125.

27 *Ecce Homo*, 97. In the German edition: '*Bewusstsein ist eine Oberfläche*' (294).

28 Dickinson, 650.

29 Friedrich Nietzsche, *On the Genealogy of Morals*, trans. Walter Kaufmann and R. J. Hollingdale, *Ecce Homo*, ed. and trans. Walter Kaufmann (New York: Random House, 1969), 265–6.

[30] *Ecce Homo*, 72.

[31] Thoreau, 91.

[32] Ibid., 90.

[33] Nietzsche, quoted in Gilles Deleuze, *Nietzsche and Philosophy*, trans. Hugh Tomlinson (London: Athlone Press, 1983), 41.

[34] Karen Horney, 'The Distrust Between the Sexes', in Harold Kelman, ed., *Feminine Psychology* (New York and London: W. W. Norton, 1973), 114–5.

[35] Donne, *Complete Poems*, 53.

[36] Ibid., 55.

[37] Donne, 'Go, and catch a falling star,' 77.

[38] *Ecce Homo*, 89.

[39] Ibid., 124. Nietzsche was notoriously hostile to feminism, which he almost inevitably saw as a species of *ressentiment*, pouring scorn on 'the "emancipated", who do not have what it takes to have children' (ibid., 105). Nevertheless one has to set against this his warm equable references to *particular women*, such as Cosima Wagner and Lou Salomé, and his embrace of the mythological figure of Ariadne. Nor is it going too far to suggest that his feeling that he was—as Kaufmann's translation of *Ecce Homo* has it—'6000 feet beyond man and time' (295), might be considered as comprehending, by definition, a soaring above everything that had previously passed for manhood.

[40] Stanley Cavell, 'Finding as Founding: Taking Steps in Emerson's "Experience"', repr. in David Justin Hodge, ed., *Emerson's Transcendental Etudes* (Stanford: Stanford University Press, 2003), 127, 130.

[41] *Ecce Homo*, 128.

[42] Friedrich Nietzsche, *The Will to Power*, ed. Walter Kaufmann, trans. Walter Kaufmann and R. J. Hollingdale (New York: Random House, 1968), 3.

[43] *Ecce Homo*, trans. Kaufmann, 259.

[44] *Ecce Homo*, 83.

[45] Emerson, 'Circles', 413. Cheerfulness (*Heiterkeit*) is exactly what Nietzsche finds in Emerson in a wonderfully perceptive paragraph in *Twilight of the Idols* (198–9). Compare it with the 'cheerfulness' of Nietzsche himself: 'Anyone who saw me during the seventy days this fall when, working without a break, I created things of only the highest calibre, things that nobody will surpass—or anticipate—with a responsibility for all the millennia to come; nobody who saw me then would have noticed a single trace of tension, but rather an overflowing freshness and cheerfulness' (*Ecce Homo*, 99). It is precisely in the way that Nietzsche seems compelled to project an audience for himself ('Anyone   .   .   [or] . . . nobody who saw me'), even while he abjures an audience—this restless antipathy—that we can we see how far he strays from the 'blithe air'

surrounding Emerson. 'When I compare myself . . .', he says, contradicting his brilliant advice to, 'Beware of picturesque people!' (ibid., 98–9).

[46] *Ecce Homo*, 96.

[47] Nietzsche presents what he calls the happiness of his existence in the form of a riddle: 'as my father I am already dead and as my mother I am still alive and growing old. This *double birth*', he writes, 'explains that neutrality, that free-dom from partisanship in relation to the overall problems of life, that is, perhaps, my distinction' (*Ecce Homo*, 74–5, my emphasis). For his championing of 'life', 'nature' and 'sexuality', see the penultimate section of the book (148–9).

[48] It would be interesting to know whether Basil Bunting recalled this passage when describing the two young lovers in *Briggflatts*: 'Naked / on the pricked rag mat / his fingers comb / thatch of his manhood's home.' Basil Bunting, *Collected Poems* (Oxford and New York: Oxford University Press, 1978), 41. In a much earlier poem, which he addressed to Loy, Bunting used the image of a closed door to evoke distance, admiration and the longing that still flickered from afar: 'Very likely I shall never meet her again / or if I do, fear the latch as before' (Bunting, 91).

[49] *Ecce Homo*, 134.

Adolescent Prosody

Geoff Gilbert

'Faces express the labor of perceptual mimesis; flowers seem to express its ease'.[1]

In 1938, Brecht asked: 'what about realism in lyric poetry?'. The question is a live one. What does the specific grasp of lyric poetry on the world, at once deep and flimsy, offer in the way of realism?[2] How do we make life in this world out of lyric poetry? Mina Loy's 1942 poem 'Mass-Production on 14th Street', written when she was sixty and living in poverty in New York's Lower East Side, will be the focus for this essay. Prosody, the specific work and the specific matter of lyric poetry, will be read as a kind of living. Lyric poetry enacts a resistant account of positions in life (positions close to its authorship like woman, bum, and poet, and apparently more distant ones like 'adolescent'), where prosody works against the sociological reductions in these terms which would submit bodies weakly to the world.

In her 1925 essay on 'Modern Poetry', published in the fashion journal *Charm*, Loy gives us a sketch of what a lyric realism might be. There is nothing very unusual about her statement; we can find versions of it throughout modernist poetics. She notes that 'Modern poetry, like music, has received a fresh impetus from contemporary life; they have both gained in precipitance of movement. The structure of all poetry is the movement that an active individuality makes in expressing itself' (*LLB II* 157). But unlike 'the new music of unprecedented instruments', the 'new poetry of unprecedented verse' has not been recognised as bearing 'the collective spirit of the modern world.' She sees this failure of recognition as emerging from the 'silent sound' of the 'cold barrier of print', which requires a concentrated voluntary attention, if the movement of 'active individuality' in the poem is to be grasped into spirit, and is thus to enchant contemporary life (*LLB II* 157).

In his remarks on realism, Brecht was responding to the project of Georg Lukács, as it had developed in the 1930s. Lukács, in a series of essays on contemporary novelists, had everywhere diagnosed decline; for Brecht, he is 'unable to find in them a realism equal to that of the classical novelists in depth, breadth and attack'; and the inventiveness of the writers he discusses (Joyce, Gide, and Musil are the worst culprits) has become distressingly alien, a kind of visible technicity. What Lukács wants is simple: a narrative which is at once about the contemporary world and of it, and which invokes 'a rich life of the spirit', and which thereby will 'hold back the pace of events by a slow narrative', and 'bring back the individual to the centre of the stage'.[3] While, for Brecht, Lukács's ambition is impracticable in the context of the gathering speed and alienation of contemporary capitalism; and while, for Adorno, Lukács's formulations are ideological in origin, I can understand the value of what he hopes to imagine: a writing which would image the human subject, in its integrity, as the agent of history, in its totality, such that that written figure can provide mediation for the political subject. Through such a figure, we can model and animate the 'concrete possibility' of human action as historically productive; against this, contemporary writers, particularly 'modernists', imagine only 'abstract possibility'. The position from which they write only exists theoretically or psycho-pathologically; it is withdrawn from human society and historical process.[4]

Paul Ricoeur, in his work on the hermeneutics of narrative, may help to provide respectable and independent support for Lukács's impracticable ambition, or rephrase his compliance with Stalinist doctrine. Narrative, relatively autonomous in that its schematization of human action draws on formal systems, systems of mythos, which are not of or in lived time, is an important basis, from which ground the lifeworld (the humanly arranged *umwelt*, or context, consisting both of objects and of the resources on which we draw as we negotiate the *umwelt*) can be enchanted and transformed into *welt*, a world. That is, the act of reading narrative is part of a process through which our context is grasped as a world, rather than as a situation. Real lives are lived here, because there was realist fiction.[5]

Neither Lukács nor Ricoeur is critical. Ricoeur's realism is not critical because the space of form, of mythos, is imagined as 'out of history', as a transcendent schema. Lukács, for Brecht, and later and more trenchantly for Adorno, is not critical because the mediating narrative form is transcendently ideological.[6] We might say the same about Loy, in 'Modern Poetry'. Her vision of the 'poet' and her 'active individuality', and even her vision of the will that would drive a 'voluntary attention', seem to originate outside the historical processes that operate in and against the 'precipitance of contemporary life'. Her poetics, in one statement, finds its proper place outside the world: 'surely if there were a heaven it would be where this horrible ugliness of human life would arise self-consciously as that which the poet has made of it' (*LLB II* 159).

There is a persistent strain of mysticism in Loy's life and work with which her account of modern poetry could be aligned. But more importantly, the actually mediating, formal space of poetry, 'the silent sound' of the 'cold barrier' of written language, is given *material* genesis, rather than descending from heaven or cthonically emerging as *mythos*. There is a figure in the essay who stands I think for this meeting of precipitance, will, and alienated language:

> You may think it impossible to conjure up the relationship of expression between the high browest modern poets and an adolescent Slav who has speculated in a wholesale job-lot of mandarines and is trying to sell them in a retail market on First Avenue. But it lies simply in this: both have had to become adapted to a country where the mind has to put on its verbal clothes at terrific speed it if would speak in time; where no one will listen if you attack him twice with the same missile of argument. (*LLB II* 159)

I like the cut of this adolescent Slav. His language is immigrant, idiomatic, and improvised. It appears to offer him an entry into a life in capitalism, but it operates as a demand for a modern listening. No phrase can be repeated, and he will not be formed durably in language under capitalism, and *welt* will not be formed; but something of him is made there in his prosody, among the mandarines that came cheaply, and will rot if he does not sell them.

1. Of the garment-worker

'Mass-Production on 14th Street' is not an easy poem. Carolyn Burke, Loy's biographer, sees it as one of 'her most successful poems of the 1940s', but then gets it, I think, a bit wrong, seeing it as an integrative and picturesque construction, in which the poet, positioned as observer, finds identity with the 'femina' she aesthetically arranges, and nourishes herself on the scene (*BM* 397–8). And Susan Dunn, in a very interesting account of the poem in relation to the context of consumerism, doesn't account for the processes of production that provide the poem's title.[7] As I don't find it an easy poem, and at the risk of making a lot of very obvious statements, I want first to attempt a prose summary and commentary: a reading of the poem, more or less line by line (I'll be more thorough with the first part of the poem, where its modes are laid down, and very rapidly skate over the rest).

The opening couplet, set off in apposition to the rest of the poem by a colon, makes a first stab at the terms of the poem as a whole. It offers a paradoxical temporal structure, an opening of an ocean to flower that is aligned with a 'closing hour' (this alignment is sealed and confused by the rhyme of hour and flower, and its awkward pressure on indecision about whether hour is a diphthong or not). This structure offers us an image — the traditional image — of aesthetic beauty and form: the flower, growing and passing in time but holding that time within its form (the ocean is in flower, not in flow); and it is aligned with its content, the oceanic surge of people liberated by the hour of closing, when shops perhaps or factories close. The ocean is pedestrian, material and mundane; but it has an undertow, a potentially treacherous current that moves in an independent direction. This complicates considerably our flower, the flower we want to stand for form, for closing *as* opening. The image is material, and thus it is both simple and complex. The undertow to the oceanic movement is provided by the form of the legs of the pedestrians, motor of the flow, enclosed in rosy hosiery (rosy both like flesh and like flower). The legs act as scissors, snipping the continuous space of and under the crowd into triangles of particular intention. A 'racing lace' is given here as the work which overlays and undermines the aesthetic generalizations which enclose this mass-movement as form. As texture and fabric, this lace can be draped decoratively over that form, but as a trace of production, it operates also against it.

This first sentence of the poem is completed by a single line, set off from the rest of the stanza: 'in an iris circle of Industry'. This 'in' here is the fourth, and by no means the last, arresting preposition of the poem: it wants to contain what has gone before within the 'iris circle', as the same preposition wanted to range 'ocean' *inside* the idea of flower. But any gesture of containment looks less than secure: the 'commodious' space that will open after this line allows what is placed inside it to rattle with a certain autonomous resistance. The lace which has been produced in and against the generalized ocean may well now be taken into the circus, the circular form, of the iris — both part of the eye and another flower — but it has enough space there to do its independent bidding. Relations are good and rich here: the lozenges of the eye (or the multiple faceting of the bee-eye which appears later) are formed of triangular snippings of generalized space, but the integrative movement which would allow the eye to own those fragments entirely as form is not complete. Remember that the Iris is a flower named for the rainbow and the hexagonal crystal, for their prismatically separated light, and that this mode of separation is tied to the figure of Iris, the messenger of no specific myths.

The movement of vision which would integrate both the ocean and its lacy undertow is *of* 'Industry'. The term is capitalized. Raymond Williams describes the nineteenth-century shift in the meaning of the word 'industry' from signalling an inalienable human attribute — skill, perseverance, *my* industry — to referring to the institution through which labour is alienated from itself. 'Art' follows a complementary trajectory, from inalienable human property to ineffable institution, as though to compensate for that alienation.[8] This sense that integration is coordinated with alienation is confirmed by the characterization of the eye — the iris circus — as a 'commodious bee', the traditionally industrious creature, whose industry absorbs and enables the sex of flowers. The eye-bee is commodious because it has space for all that is gathered into it, and it is commodious because it profitably serves industry (commodity is, among other things, the property of being commodious), here the Industry of aesthetic or generalizing perception.

What this bee-eye does is to gather things which are unlike, facets of faces, together. It works against the diamond flesh of adolescence. Flesh is difficult to dissociate from flash: the two temporalities, of organic growth and decay, and of immediate inorganic brilliance, compete here, as they do in Pound's 'In a Station of the Metro', or often in Baudelaire. The diamond is compounded of faces and facets, which are record of the work — not quite snipping triangles, but not quite *not* that either — through which its status as commodity is produced. The tension is nice here, infinite singular faceting and faces inscribe one kind of work; the gathering of these under the commodious bee-eye of the iris Industry circus describes another, through which the initial laborious process is effaced. Unlike faces and adolescent flesh are processed as we move towards integrative aesthetic sight. We 'slop[e] towards perception', in a form of movement which is furtive and shamed (one slopes off without paying the bill), as it follows the sloping facets of the diamond towards commodity. The eye traduces the object, as it comprehends facets into images.

In an exquisite argument about 'perceptual mimesis', Elaine Scarry argues that the flower, presented in words, makes imagination easily possible in two ways. First, it *fits* the imagination, it lifts itself into our head, by virtue of its beauty: its rarity and form and scale. 'When a poet describes a flower, even (I think) when a poet merely names a flower, it is always being offered up as something that after a brief stop in front of the face can immediately pass through the resisting bone and lodge itself and light up the inside of the brain.' Then, because it is easy to imagine, it provides itself as a support on which other forms, more difficult to perceive in the mind, can be laid out. 'The poet gives us the easily imaginable flower [. . .] and does so in order to carry onto that surface other, much less easily imaginable images.'[9] This process, a perceptual mimesis that we learn from the flower, is grounded in our physiological kinship with the flower, a homology between our organs of perception and the sentient, reactive, patterns of growth and movement of and in the flower. We love *towards* the flower in a cross-species erotics, and that loving relationship, with a beauty that grows in us to inform our capacity to perceive beauty, enables other imaginative relations:

> Flowers can be taken as the representative of the imagination because of the ease of imagining them. That ease is in turn attributable to *their* size and the size of our heads, *their* shape and the shape of our eyes, *their* intense localization and the radius of our compositional powers, *their* rarity that lets them rise and enter our brains and our willingness to receive them as the template for the production of other, more resistant compositions. It is clear, we were made for one another.[10]

Much in Scarry's strange strong argument is germane to a reading of Loy's poem. But there is a gathering objection which we can direct from Loy towards Scarry, and which concentrates in that final phrase: 'we were made for one another'. Loy's poem will not allow the easy passive here: *who* made us? How are the complementary institutions of art and industry under capital arranged within this making; how do we read the institutions and Industries, as well as the intuitions and industriousnesses, of the perception of beauty?

My answer, which I'll develop below, begins in the adolescent: the adolescent flesh signals a competing image of aesthetic form to that of the flower, and within that of the flower, with a different temporality, a different integrity in relation to the social, and a different prosody. Flowers multiply at this stage of the poem, laid on one another to form a 'corolla of complexion', where a corolla again is an intimate part of the flower, a little crown of petals or leaves which form the inner envelope of the flower, as well as calling for its corollary, a gratuity or supplementary payment for garlands and decoration. Complexion, the revelation of the humours, human temperament on the surface of the face, is decomposed analytically (into the components of 'fashion's humour' at the end of the poem). The layers — wondrously arrayed in the artificial hanging-gardens — are 'of' the 'garment-worker', and as such their picturesque completion as a single effect is disharmonious with the labour that was required to arrange them.

Hyphenation becomes more than merely conventional here, as it does in certain other places in the poem (the hyphenated 'Mass-production' of the title and line 25, and the 'hand-labor' of line 35). The garment-worker is a complex compound noun, referring of course to a particular sociological category within an industrial system, but also marking the provisionality and the problem, in the conflation of clothing and person. 'Mass-production' does something similar, denoting an alienated category, and also signalling uneasily its genesis, in the perceptual production of 'the mass' in the aesthetic form of the 'ocean in flower'. 'Hand-labor', again, separates the terms of the industrial at the same moment as yoking them.

All this makes the 'all this' of the next stanza difficult to gather together. We have a further agent of productive integration, given as 'Eros', and thus not different, in its movements, from that of the bee, gathering and pollinating. Loy is a famously erotic poet, and so it is awkward for me to be reading her poem against this tendency. Kenneth Rexroth's ecstatic 1944 review of Loy's poems values her work on the basis of its erotics, and thus its importance and earnestness (set against the work of Marianne Moore's 'dehydrated levity'). Sex is real in Loy's work, for Rexroth: 'Her copulators stay copulated'.[11] But the kinds of copula (in a loose sense, as those grammatical features that link words together) that are scattered through 'Mass Production' are strongly ambivalent. The hyphens separate as well as conjoin; the prepositions are difficult to aggregate into a set of stable spatial or temporal relations which would reach out to a world; the couplets signal uneasy cohabitation. The classic and absolute form of the copula — the verb 'to be', linking subject and predicate in the mode of identity — is suppressed in many places, including here, in 'All this Eros's produce'. In fact, it is present only once in the poem, in its last couplet, as a gesture of slightly despairing literal reduction, which is overwhelmed by the dense sequence of rhymes and the halting syntactical confusion between plurals and genitives: 'Only — her buttons are clothespins / the mannequin's, harlequins'. The copula, like the clothespins, only barely holds things together. Eros, for Freud, is a binding energy, which through desire conjoins communities and species and Life. In this poem, that integrative tendency is aligned with the alienated system of Industry, and later of identity. Eros is the wrong deity for Loy's sexiness.

The flowers in this part of the poem *are* riotously sexy: carnations are returned to their fleshiness in 'a carnal caravan / for Carnevale'; fuschia [sic] is an 'audacious' mode of dress; orchids appear in the form of orgies (where orchids, by a slight morphological confusion, are cognates of the 'orchis' or testicle). But their sexiness and their intensity, the heightened sonorities of this part of the poem, are derived from a burgeoning energy of the etymological rather than an erotics of productive relation. 'Dandelion' is 'dented' here to recall the 'dents-de-lion', the lions' teeth, in the word, as much as to help us imagine the forms of the petal which the etymology underlines. If the incarnation that is one of the early possible meanings of 'carnation' opens up to a social erotic space — the Carnevale which modifies the earlier circus — that erotics is doubled by a sexy energy in the materiality of words. This energy of (diamond?) flesh is partly resistant to integration; it sits over and against the background foliage of mass-production, against that which is mass-produced and that which produces the mass; it is wastefully 'tossed'. Here too, we might worry about Rexroth's characterization of Loy's work as 'earnest' in its erotics; its important wastefulness works at least partly in the mode of levity.

These orgiastic flower-words are more like those of Brecht's favourite poet Arthur Rimbaud, in 'Ce qu'on dit au Poète à propos de fleurs' (1871), than they are like Scarry's rare matter for the imagination. Flower-words here don't enable a direct vividness of imagination, but rather decompose it into energies that are difficult to hold together. Rimbaud's poem, aggressively addressed to Théodore de

Banville, accuses the Parnassian writers of a picturesque inability to
see flowers, so caught up are they in a mimetic process of perception
by which flowers serve a binding construction of beauty (the model
flower here is the *lys*, a form of iris, and emblem of the monarchy).
Kristin Ross has read this poem in relation to the Paris Commune.
Its odd lexical shocks, its introduction of industrial, technical, political, and economic vocabularies into the picturesque space of the
poetic flower, operate against an easy assimilation of poetic perception to an elite position in social and political structures. But these
terminologies, estranging the flower from 'the aesthetic' with their
new combinations, won't serve either any 'smooth ideological agenda
[. . .] associated with a vocabulary of utility'. Thus the exorbitant
potential this poem forces on flowers, concentrated for Ross in the
line 'Trouve des fleurs qui soient des chaises!' ('Find flowers that shall
be chairs!'), is also a demand for a new social and spatial formation,
which is objectified in the Paris Commune. In the material *bricolage* of
barricades, and the wider improvisation of the material and political
languages and structures of the commune, objects and words are
wrested from their original functions, are *détournés*, in a 'tactical
mission of the commonplace'. This mission enacts a kind of seeing
which refuses the traps of the human eye or the pleasing resolution
of *umwelt* into *welt*: 'Rimbaud's *target* is the closure of the fields of
socially available perception [. . .] Grotesque, hyperbolic, extraordinary, superhuman perception is advocated in opposition to what capitalist development is at that moment defining (in the sense of setting
the limits) *as* human, as *ordinary* perception.'[12]

It is more difficult to attach the lexical shock and the analysis of
vision in Loy's work to a sense of historical project, for she has no
Commune. Her work against the closure of the fields of socially available perception is ruled by a formal stasis which is harder to locate
than is Rimbaud's mapping of colonial geography and politicised
strike. The three sentences of 'Mass-Production on 14th Street' that I
have discussed so far all arguably function as noun phrases. The
obstruction of the work of the verb is reinforced microcosmically by
the fact that the line endings compete with the syntax which would
work across them. This is occasionally reinforced by the shadow of a
strong two-beat rhythm, where the second beat often falls after the
line end. The next sentence, though, *has* an active verb, and the line
endings entirely support the syntax, doing easily the work of the

absent punctuation. An element of undeniable narrative has been introduced within the oceanic pedestrian mass. *The consumer jostles the sempstress.* It's a miniature Baudelairean scene: the revealing shock of anonymous contact in the crowd (Loy's poem shares the trappings of fashion and the failure of connection with 'A une passante'). But the revealing modern shock has labour rather than gender as its scene. The sempstress is the 'auxiliary creator' of the consumer in two senses: first, because the two figures are alienated and thus related by a mode of production, by the Industry which has been defined by the poem as the logic of aesthetic perception. The consumer cannot be a consumer without the 'hand-labor' of the sempstress, and this division of labour is what the eye will miss in its construction of the crowd as an aesthetic form. Second, the sempstress has literally produced elements of the consumer: the statue of the daisy in her hair, immediately here; but also previously, in the layering flowers that build her very complexion. And this production is pointedly 'auxiliary' to a larger structure of creation; 'hand-labor' is not a nostalgic point of resistance to 'mass-production', but one of its alienated components. Perhaps we have a shadow too of the *grammatical* auxiliaries that the poem so strangely foregrounds, the prepositional difficulty that won't quite simply serve the overall process of communication?

The second half of 'Mass-Production on 14th Street', which I shall deal with in a fairly summary fashion, develops these notions (the separations and relations within the Industrial production and commodious perception of beauty) in a more narrative mode, and within the field of consumption. Mannequins in shop windows and window shoppers reflect one another, such that the relations of production are overwhelmed by the process of representation, such that the tidal life of the crowd is fixed ('in chic paralysis') as a 'mobile simulacrum' of its commodities; and a composite identity 'Femina' is derived from this appearance by a further fashion-industrial agency, the 'ironic furrier, in the air'. This uncanny combined creature of the thoroughfare completes vision as identity, and that completion depends upon the effacing of the 'garment-worker'. The pathos of this process is concentrated, under a neon glow, after the closing hour is over, as the light has faded, in the figure of two — homeless? — lovers, the clothes of one of whom — her buttons are clothespins — mark her as outside the fashion system. Their perception of the products in the shop window is light and pointedly improvised, it is a sweet conjecture (conjecture from *conjectare*, throw together), which aggregates them humanly (they are 'crushed together' by their looking and thinking. But she and her lover are also the closest thing to an originator, beginning outside the systems which the rest of the poem has described. They are rhymingly 'alone' in a space that has become material, as the thoroughfare has 'returned to stone', and her clothes are the original creation of which those in the window are only a 'replica'.

2. The nascent/static: adolescence, iridescence, opalescence

The words 'adolescence' and 'adolescent' appear with slightly unusual frequency in Loy's poetry. Their semantic force is closely articulated, I want to suggest, with their prosodic energies. Even in isolation, it is hard to know whether the main stress should fall on the first or the third syllable, whether the root or the suffix is primary. Indeed, it both performs and conceptualizes a prosody which informs its account of what an 'adolescent' is, and what she or he can do.

In the poems collected in *The Lost Lunar Baedeker*, the adolescent appears thematically within Loy's awkward relation to temporal categories of life. Her poems place maternity, marriage, and babies, and youth and ageing, somewhere within the general movement of 'life'. 'Parturition' and 'Babies in hospital' import a gravity to the developmental roll of temporal and physiological processes, 'The was-is-ever-shall-be / Of cosmic reproductivity' (*LLB II* 7). But then they also step away from it, here with the jingling rhyme, and generally in the name of a knowledge (acquired through the pain of birth in 'Parturition'; imposed as gender and war in 'Babies in hospital') which cannot be part of that life. 'I cannot be your mother / There are already / So many ignorances / I am not guilty of.' (*LLB II* 26)

This knowledge that holds life apart from itself enters life again, awkward, uneasy, as adolescence. In 'Giovanni Franchi', the mode of knowing is pointedly trivial. 'His wrists explained things / Infectiously by way of his adolescence', and those wrists have a happy life, they 'flicked / Flickeringly as he flacked them' (*LLB II* 27). This adolescence 'was all there was of him', but, for the poem, that jaunty ontology (aligned with the narrative statement that 'Some think [Florence] is a woman with flowers in her hair / But NO it is a city with stones on the streets' (*LLB II* 30)), is surrendered to a pretentious romance of learning. He is ecstatic about the 'imposing look' of books, although, as the narration suggests: 'No book ever explained what to be young is / But they look so much more important for that' (*LLB II* 29). In 'The Black Virginity', adolescence is 'subjugated' in a movement from the mysteries towards education, which inscribes us on 'Parallel lines', rather than allowing relation (*LLB II* 43); in 'Songs to Joannes', again, adolescence is a kind of hidden learning, performed, against the will of the jealous guardian of candles, in the 'nascent / Static / Of night' (*LLB II* 60). In 'The Dead', which compresses all stories of generation into an exceeding of self which is gathered as 'our' death, 'your' adolescences are disappointing in their lack of resistance, in being 'So easily reducible' (*LLB II* 73).

There are other adolescents and adolescences in her work, but perhaps these will serve.[13] The place from which life is known — or more often could have been known — both in and outside its processes, is named 'adolescent'. There is something mystical about all of this, a kind of knowledge which we cannot have, like the 'evanescence' about which Joseph Cornell writes to Loy. He tells her about a visual experience, a flash of recognition, which has troubled him and made him think of her: 'The image and his thoughts about it, he continued, seemed "so evanescent and nebulous that I have never mentioned the trifle to anyone." As if they had been enjoying tea and marzipan, he asked her, "Terms like 'evanescent' and 'nebulous' are defeatist, are they not, to those who like ourselves are tortured most of the time by their reality?"' (*BM* 408).

The reality of evanescence is not only mystical (in)carnation; it is economic too, for Loy. Money means that material things tend to leave her, or are made to be sold, or are hastily improvised and rapidly replaced. She attempts in concentrated bursts at several points in her life to make or to conserve money, by inventing and by decorating, sometimes with some success. Her occupation of the position of the adolescent Slav, hustling idiomatically in the retail market, develops a very singular pattern, which ties her entrepreneurship closely to her poetics. For Caroline Burke, the original scene of her creativity outside poetry and the visual arts is defined in her selling off good solid valuable furniture after her separation from her husband Stephen Haweis, and creatively decorating cheap and flimsy things with silk petticoats; and it is reinforced in the pathos of comparing her own improvisations to the wealth incorporated in the depth of the *real* old things in her rich friends' homes. This scene is repeated when she incompletely masks the ugly orange, silver and green wallpaper in her Paris apartment with sheets of soft grey paper. We might add the lead dust she, rather horrifyingly, had her daughter Joella rub into the cracked enamel in her Paris shop, producing an unevenly variable soft shine. Burke describes this as a capacity to evoke 'the sublime from the ridiculous'; I want to see in it a peculiar relation to depth and solidity, to luminous, thickly translucent, complex surfaces, performed among economic determinations (*BM* 190, 176, 326–7).

That relation is best evoked by the terms 'opalescent' and 'iridescent'. The lamps she makes of opaline and cellophane in the 1920s, and then later from the new substances 'crystal lux' and 'rhodoid', are inspired by Lalique's *bibelots lumineux*, made of new opalescent materials, which she sees at the 1925 Exhibition of Decorative and Industrial Arts. Her favoured substances are modern, they both transmit and reflect light, and their surfaces are changeable. Like Brancusi's golden bird in Loy's poem, whose 'incandescent curve' begins a relation to 'aggressive light' which allows the 'significance' of the artwork to 'occur' in the form of 'gorgeous reticence' (*LLB II* 79–80), something of light is held back into the surface. We could cite also her early scheme to offer 'expensive' initiation to the science of 'auto-facial-construction', by which the harmonious 'facial contours' of the adolescent can be regained (*LLB II* 165). The last of her experiments in this mode is the unrealised invention in the 1940s of 'Chatoyant', a synthetic material combining brilliant coloured foil with plaster or glass to create a silvery or cloudy surface (the term is from the eighteenth century, and refers to the changeable lustre which is like that of a cat's eye) (*BM* 396).

Loy's evanescent invention, her opalescence and her iridescence, are responses to the market. This is hand-labour, which through its distinction from mass-production creates a value which capitalism can then absorb, at its price. Her calla-lily lights (*BM* 365), made of rhodoid, offer themselves up commodiously to the Iris-eye of the mind and the market, as willing and finally as dispensable as Scarry's delphiniums (it appears that none of her lights has survived). But their incorporation of the momentary disaggregation of labour from commodity is arranged in Loy's living, and in their materiality, according to another logic entirely. Despite her mystical and financial fantasies of transcendence of or escape from mundane determination, the flimsy persistence of these objects has its life within her prosody, which grasps the world and her writing together, and provides the realism of both. In a very lovely essay on the 'temporal texture of queer adolescence', Dana Luciano suggests, referring here to Todd Haynes's film *Velvet Goldmine*, that a textural sensibility can operate both with and against transience; it can help us to feel our way back to familiar forms, or, where their textural register is damaged or insufficient, can open towards a 'consciousness that enables critique and the operation of corporeal knowledge disenthralled from the symbolic repetitions of capitalism'.[14] Adolescent flesh persists within the production of commodity, and texture softly insists against the processes of vision and conception that would englobe and symbolize, that would link 'art' irreparably to 'Industry'.

In the adolescent, the iridescent, and the opalescent (not to mention the incandescent, the mollescent (!), the pubescent, and the liquiescent [sic], which also appear in Loy's poetry), there is an energy at once semantic and prosodic, which ties her damaged life and this poetry together. The '-escent' and '-escence' suffixes bear unusual semantic weight (which means that it is hard to form new words with them). They carry the sense of 'beginning to assume a certain state', and thence (perhaps *via* 'iridescence') in some cases describe a play of light or colour. And the state that is beginning to be assumed is itself generally not stable (the putrid, the liquid, the iris). 'Adolescence' is formed from 'ad- and alescere', to grow up. When we feel the suffix, as we do in Loy's work, it wants to mean 'to begin to assume the state of growing'. Her revealed preference for these words, and for those surfaces, is part of a potentially decadent interest in Latinate vocabulary and preference for rich-cheap surfaces over aged solidity (for non-admirers this is evidence of degeneration, or, in the French, 'dégénérescence'). From the beginning to the end of her career, these terms block smooth progress through her poems, coordinating with her strong cut line endings to compete with syntactical arrangements of meaning. The state of growing is always only beginning laboriously to be assumed, and her life and her work stop and persist there. The effect is both arresting and trivial, as it is both arresting and trivial to hold a modern life together by the sheer force of prosody.

Christopher Nealon, in a discussion of recent work by post-language writers Kevin Davis, Lisa Robertson, Joshua Clover, and Rod Smith (all writers who learn from Loy, as Nealon does, in a mode of 'adolescent learning'), describes their stance, their campy 'polemical affection' for a 'good house' or a 'feminist sky', as grappling with a cultural problem, 'which is the problem of how to have a live relationship to a material world whose temporal-spatial character is almost unreadable: an obsolescence on top of an obsolescence'.[15] Obsolescence on obsolescence, opalescent flower over opalescent flower: the complexion of the *welt*, fashion's humour, is decomposed here through a persistent labour, and then grasped again, as life, in the realism of adolescent prosody.

Notes

[1] Elaine Scarry, 'Perceptual Mimesis (Particularly Delphinium)', *Representations* 57 (Winter 1997), 92.

[2] Bertolt Brecht, 'Against Georg Lukács', in *Aesthetics and Politics: Ernst Bloch, Georg Lukács, Bertolt Brecht, Walter Benjamin, Theodor Adorno*, trans. Ronald Taylor (London: Verso, 1980), 70.

[3] Bertolt Brecht, 'Against Georg Lukács', 68, 69.

[4] Georg Lukács, *The Meaning of Contemporary Realism* (London: Merlin, 1957).

[5] Paul Ricoeur, 'The Model of the Text: Meaningful Action Considered as a Text' and 'Imagination in Discourse and in Action', in *From Text to Action, Essays in Hermeneutics, II* (1986; repr. Evanston IL: Northwestern University Press, 1991) 144–67; 168–87.

[6] Theodor Adorno, 'Reconcilation under Duress' (1961), trans. Rodney Livingstone, in *Aesthetics and Politics*, 151–76.

[7] Susan Dunn, 'Fashion Victims: Mina Loy's Travesties', *Stanford Humanities Review* 7 no. 1 (1999), www.stanford.edu/group/SHR/7–1/html/body_dunn.html [accessed September 2006].

[8] Raymond Williams, *Culture and Society: Coleridge to Orwell* (London: Hogarth, 1958), xiii-xx.

[9] Scarry, 94–5.

[10] Ibid., 105.

[11] Cited in *BM*, 403.

[12] Kristin Ross, *The Emergence of Social Space: Rimbaud and the Paris Commune* (Houndmills, Basingstoke: Macmillan, 1988), 83–93, 43, 36, 102.

[13] I make some more general points about modernist adolescent knowledge in 'Boys: Manufacturing Inefficiency', in *Before Modernism Was: Modern History and the Constituency of Writing* (Basingstoke: Palgrave, Macmillan, 2004), 51–73.

14 Dana Luciano, 'Crushed Velvet: Todd Haynes and the Temporal Texture of Queer Adolescence' [unpublished paper delivered at the Queer Matters conference, Kings College London, 30 May 2004].

15 Christopher Nealon, 'Camp Messianism, or, the hopes of poetry in late-late capital', *American Literature* 76 no. 3 (September 2004), 579–602.

Loy and Cornell: Christian Science and the Destruction of the World

Tim Armstrong

It is often suggested that spiritual values and religious belief do not find a ready place within modernist aesthetics. The centrality of processes of secularization to modernity; the consequential stress on negativity, irony and fragmentation in modernist writings — all these seem to marginalise the world of religion to conservative groupings within the period. This is a view which must be contested, however, since there are significant lines of influence connecting the exuberant religious innovations of the late nineteenth century to the abstraction of the twentieth. The influence of Theosophy is perhaps the best example: for painters like Kandinsky, Malevich, Mondrian and Bisttram, the hidden truth described by Madame Blavatsky helps their art release itself from the burden of representation; colours take on a symbolic weight and flood the eye with meaning. The music of Scriabin and Schoenberg shows similar impulses; and Theosophical notions of religious syncretism and vibrational energy enter literary modernism via Yeats, Jessie Weston and others.

This essay investigates what is for a number of reasons a difficult aspect of the subject of religion and modernism: Christian Science in the works of Mina Loy and Joseph Cornell. I say 'difficult' because Christian Science offers, for the outsider, a resistant discourse. The first major religious sect founded by a woman, Mary Baker Eddy, at its peak in the first three decades of the twentieth century Christian Science seemed to represent the future of religion, de-mythologised into a Hegelian idealism in which Christianity is folded into divine Mind. It expanded massively in America and Europe, garnering a largely middle-class constituency; it built large churches and attracted commentary from many admirers and sceptics (the latter famously included Mark Twain and Sigmund Freud; Aldous Huxley's satire in

Ape and Essence is less often noted).[1] But it represents a highly conservative form of middle-class idealist piety, frozen into interpretive stasis by the peculiarly restrictive strictures issued by Eddy — who controlled its structures, scriptures, and forms of worship; attempting, with a fair degree of success, to prevent its development of a *midrash*, a living interpretive tradition.[2] Its writings are stultifying; formulaic; almost impossible to read for outsiders — indeed, they have a peculiar negativity which will be one topic of this essay. Moreover, for the artist a tension exists between Christian Science and iconography, since the sect de-emphasises the actual body, whether that of Christ or the body of the person, and the material world generally. It seems indicative that a recent collection on *The Visual Culture of American Religions* does not have a single reference to Christian Science.[3] Given this unpromising set of premises, what is its significance for these two artists?

I will discuss Loy and Cornell in the years around the end of World War II — the period which sees the inception of the nuclear age. It is the period of Cornell and Loy's most intense friendship, with the exchange of letters, books and ideas; and some degree of mutual artistic influence (involving Cornell, for example, providing material for Loy's assemblages and a shared interest in *mappemodes*). For Cornell, Loy was one of his valued woman intimates; people with whom he could extend his dialogue with himself. She was the addressee of a letter often seen as central to his self-explanation, in which he described his largest and most important dossier of materials, the 'GC 44' (or Garden Centre 1944) folder.[4] The artists were brought together, at least in part, by Christian Science, which seems to have cemented existing linkages through the New York art world of Duchamp and the Surrealists.[5] Cornell was a devote Christian Scientist; from his membership application in June 1926 until his death, his diaries record readings of weekly lessons and exchanges with practitioners.[6] Loy, who first made contact with the sect in Florence in 1912, placed its beliefs within a more eclectic understanding of the spiritual in which different elements compete; but certainly her work after her return to New York in 1936 begins to show a more intense interest in spiritual issues (her biographer reports that in the late 1940s she corresponded with the dissident Christian Scientist Joel Goldsmith) (*BM* 414–16).[7] Yet there are significant tensions in their adherence to the faith: Cornell, the obsessive collector and classifier of everyday materials; Loy, the poet whose work is often seen as expressing an embodied poetics. How is art reconciled with a religion which dismisses mere physical existence?

1. The object-world and a poetics of reverie

One answer to that question involves seeing that Christian Science does not so much abolish the object as replace it with something different: a transfigured reality. In the most careful consideration of Cornell's Christian Science to date, Richard Vine relates the faith to a stress on the timeless, on a hidden order in which the clutter of the world may be reconciled in the mind of God. Vine suggests that Cornell's boxes carry an all-pervasive spirituality; a fascination with spiritual avatars like the actresses and shop-girls he worshipped; and with the transient, providing a memorialisation which is 'a preparation for his inevitable forfeiture of the world itself'.[8]

This seems right: transience is a quality we readily associate with Cornell's art, since his boxes incorporate the effects of weathering and often have a kinetic element (rattling balls, falling sand, drawers which demand to be opened). At the same time, his careful arrangements seem to retrospectively formalize and stabilize experience; representing the traces of mind as a fossilized representation of personal and historical memory. This method too may be enabled by religion. In the section of *Science and Health* entitled 'Christian Science versus Spiritualism' Eddy writes of what she calls 'Images of Thought', opening up a poetics of reverie:

> The mind knows naught of the emeralds within its rocks; the sea is ignorant of the gems within its caverns, of the corals, of its sharp reefs, of the tall ships that float on its bosom; or of the bodies which lie buried in its sands: yet these are all there. Do you suppose any mental concept is gone because you do not think of it. The true concept is never lost. The strong impressions produced on mortal mind by friendship or by any intense feeling are lasting, and mind-readers can perceive and reproduce these impressions. Memory may reproduce voices long silent. We have but to close our eyes, and forms rise before us, which are thousands of miles away or altogether gone from physical sight and sense, and this is not in dreaming sleep.[9]

In such formulae Eddy describes the world of mind as at once a Cornell-like collocation of objects, dreaming in the embrace of the sea; and as a cinematic image-bank, able to overcome time and distance. This is an opening to what Cornell, in a 1961 diary entry, described as 'dreams ever different ever varied endless voyages / endless realms ever strange ever wonderful'.[10] His own preoccupation with flotsam and sailor's boxes reflects this Sargasso of the imagination, in which historical resonance — the lost world of nineteenth-century ballerinas, sentimental narrative, toys, natural philosophy — may be part of a reverie which, in Christian Science, is accorded an absolute reality. Thus in his letter to Loy on 'GC 44' he describes the contrast between the poverty of the present moment — the 'shabby and uninspired' reality of the delivery truck he saw a few days ago — and the same truck with its advertising logo, transfigured by layers of memory incorporating both an earlier sighting and rural wanderings dating back a decade.[11]

What does Loy make of this de-materialised and essentially retrospective poetics of Mind? Loy's work in the 1940s, which she intended to publish in a volume entitled 'Compensations of Poverty', seems to be written in a dialogue with the Christian Science view that mind can transcend the material — and indeed often suggests an intense struggle to sustain that belief. The title comes from 'On Third Avenue', which meditates on the kind of images — popular glamour; parts of mannequins stacked in a trolley — that Cornell celebrates. Loy writes of 'a ten-cent Cinema':

> a sugar-coated box-office
> enjail a Goddess
> aglitter, in her runt of a tower,
> with ritual claustrophobia.
>
> Such are the compensations of poverty,
> to see ——————
>
> Transient in the dust,
> the brilliancy
> of a trolley
> loaded with luminous busts [. . .] (*LLB II* 110)

Here is the surrealism of a redeemed object-world; a fetishism which Loy nonetheless undercuts — and this undercutting is something of a keynote of this essay — as a 'mirage'; less stable even than Cornell's arrangements, because observed in passing. The box itself is a less than celebratory image; indeed it would be quite easy to read these lines as a indirect critique of Cornell and his rituals of enclosure.

Perhaps Loy's most obviously Cornellesque poem, in terms of the capture of a resonant moment and the transfigured object, is 'Ephemerid', with its description of a girl wrapped in 'white muslin curtain', pushing a doll's perambulator erratically, seen from a distance against the iron girders of the El (*LLB II* 116–18). That this vision seems like an insect, an 'imp-fly', is intended as an illustration of how 'The Eternal is sustained by serial metamorphosis' — Mary Baker Eddy was fascinated by the butterfly as a symbol of an idealized form of reproduction, which she initially conceived in terms of parthenogenesis.[12] Loy creates of this gauzy figure a 'nameless nostalgia', a vision of 'fictitious faery' like those in Cornell's boxes. But the use of that term and the fact that the vision of the girl is self-consciously described as an overlayering of reality for the spectator — 'penury / with dream' — also suggests the obdurate weight of the material world: that which 'soars' in childish fantasy must also push a 'heavy child' in the stalling vehicle; the viewer who which wishes to idealize the child must 'kidnap' this image.

It is, perhaps, with the moving meditation of 'Letters of the Unliving' that the burden of memory is heaviest, as Loy handles her dead lover Arthur Cravan's letters, now decades old, and must declare that his failure to live renders them mere dead material:

> The present implies presence
> thus
> unauthorised by the present
> these letters are left authorless—
> have lost all origin
> since the inscribing hand
> lost life ——— (*LLB II* 129)

This is a position no elegist — no human, perhaps — can sustain, and Loy goes on to consider what traces of desire *are* contained in what is dryly described as 'this calligraphy of recollection'. She does so in dialogue with the Christian Science belief in the persistence of spirit. Eddy writes: 'Though individuals have passed away, their mental environment remains to be discerned, described and transmitted. Though bodies are leagues apart and their associations forgotten, their associations float in the general atmosphere of human mind'.[13] Loy asks why she should be forced to communicate with a lover frozen in the past, since 'This package of ago / creaks with the horror of echo / out of void' (*LLB II* 130). The bodily metaphors seem to negate the Christian Science belief that Spirit transcends fleshly reality, offering healing for any ill: 'No creator / reconstrues scar-tissue / to shine as birth-star' (*LLB II* 131).

In the period we are examining, the most compelling example of the pressure of the reality is of course World War II. Christian Science was generally pacifist in tendency, seeing war and its polarisation of the world as a failure of understanding. While the *Christian Science Monitor* reported the war assiduously, the in-house magazine, the *Christian Science Sentinel*, referred to it only sporadically, and while it eventually included a column of reports of healing in the armed services alongside general testimonies, the effect was to distance the war; to stress the business of healing as usual. Again there is something of a contrast between Loy and Cornell here. Cornell makes few comments on it, whereas its horrors are registered by Loy in various poems. They include 'Aid of the Madonna', which she sent Cornell in 1943 (*LLB II* 209). Madonnas, the poem suggests, are symbols of motherhood outside time, offering a respite for those who have begotten heroes who have fallen into war, into 'skies once ovational / with celestial oboes' which now see 'in clamour / of deathly celerities, / the horror / of diving obituaries' (*LLB II* 115). If the idea of the Madonna as an 'island in memory' appealed to Cornell, Loy was in contradistinction indicating, I think, the islanded nature of such ideas; the fact that in a world in violent conflict an enclosed box might be their only suitable locus. A difficulty in dealing with the violent presence of history is, I would suggest, visible in Cornell's distant reaction to the war, and eventually in Loy's way of reading his work — a reading which takes up the issue of nuclear energy raised by the end of the war in the Pacific.

2. Denial: 'the nothingness that it really is'

The second and more important aspect of Christian Science I wish to focus on is denial — a topic generated by Eddy's absolute insistence of Spirit's transcendence of the material, and a curious set of attitudes it engenders. Christian Science is founded on the notion that pure Spirit is the only important aspect of existence; sickness is a mistake founded on misapprehensions about embodiment. In Eddy's writing and in Christian Science periodicals there is a constant preoccupation with what is labelled 'error': error about the origins and authorship of Eddy's writings; about mesmerism or animal magnetism; about 'suggestion' as a mechanism for cure; about understanding of doctrine; and above all about the material itself.[14] Errors are constantly and voluminously cited and denied in the correspondence of the *Christian Science Sentinel*; errors which Eddy would return to obsessively while also issuing rules about not repeating 'untruth' any more than was needed for its refutation (the negative error — the error in correcting an error — was something of a specialty for Eddy). The terms covering this semantic field in Christian Science are suggestive: error (materialist explanation) is *denied, repudiated* or *refused*; it is *uncovered, banished* and *excluded*; it is even *annihilated* or *destroyed* — though it constantly returns as attack from outside the movement or backsliding from within. As an article entitled 'Denial in Christian Science' attested in 1924, the negative is a central principle of the movement.[15] At the limit, what must be denied is connection with the world and with others.

Yet paradoxically, despite the denial of the importance of physical life in Christian Science, the body is the ground where its power must be proved — the body must, to adopt Freud's formula from the *Studies on Hysteria*, 'join the conversation' (*mitsprechen*); it must, in its return to health, testify to the primacy of Spirit, to its own finitude and negation.[16] Denial in this context is close to the Freudian mechanism of 'disavowal': not doubt or repression, but a negation which does not allow the 'real' to be admitted to consciousness, which refuses to even repress it. You are not ill or infirm, the Christian Science practitioner insists; you only think you are; and if you can only understand your error the illness will go away. In this paradoxical situation, the subject both knows and does not know about the status of her body; its materiality is both transcended and returns as evidence. One could see both the workings of Cornell's boxes and poems like Loy's 'An Aged Woman' in this way: on the one hand the boxes offer a perfected arrangement of the image-world; on the other they contain worn, broken, rattling objects and cracking paintwork, like the ageing body.

The negativity which is so central to Christian Science can be compared loosely to one defining impulse of Surrealism: the abolition of the world in favour of a transfigured reality, a universe of desire.[17] Compare 'The Destruction of the World' as it is imagined by Pierre Mabille in an 1942 essay in which he meditates on catastrophe and deluge:

> May it cease to exist, this world of pain, may the fire of the earth, the water of oceans with an ultimate convulsion put an end to this miserable creation capable only of bringing to birth unhappiness . . . And if the terrestrial mechanism, too unchangeable in its equilibrium, cannot explode and abolish humanity, if the universe will not consent to disappear, the actual state of things, at least, must be destroyed . . . The slave knows that nothing can be saved from the ancient dwelling and its masters; the smallest objects are cursed; he feels that any contact with them will corrupt him in turn.[18]

The context here is clearly that of the war, which was to end indeed with fire and destruction, founded on the abolition of matter and its rendition into energy, at Nagasaki and Hiroshima. It is worth pausing over the meaning of nuclear weaponry. Christian Science writers often compared the de-materialised world of modern physics — in which even matter could be dissolved into energy — to the world of pure Mind.[19] Cornell acknowledged this line of thinking in a note of 1947: 'Christian Science thoughts — spirituality of world of Romance of Natural Philosophy tie in with new *Einstein* ones?'[20] The atom bomb, with its destruction of matter, thus touches awkwardly on the Christian Science world-view, with its sense of an ever-present eschatology (if only we could realise that the world is Mind, the error which is material existence would dissolve before us).

In looking at the end of the war, we can begin a letter Cornell wrote on 17 August 1945 to Marianne Moore — another poetic correspondent interested in Christian Science. He refers to his worst moments, and adds: 'but in spite of the compensations of moments of deep peace and beauty in the midst of this oftentimes cruel claustrophobia there are occasions enough when its whole illusory mesmeric nature is exposed for the nothingness that it really is.'[21] 'Mesmeric' here places the text in the Christian Science mainstream: for Eddy, 'mesmerism' represented the disavowed origins of Christian Science in nineteenth-century Spiritualism; 'Malicious Animal Mesmerism' (MAM), the subject of a chapter of *Science and Health*, became a source of paranoid concern in her later life, when she thought she was under attack from enemies using MAM.[22] Mesmerism represents the obsessive return of the body; the idea that what might be involved in Christian Science healing is a kind of occult biology rather than the operations of Spirit or Mind; she characterizes it typically as 'mere negation', a denial of truth.[23] Cornell had already used the term 'mesmerism' in an earlier letter to Moore, in May 1945:

> Let me say simply that if the welter of the material that I work with (matched too often by a like confusion of mind) seems too often like endless and hopeless chaos — there are times enough that I can see my way through this labyrinth and feel at home enough among its many 'by-paths of romance' (to quote your apt phrase) to be grateful. When I think of the unspeakable things that have been visited upon so many countless thousands during this same period of time I don't have too many misgivings about not having 'produced' more. While realising that this thought is not a solution to my problem, still it has not been so easy to stay free of its mesmerism.[24]

Here again 'mesmerism' represents the influence of the world; a dwelling on the traumatic actuality of outside events. 'Unspeakable things' include the war with Japan, and Cornell's ambivalence about Japan can be gauged by his quite frequent positive references to 'Japanese qualities'; and the feeling of the 'Japanese masters'— associated with an art of nuance and self-effacement.[25]

The 17 August letter was written two days after the ending of the war in the Pacific, as Cornell notes in his diary entry that morning ('Christian Science Holiday — second V-J Day'). The diary records:

> A beautiful feeling of gratitude for atmosphere of garden and woods in the back of garage and of being rid of a feeling or always wanting to be somewhere else. Observed tiny insect like a miniature darning needle but wings (transparent) more like a butterfly. Tiny ball shaped head red — undulating black tail — only about an inch long — maybe Miss Marianne Moore will know its name — rare feeling of calm similar to morning a week ago Sunday when this spot as alive with birds — went through the whole lesson on SOUL in Christian Science Quarterly and enjoyed it more than I can remember a similar session.[26]

This is followed by 'One of most transcendental experiences [I] ever remember', an account of watching a young girl riding her horse bareback. Being where one is; rejecting the nothingness that is — between these formulae is the space of Cornell's work, a space in which mind, in binding material into remembrance, achieves a balance. The 'gratitude' here is part of a pattern constantly reiterated in Cornell's Christian Science lexicon — 'tension' or a 'crowded' mood resolved in a 'clearing' followed by 'gratitude' (most baldly 'Gratitude for MIND')[27].

Denying mesmerism; denying the tug of the world; of events — the necessity and difficulty of negation in a turbulent world is registered in these letters. Consider the following meditation on reality and memory, written a few years later in the autumn of 1947:

> Going through the G.C. notes <u>without</u> enough <u>enthusiasm</u> to get into the spirit or catch up the thread noticed to-night (Oct. 4.47) the notation of Psalm 31:7 on 'the little dancer section' lying open on my bible at exact place but not with relationship to all this. Last section of the lesson in the Christian Science Quarterly and had not been closed. Subject: UNREALITY. Little 'coincidences' are so often the occasion of making these experiences <u>live again</u> in the present in a way most pleasurable and significant in their unexpectedness + appropriateness.[28]

One link to 'G.C.44' is suggested by the 'responsive reading' specified in the lessons for that week printed in the *Christian Science Quarterly*, Isaiah 41: 15–16, with its apocalyptic references to threshing: 'Behold, I will make thee a new sharp threshing instrument having teeth: thou shall thresh the mountains, and beat them small, and shall make the hills as chaff. Thou shall fan them, and the wind shall carry them away . . . '[29] The threshing of grasses down to their 'pulverised essences' was an important part of the preparation of Cornell's Owl boxes in this period, described in his diaries as a re-creation of the tactile immediacy and sense of Keatsian fruition of the original experience: 'the transcendent experiences of threshing in the cellar, stripping the stalks into newspapers, the sifting of the dried seeds, then the pulverising by hand and storing in boxes.'[30] As the world is harrowed, destroyed, revealed as 'the nothingness that it really is', it falls into shape in the retrospection of art. In this sense, the avaries represent both a negation of and a response to the war, offering destruction and recovery held at an allegorical distance.

3. Loy and actuality

We will deal with Loy's response to Cornell's aviaries in a moment. It is worth noting, first, the traces of mesmerism in her own work. It permeates her novel *Insel*, written in the 1930s, for example. As David Ayers suggests in this volume, Christian Science inflects the description of the eponymous central character in terms of the 'magnetic tides' which surround him. Ayers argues that her usage of these terms is eclectic and seems to evoke a more general context of mind-cure discourse and popular thinking about radioactivity (the 'rays' emitted by Insel). But the negative depiction of mesmerism in the novel has, I would suggest, a fairly direct relation to Christian Science, for which mesmerism represents the dangerous leakage of energy between bodies — as opposed to the desired direct relation of the (disavowed) body to God. Also rejected, again as in Christian Science discourse, is the notion of mesmeric sympathy and flow: the novel's progress involves the narrator gradually realising 'how unsuccessfully I had succoured him' and refusing any further exchange of bodily energies (*I* 138). Similarly in Loy's poem 'Revelation' we have the rather orthodox Christian Science thought that sin is error:

> The agony of Gethsemane
> was that hour when Genius
> disillusioned   comprehended
> the incommensurable idiocy
> (as you would say,
> sin) of the world.   (*LLB I* 203)

The way in which *Insel* repudiates its central character and the movement from Insel's death-obsessed 'Sterben — man muss' to the narrator's declaration of self-reliant health 'Man muss reif sein — One must be ripe' is, as Elizabeth Arnold notes, central to the novel; it is also central to Christian Science.[31]

Like Cornell, Loy could depict the fall into history as a succumbing to a kind of mesmeric influence, as in 'Hilarious Israel', her rather ambivalent poem about the Jewish musical hall. Here the title figure is described as

> Magnet to maniac
> misfortune
> History inclines to you
> as a dental surgeon
> over the sufferer's chair. (*LLB I* 207–8)

Given the Christian Science distrust of health professionals, this seems to characterize history as error. In contrast, 'Hilarious Israel' investigates the 'self-sought anaesthesia' of the music hall; a description which recalls the song which 'anaesthetizes all sense' of Loy's poem for her daughter, 'Maiden Song' (*LLB I* 237). We could relate that aesthetic anaesthesia to a recurrent term in Loy's poetry in the 1940s: *coma*. There is the 'coma of logic' of this poem; the 'coercive as coma' of 'Moreover, the Moon —'; the 'state of animated coma' in 'I almost Saw God in the Metro'; and the 'lenient coma' of 'Letters of the Unliving' (*LLB II* 146, 248, 132). Coma signals a desired escape from the pain of memory; it represents the flesh which cannot be escaped or transcended; it could even be described as a state of pure embodiment; embodiment without mind. As a term for the suffering of the Jew, 'anaesthesia' is anything but the serene transcendence aimed for by the Christian Scientist.

One might also see a Christian Science inflection in Loy's 'Hot Cross Bun' (1949), her major sequence of the post-war years, describing bums and winos in the Bowery. The poems are linked to the sculptural assemblages depicting street life she made in the period — which themselves insisted on including 'dirty' reality spilling from their surfaces, in contrast to Cornell's fastidiously alienated items.[32] A central stylistic characteristic of the sequence is an Eddy-like stress on negatives, often formulated as obscure neologisms: Loy uses 'irrhythmic', 'inideate', 'irreal', 'illenience', 'indirigible', 'unavailing', 'infamous', 'impious', 'indecision', 'impersonal', 'inattentively', 'unfuture', 'inobvious'. This stylistic habit is to some extent shared by other poems of the period, as in the 'uncolor of the unknown' of 'Ephemerid'. Cumulatively, these terms suggest an area of creative negation akin to that of Cornell's boxes: the Bowery as the zone of exclusion, in which the workaday world of reality is annulled, language reduced to babble.

But here I think we need to register an important difference between Loy and Christian Science, and arguably also between Cornell and Loy. Instead of stressing the 'error' of any belief in the material, Loy retains a fascination with the actuality of her subjects; their refusal of the kind of transience which signals another reality. The characteristic movement of 'Hot Cross Bun' is upward-downward, ecstasy-disgust, sky-street — a transcendence, that is, paradoxically rooted in the waste and presence of the body. One of the sequence's main topics is a refusal of distance; a stress on the 'close-up of inferno face' (*LLB II* 139) as opposed to the 'down-sight from tall tower' in which the nobility of the bum is (in another curious negative) lost 'in grey dis-synthesis // of our adamic insects' / collision with confusion' (*LLB II* 140). The distant view which might cleanse the bums of detail is rejected. Indeed, Loy, in 'On Third Avenue', seems to willingly join these bodies, just as she joined the bums below her New York apartment, seeking 'to share the heedless incognito // of shuffling shadow-bodies' (*LLB II* 109).

'Hot Cross Bum' allows us to explore this ambivalent, paradoxical relation to the body and reality generally. As we have seen, her work of the war years and immediately after seems to resist the Christian Science tendency to privilege mind or spirit over the illusory real. The poem has a steadfast insistence on the real, while also registering the attraction of exchanging it for a alcohol-fuelled dream:

> Bum-bungling of actuality
> exchanging
> an inobvious real
> for over-obvious irreal   (*LLB II* 134)

In such formulae, Loy celebrates the 'shrunken illuminati' (*LLB II* 139) of the Bowery, who rightly reject the world but fail to rise to a proper alternative. The 'exoteric redemption' and 'illenience' of Catholicism is rejected for a future reconciliation. It is only 'Evolution' — an orientation towards the future — that will solve this conundrum, breeding people 'more amenable / to ecstasy' — more able to reconcile pleasure and discipline.

At the end of the period we have been considering, in December 1949, Loy visited Cornell's exhibition of Avaries at the Egan Gallery in Manhattan; a visit which produced the short unpublished prose piece 'Phenomena of American Art'.[33] Loy's essay might be considered a summation of many of the somewhat paradoxical issues examined above: it represents a response not only to Cornell's work in a Christian Science context, but to the fact that time has been fractured by the nuclear age, its progressive impulse shattered, leaving the artist with the kind of isolated, spatialized perception one might place in a box.

Loy firstly praises Cornell for moving beyond the 'ingenuity of Evil' and the 'finale of figuration' she associates with Surrealism; and for reintroducing the sublime (which 'does not solidify') into the everyday. The result is an 'Optic music'; something akin to the 'anaesthe-sia' of music in Loy's poems: 'Music is the only transcendancy communicable to us all, here in this bird cage diocese prevailed an optic music sedative as juvenile voices of Bach choristers'. Cornell achieves this by replacing making with an art of Mind, working under the sign of reverie: 'A contemporary brain wielding a prior brain is a more potent implement than a paint-brush'; or again, 'the birds in the Aviary, had not to be made by Cornell, they were elected by Cornell, <u>located</u> by Cornell'.[34]

Loy also, crucially, sees Cornell's work as a rupture with the dialec-tical development of art, in which the 'great sculptures formed in the dim past were vast enough to absorb the centuries of their duration'. In this classicizing view, all art derives from the ancients, and is measured by their standards. In contrast, Cornell's work represents an leap into the future, paradoxically 'placing' all previous art in its retrospective gaze. His works represent a stabilized temporality, 'outlasting all passing, instantaneously returning to the potential emptiness of their status quo'. Why has this 'evolutionary mutation' happened? The reason Loy gives is the coming of nuclear fission. She writes: 'Man's scientific use of the creational "natiere" as a medium for smashing creation has reduced the future to a hypothesis'. The result is a fundamental set of questions: 'What knowing? What making?'[35] Cornell's art of mind answers this call, bypassing the monumental art of the past for an 'evolutionary conscience' (Loy is using the word in the French sense, I think: consciousness) which, as prophesied in 'Hot Cross Bum', might be 'more amenable / to ecstasy'. Art in this view might begin to achieve a realisation of the pure mind, and the reduction of matter to mind, prophesied by Mary Baker Eddy.[36]

Loy analyses Cornell's art in terms of the end of art — in so doing returning it to the history of the twentieth century, and its destruc-tion of the both matter and the future. She gives us a way to read Cornell as presenting the stabilized world of Christian Science, a world held still in the reverie of mind. In terms of her own work, we are left with a fascination with the ideal categories of Christian Science, in which the world might fall away into illusion. But both as poet and as critic Loy also registers, more acutely than her friend ever does, the persistent, seemingly ineradicable linkage between that hope and the 'coma' of nescience, and the presence of both historical reality and the obdurate actuality of the body in the margins of the text.

Notes

[1] A psychoanalytically-inflected reading of Christian Science would need to note both Freud's preoccupation with the movement's success, and his diagnosis of its failings in terms of denial: for example in his comments in 'The Question of Lay Analysis' on it representing 'a regrettable aberration of the human spirit' in its denial of 'the evils of life'.

[2] The most recent assessment of Eddy is Gillian Gill's *Mary Baker Eddy* (Cambridge, MA: Perseus Books, 1998). The movement's recurrent internal fractures have often concerned the place of Eddy in its theology, the status of her will, and the extent of the persistence of her influence.

[3] David Morgan and Sally Promey, *The Visual Culture of American Religions* (Berkeley: University of California Press, 2001).

[4] In fact there are two letters, since Cornell revised and expanded the 1946 version in 1950. They are dated 21 November 1946 and 27 February 1950 by Lindsay Blair in *Joseph Cornell's Vision of Spiritual Order* (London: Reaktion Books, 1998), 54; the 1946 letter appears undated in the November 1946 section of *Joseph Cornell's Theatre of the Mind: Selected Diaries, Letters and Files*, ed. Mary Ann Caws, foreword by John Ashbery (New York: Thames & Hudson, 1993), 135–6. 'GC 44' is a folder over 1,000 pages long relating to various epiphanies Cornell had while working in a garden centre in Flushing, NY in 1944.

[5] As Carolyn Burke points out they were connected before they met via Loy's son-in-law the art dealer Julian Levy; Loy and Levy had searched for watch-parts for Cornell in Paris and Cornell had seen Loy's paintings. *BM*, 379, 404.

[6] On Cornell and Christian Science, the best study is Richard Vine, 'Eterniday: Cornell's Christian Science "Metaphysique"', in *Joseph Cornell: Shadowplay Eterniday* (New York: Thames & Hudson, 2003), 36–50; Cornell's devotion is also discussed by his biographers Lindsay Blair, *Joseph Cornell's Vision of Spiritual Order* (London: Reaktion, 1998) and by Sandra Leonard Starr in *Joseph Cornell: Art and Metaphysics* (New York: Castelli, 1982).

[7] Writings on Loy and Christian Science include Maeera Shreiber, 'Divine Woman, Fallen Angels: The Late Devotional Poetry of Mina Loy', in Shreiber and Tuma, eds., 467–83; Richard Cook, 'The "Infinitarian" and her "Macro-Cosmic Presence": The Question of Loy and Christian Science', ibid. 458–65; and David Ayers's piece in this collection. Goldsmith — in this period at least — remained a fairly orthodox Christian Scientist, and I can see little argument for a specific influence from his rather bland writings.

[8] Vine, 'Eterniday', 44.

9 Mary Baker Eddy, *Science and Health, with Key to the Scriptures* (Boston: First Church of Christ, Scientist, 1994), 87–8. The text was stabilized in 1910 and later editions are printed with the same pagination.

10 Cornell, *Theatre of the Mind*, 285; also in Joseph Cornell, 'Some Dreams, 1947–1969', Surrealist Painters and Poets: An Anthology, ed. Mary Ann Caws (Cambridge, MA: MIT Press, 2001), 485.

11 Cornell, *Theatre of the Mind*, 135–36.

12 The importance of parthenogenic thought — that is, the presence of unassisted, idealized motherhood — in Christian Science is noted by Frank Podmore, *Mesmerism and Christian Science: A Short History of Mental Healing* (London: Methuen, 1909), 295. Editions of *Science and Health* up to 1906 claimed that 'generation rests on no sexual basis' and provided the butterfly, bee and moth as examples.

13 Eddy, *Science and Health*, 87.

14 The central example is the much-revised 'Animal Magnetism' chapter of *Science and Health*, but other texts also provide plenty of evidence of the preoccupation with error, for example the many corrections issued both to the church and its critics collected in *The First Church of Christ Scientist and Miscellany* (Boston: The Trustees, 1913).

15 M. J. Turner, 'Denial in Christian Science', *Christian Science Sentinel* 27 no. 11 (15 November, 1924), 207.

16 Sigmund Freud, *From the History of an Infantile Neurosis. Case Histories II*, Penguin Freud Library, vol. 9, ed. Angela Richards (London: Penguin, 1990), 312.

17 See Peter Nicholls, *Modernisms: A Literary Guide* (Basingstoke: Macmillan, 1995), ch.12.

18 Pierre Mabille, 'The Destruction of the Word' (1942), *Surrealist Painters and Poets*, 273–4.

19 For examples see Robert Peel, *Christian Science: Its Encounter with American Culture* (Harrington Park, NJ: Robert H. Soames, 1958).

20 Cornell, *Theatre of the Mind*, 138.

21 Ibid., 122. My attention was directed to this passage by reading an abstract of Philip Cowell's paper 'From Joseph Cornell to Marianne Moore: Negation, Nothingness and the Art of Not Saying', delivered at the 2003 UEA Cornell conference, which also examined negation in Sartre.

22 See the chapter on MAM in Gill, *Mary Baker Eddy*.

23 Eddy, *Science and Health*, 102.

24 Cornell, *Theatre of the Mind*, 123.

25 Ibid., 108, 153.

26 Ibid., 120.

[27] Ibid., 454.

[28] Ibid., 146.

[29] *Christian Science Quarterly* 58 no. 4 (1947), readings for Oct. 5, 1947 (subject: UNREALITY).

[30] Cornell, *Theatre of the Mind*, 130, 117.

[31] Elizabeth Arnold, 'Afterword', *I* 187.

[32] Because Loy's artworks are not in public collections, and are accessible only in poorly-reproduced illustrations in the texts of Burke, Conover and others, I have not discussed them here — though certainly they were produced in dialogue with the collage-assemblages of both Duchamp and Cornell.

[33] This exists in different versions. I am using that in the Loy Papers, YCAL MSS 6, fol. 172 (11pp, mixed TS and MS); by page number. I am grateful to Alex Goody for allowing me to consult her transcription of this essay.

[34] Loy, 'Phenomena', 2, 3, 6, 3, 4, 5.

[35] Loy, 'Phenomena', 5, 11, 5, 6.

[36] 'Consciousness' (rather than Spirit or Soul) is the term stressed by the Christian Science writer Peter V. Ross, whom Cornell read, seen as a form of artistic *making*: 'Consciousness is not only the builder but the building material. It is at once the sculptor and the marble. Serene in tempo and possessed of divine substances — integrity, animation, wisdom, affection — consciousness becomes spiritual and thus is equipped to rear a princely structure'. Peter V. Ross, *Lectures on Christian Science* (New York: Hobson Press, 1945), 215–6.

Mina Loy's Insel *and its Contexts*

David Ayers

Mina Loy's *Insel* is the fictionalized account of her own relationship with the painter Richard Oelze, published only in 1991 under the editorship of Elizabeth Arnold. It is a text concerned with power and art. It is about the relationship between an older woman and a younger man, and the gradual shift in emotional power relations between them. It is about the relationship between an art dealer and an artist, and is therefore about the difference between economics and creativity. It is also about the relationship between one artist and another, and about the relation of each to the background of Paris art and the dominant movement of Surrealism in the mid 1930s. It is also about the confrontation of two different arts, writing and painting, and about male and female creativity.

In what follows I have mapped out several major areas of the text, supplying some background information and highlighting aspects of *Insel*'s systematic organisation. In doing so, I have tended to dampen speculation in the interest of introducing an element of political realism in the reading of this text. That said, what I present here is intended as a clarification, and sets in place material that might readily be given a more affirmative speculative twist than I have sought to do in this context.

The first section deals with the central notion of healing and asks how this might draw on Christian Science and other available vocabularies; the second section introduces, in a condensed fashion, the figure of Richard Oelze, and recognises some of the difference between Oelze and Insel; the third section compares *Insel* to *Tarr*, by way of articulating illuminating similarities and recognising important differences between Loy and Lewis; and the final section compares *Insel* to Breton and the project of Surrealist literature, in order to articulate *Insel*'s notion of creativity and the function of art.

1. Rays, healing and Christian Science

Loy's relationship to Christian Science continues to present interpretative difficulties to her commentators, not least because the nature of her commitment to the beliefs of the movement is not well documented. Carolyn Burke's biography of Loy includes occasional references to Christian Science which are enough to establish Loy's continued interest, but which frustratingly reveal little about the nature of the movement or about Loy's orientation within it.

Christian Science had been founded by Mary Baker Eddy in Boston in the 1870s. Its founding document was Eddy's *Science and Health* (1875) and its reach was consolidated by the establishment of *The Christian Science Journal* in 1883, *Der Herold der Christian Science* (in German and English) in 1903 and of *The Christian Science Monitor*, in 1908. The Herald appears to have responded to an upsurge in interest in Christian Science throughout Europe in the immediate aftermath of the War, with the publication of a French edition (*Le Héraut de la Science Chrétienne*) in 1918, and reflected in the testimonies of ex-combatants in letters published in the various journals of the movement.[1] As well as generating a growing literature, the spread of Christian Science prompted a series of rebuttals, notably from Mark Twain in *Christian Science* (1907), and including, in England, Frank Ballard's mockingly titled *Eddyism* (1909) and H.A.L. Fisher's *Our New Religion* (1929). In Germany, Ernst Toller and Hermann Kesten made Eddy the subject of *Wunder in Amerika* (1931), a Brechtian *lehrstück* intended to expose the workings of charlatanry, which was staged in London as 'A Miracle in America' in 1934. Loy, who adopted Christian Science in 1909, would have been aware that her new religion was viewed by many as the product of cranks and charlatans.

Central to Christian Science are its doctrines concerning healing. These ideas stem ultimately from mesmerism, although with a significant transformation. Eddy herself was healed by Phineas P. Quimby, who believed that illness was caused by the mind. He is quoted as saying that 'all sickness is in the mind' and 'the truth is the cure.'[2] Quimby's practice was really a derivation of mesmerism with more emphasis on conscious explanation to the patient of traumatic origins of their illness, and on physical manipulation.[3] Despite this difference, Quimby's thinking retained elements of Anton Mesmer's pseudo-scientific theory of animal magnetism (as outlined in his 1779 'Propositions Concerning Animal Magnetism') and his practice included variants of the ritualistic elements which Mesmer had employed. Like Quimby, Mary Baker Eddy claimed that the body was dominated by the mind. Unlike Quimby, she claimed that her knowledge of healing was a direct revelation from God, and set about distinguishing her approach from the contemporary alternatives, especially animal magnetism.

Eddy's beliefs, as set out in the rambling *Science and Health* and consolidated in her *Miscellaneous Writings: 1883–1896* (1896), contained a variety of home-spun theological assertions. Among these tenets, Eddy's emphasis on the subordination of matter to mind, and, consequently, on the unreality of matter, seems as if it ought to have major implications for Mina Loy's beliefs and aesthetics. The following extracts from *Science and Health* are only selection of Eddy's extensive reiteration of this doctrine:

> To be on communicable terms with Spirit, persons must be free from organic bodies; and their return to a material condition, after having once left it, would be as impossible as would be the restoration to its original condition of the acorn [. . .] Spirit never entered matter and was therefore never raised from matter.

> Man is not matter. He is not made up of brain, blood, bones, and other material elements. [. . . M]an is made in the image and likeness of God. Matter is not that likeness. [. . .] Man is idea, the image, of Love; he is not physique. [. . .] Man is incapable of sin, sickness, and death.

> Christian Science reveals man as the idea of God, and declares the corporal senses to be mortal and erring illusions. Divine Science shows it to be impossible that a material body, though interwoven with matter's highest stratum, misnamed mind, should be man [. . .].

> When the substance of Spirit appears in Christian Science, the nothingness of matter is recognised.

> Material sense never helps mortals to understand Spirit, God.

> Sickness is a belief, which must be annihilated by the divine Mind. Disease is an experience of so-called mortal mind. It is fear made manifest on the body.[4]

This repudiation of the flesh echoes Calvinism, and culminates, in Christian Science, in the doctrine that not only sickness, but even death, are illusions of the mind. Contemporary readers of Loy are likely to be Nietzscheans who elevate the surface of appearance over the depths of mind, or perhaps Hegelians who see mind and matter as existing in a dialectic. Such readers might find it counter-intuitive, or at the very least unproductive to read Loy in terms of this doctrine of the priority of mind. It might be easier to believe that Loy embraced Christian Science for its healing doctrines while disregarding its theology. Yet as a contemporary noted, there was no shortage of alternatives to Christian Science for those who sought alternative routes to health: 'From the first the Founder of Christian Science was encompassed by rivals [. . .] by mesmerists, spiritualists, apostles of the New Thought [. . .] who were directly competing with her in her own market [. . .].'[5] 'New Thought' was the umbrella term given to alternative healing doctrines which in many cases were advocated by former disciples of Eddy. In general, the New Thought was far more liberal in outlook than Christian Science, embracing an eclectic variety of beliefs and practices while mocking Eddy as a papal figure for her insistence on theological orthodoxy.[6] Since the promise of mind healing would have been available to Loy without the rigid theological framework of Christian Science, we should conclude that Christian Science theology, and not merely its healing practice, was accepted by Loy. However, once we refer to the presentation of healing in *Insel*, important reservations appear.

Loy's narrator several times identifies Insel as a healer. In this passage, the suggestion is given and retracted before it is uttered:

> Now I had found another profession for him — magnetic healer. Suddenly I foresaw the fear my physician would inspire nullifying his therapeutic value, and I did not suggest it to Insel. (*I* 77)

Insel the death's head would terrify his clients. The narrator's idea of finding Insel a profession is related to the recurrent theme of Insel's poverty and the narrator's economic realism. "Magnetic healing" is another term for Mesmerism, which relied on the ability of the healer to influence the magnetic flow of the patient. Although the reference here is couched with comic irony concerning both Insel's ugliness and the narrator's excessive pragmatism, it is one of a number of references to healing in *Insel*, references which are reinforced by the use of vocabulary related to other aspects of the pseudo-science of healing and which apparently contradict the Christian Science emphasis on spirit.

The frequent use of the term 'rays' is closely related to the reference to mesmerism. In accounting for his attraction to her, the narrator several times speaks of Insel's rays:

> Urged to cross the frontier of his individuality, I got in the way of that faintly electric current he emitted. His magnetic pull steadily on the increase, the repulsion proportionately defined, threw me into a vibrational quandary [. . .]. (*I* 65)

> [H]is magnetic rays drawing some other girl out of bed on to her balcony whenever he passed below at night. (*I* 67)

> His eyes now pacified in a steady human mesmerism smiled cosily into mine. (*I* 94)

> But as if his astounding vibratory flux required a more delicate instrument than the eye for registration. Some infrared or there [sic] invisible ray he gave off, was immediately transferred on one's neural current to some dark room in the brain for instantaneous development in all its brilliancy. So one saw him as a gray man and as an electrified organism at one and the same time — (*I* 96)

> The storm must have completely disintegrated his exceptional electrification. (*I* 98)

> cocoon of his magnetic rays, introvert, incomparably aloof, 'They're mine,' he exulted [. . .]. Too simple to fully imagine the effect of these rays, he had, it would seem, only an instinctive mesmeric use for them. (*I* 144)

As well as reference to magnetic rays, there is also reference to electricity and infrared. It is notable that magnetism is presented as rays, since in the vocabulary of Mesmer magnetism is presented as a fluid. This is likely to be a reflection of a new emphasis on rays, following the discovery of x-rays and radioactivity in the mid 1890s, in the contemporary science and pseudo-science to which Loy was probably exposed. In the decade following the War, 'Violet Ray' appliances were widely marketed, promising curative and beautifying effects justified by vague but impressive reference to the role of electricity on bodily health.[7] Albert Abram's *New Concepts in Diagnosis and Treatment* (1916) theorized that ill health resulted from the disruption of electronic vibrations in the body. His thesis received little scientific support, however its appeal evidently rested on the combination of science and mysticism in Abram's loosely synthesized vocabulary of electricity, magnetism, radioactivity, energy, vibration and aura.[8] Loy uses the term aura in a manner which reflects both occult and pseudo-scientific uses:

> Between the shrunken contour of his present volume his original 'serial mold' was filled in with some intangible aural matter remaining in place despite his anatomical shrinkage. An aura that enveloped him with an extra external sensibility. (*I* 64)

We might be more impressed by this passage for its carefully weighed conceit than for its occult reverberations, and we may well feel that the connection with Walter Benjamin's use of aura (as recommended by Miller[9]) yields greater speculative leverage on this text than any attempt to return its terms to a fading history of error. However, Loy's use of these terms is sucked back by this history, and the trope I have just identified, in which matter is replaced by aura, is a governing notion of *Insel*.

Insel's personal power — as electricity, magnetism, aura or rays — increases in proportion to his physical decay. The narrative follows the increase in his power and near-approach to death, which culminates in his apotheosis into the 'man-of-light':

> Shaken with an unearthly anxiety, this creature of so divine a degradation, set upon himself with his queer hands and began to pull off his face.
> For those whose flesh is their rags, it is not pitiable to undress.
> As Insel dropped the scabs of his peculiar astral carbonization upon the table, his cheeks torn down, in bits upon the marble — one rift ran the whole length of his imperfect insulation, and for a moment exposed the 'man-of-light.'
> He sat there inside him taking no notice at all, made of the first jelly quivering under the sun and some final unimaginable form of aereal substance, in the same eternal conviction as the Greek fragment — (*I* 97)

The inclusion of 'man-of-light' in inverted commas implies a specific source, but I find nothing in Christian Science (or in discussion of Oelze) corresponding to this, and while the term seems likely to have an origin in a religious or mystical text, the parallels I have found (in

Sufism and in the Coptic Gospel of Thomas) seem unstable. While light, plainly, is a widely used metaphor in mystical contexts, the 'man-of-light' has proved harder to locate. As Insel recovers from his tran-scendent moment, the text recalls — not for the only time — Conrad's *Heart of Darkness*:

> At last Insel's eyes dying of hallucination, stared suddenly into the filtered day. Horrified almost to blindness he complained, '*Es ist zu hell*'. He sounded as if deliberately quoting 'it is too light' — (*I* 97)

If this is a quotation it remains unidentified. While it is a pity that some central reference appears to elude us here, it is clear, above all, that Loy's vocabulary is eclectic in its combination of mysticism, magic and healing science (as well as alchemy and other terms), and does not appear to share the outright rejection of animal magnetism and other healing doctrines found in Eddy's work.

Healing works both ways in *Insel*: the narrator attempts to save Insel from starvation and restore him to productive health, while his seductive rays offer to heal her:

> The *grand sympathique* (which eventually turned out to be a duodenal ulcer) must inevitably go on the rampage again. Very soon it did. There was no resource to Insel's healing *Strahlen*. (*I* 137)

Here, Insel's rays are unable to heal physical illness. Later a healing which is a form of psychic transfer occurs — a culminating moment again not unlike the transfer of Kurtz's struggle to Marlow:

> The rays that Insel had so busily been spinning around himself in an immeasurable tenderness released, attained once more to me.
> Instantly all pain vanished. I sprang up elasticized. [. . .]
> The painless buoyancy lasted well into the night when, as I sat calmly at work in my hotel bedroom, I unexpectedly disintegrated. [. . .] The life force blasting me apart instead of holding me together. It set up a harrowing excitement in my brain. [. . .] I cognized this situa-tion as Insel's. A maddening desire for a thing I did not know — a thing that, while being the agent of his — my — dematerialisation alone could bring him together again. A desire of which one was 'dead' and yet still alive — radial starfish underpattern of his life. (*I* 149–151)

> I felt that for dabbling in the profane mysteries I had got more than was coming to me. (*I* 155)

These passages, regarding the psychic transaction between the narrator and Insel — if we wish, between Loy and Oelze — seem clearly to confirm an emphasis in Loy on spirit or *psyche*, and illuminate an emphasis in her work on an eclectic range of mystical frameworks including that of magic, which is several times evoked elsewhere in the text. The narrator notes that 'there's something fundamentally black-magicky about the surrealists' (*I* 21) and presses Insel to confess to practicing magic: 'Are you one of those surrealists who has taken up black magic?' (*I* 42) Elsewhere there are references to alchemy ('Insel remained — a mess of profane dross'[*I* 102]), the séance ('his mediumistic world' [*I* 66]; 'my veritable séances with Insel' [*I* 95]), astral levels ('his astral Venus' [*I* 91]), and ritual initiation ('truly initiate acolytes' [*I* 106]).

The relationship culminates in this moment of transfer for the narrator, but in a loss of power for Insel. 'Unquestionably I had cured him' (*I* 166): his voice has changed and their positions are 'reversed', he now regarding her as a strange object as once she had him. He has lost his magic and his hold of fascination over her.

Before further unpacking the content of this psychic transaction, and having identified an emphasis on the spiritual over the material consonant with Christian Science but transformed by eclectic mystical interests, it is useful to review the figure of Richard Oelze himself.

2. Insel and Oelze

Aficionados of Mina Loy have commonly found in her work a stringent materialism, as testified for example by her penchant as an author for linguistic quiddities, and by her involvement in various branches of art and design. In relation to *Insel*, the manner in which matter might be interpretatively at stake in the novel can be seen in Elizabeth Arnold's claim that:

> [. . .] the narrator's final victory over Insel — the definitive moment of the book — coincides with her success as a writer. By the end of the novel she has reached the necessary compromise for the practising artist: to make the most of the flawed human condition, to refine as much as possible the imperfect media available to the artist in this world.[10]

As an interpretation this is of course contestable, not merely because it replicates the dominant critical tendency to read women's writing as a string of wishful textual victories over men, but because, in its assumption of the validity of Loy's matter-of-fact materialism, it plays down the narrative trajectory of the novel, in which Insel's hold over the narrator is weakened by the breaking of his artist's block and the actualization of the work which the narrator had first experienced as potential. Nevertheless, Arnold's version of Loy as committed to the practical and particular has large general resonance among her readers. Tyrus Miller's comment on *Insel* takes a different tack on particularity, locating the narrator's disenchantment with Insel in the loss of aura which ensues from the commitment of his work to photographic realism, a commitment which, in Miller's account, is adopted defensively and results only in an adaptation to technology and the loss of the artistic individuality which technological reproducibility has threatened — the very result the adaptive strategy was designed to avoid.[11] Setting aside the connection with Benjamin, whose 'Work of Art' essay is itself a thesis about the consequences of increasing mastery of the particular and the ability to 'bring it closer', it can be confirmed that the historical Oelze did make especial use of naturalistic detail in certain of his works. This element in Oelze's art stemmed from his time in Dresden, before the move to Paris, and reflected a particular debt to the *Neue Sachlichkeit* of Otto Dix and, in particular, to the naturalist meticulousness of Richard Müller, described by Oelze in later years as 'water drops on a cucumber'.[12] These influences had an impact both on the figural works and on the landscapes of Oelze's Paris years. Wieland Schmied argues that, in the work which began to emerge in the Paris years, Oelze combined the realism of Bauhaus and Neue Sachlichkeit with the dream content of Surrealism, in a dialectic in which the artist ceded authority over the content of his work (dreams) but asserted control over the means.[13] This dialectic, which Schmied calls the 'precision of the vague', makes the relationship between objectivity and subjectivity, the detail and the vague, the rational and the irrational, into the very content of Oelze's practice. According to Schmied, detail in Oelze conflates thingliness and abstraction, the real and the fantastic.[14] It is not possible here to take responsibility for the actual or possible development of Schmied's claims, though these are a promising basis for further comment not only on Oelze but on his Surrealist contemporaries. In the context of *Insel*, this brief discussion of Oelze shows

that Loy's narrator does not exhaust interpretation of Insel's stance in
what Miller presents as her rejection of the photographic quality of
his work. We might add in passing that the notion of the defeat of the
artist at the moment of the conquest of nature in the dialectic of
Enlightenment would also, in an interpretation of Oelze if not of the
fictionalized Insel, be obliged to navigate the dialectic of the human
and nature which Oelze's anthropomorphized landscapes project.[15]
Indeed, Renate Damsch-Wiehager locates the leverage of Oelze's
work in the dialectical partnership between the imaginary, in Oelze's
term 'Inbilder', and its illusionistic objectification.[16] Again, without
attempting to take responsibility for mapping this dialectic and its
consequences for Oelze or for Surrealism in general, this brief foray
into his work allows us to note that Oelze's oeuvre is organised
around the *différance* of inner and outer, conscious and unconscious,
tekhne and *psyche*, and precisely allows for the possibility, signalled by
his own portmanteau word 'Inbilder', that the depths of mind may be
nothing more than a notional interiority projected by the 'outside'
(an argument which would follow the path of Derrida's famous
discussion of Socrates and writing in *Dissemination*).

By recruiting Oelze to confront Loy's (and Loy's narrator's) Insel, it
becomes possible to see the gap between the dialectic which Oelze's
work inhabits and *Insel*'s apparent rejection of the dialectic in favour
of one of its terms — the interior, the imagination, the potential. We
may feel bound to separate Loy from her narrator, Oelze from Insel,
Loy or her narrator in the narrative 'present' from Loy or her character in narrativised 'past',[17] and no doubt insist too on possible discrep-
ancies between implied or inferred readers and ourselves — invoke, in
other words, the machinery of the structuralist response to the problem of mapping subject positions. Yet, though we must pay attention
to this, we might finally prefer not to allow ironic deferral to have
the last word. Loy's text certainly acknowledges that the figure of Insel
is an appropriation, rather than a representation of Oelze in its
presentation of his art works. The painting of 'a commonplace woman
looking at the sky' (*I* 20) does not exactly correspond to any work of
Oelze represented in the principal sources, but with its sky, theme of
waiting, and backs, undoubtedly corresponds to the most commented
work of Oelze's Paris period, 'Erwartung'[18], with a single female substituted for the crowd, perhaps to point up Loy's own identification with
the piece as an individual rather then a crowd member (indeed the
painting, modelled on a photograph of a crowd waiting for the arrival
of Charles Lindbergh's first transatlantic flight in 1927, has been inter-

preted in context as a political criticism of crowd behaviour[19]). The general discussion of the 'elementals' in Insel's new paintings (*I* 102–3) corresponds to several of the works of the Paris period, especially 'Tägliche Drangsale'[20] with its 'cerebral abortions of cats' (*I* 103). The longer discussion of 'Die Irma' corresponds closely to the drawings 'Frieda' and 'Frieda II'.[21] This is confirmed especially by the discussion of the 'male hands' (*I* 132), and the idea that its model originates in an earlier romance of Insel's is confirmed by the dependence of these drawings on an earlier portrait of Ellen Hauschild.[22]

Whether we attribute it to Loy, to Mrs Jones, or to *Insel*, this text proceeds to map a set of oppositions *other* than, but standing in relation to, those suggested by a reading of Oelze's work.

3. *Insel* and *Tarr*

Having identified the psychic rather than the object world as the preferred domain of *Insel*, it is possible to allow this text to articulate itself further by urging a comparison with the work of Wyndham Lewis. Mina Loy and Wyndham Lewis have in common the moment of response to Futurism in their work of the 1910s and 1920s. They share satire as a favoured mode, Bohemia as a favoured topic, and as visual artists frequently privilege vision as the mimetic and tropic engine of sense. In a general manner, thematically and linguistically, it would be possible to unfold a model of parallels and similarities, a mimetic mirror-dome of mutually haunting figures and environments.

A general parallel between Loy and Lewis is suggested by shared elements in their writing style, and *Insel* notably echoes such works as *Enemy of the Stars* (1914), *Tarr* (1918/1928), and *The Apes of God* (1930). Lewis's style in these works, sometimes loosely termed 'visual', is more particularly the conscious attempt to realise a style which would be anti-mimetic and express the domination of reality by the mind, rather than the contrary, a bad artistic stance which Lewis in his *Blast* manifestos linked to Impressionism. Lewis's similes and metaphors tend to foreground that surplus of meaning which is inherent in any figural speech, drawing attention both to the medium of the art and to the inventiveness of the artist who creates it, sometimes resulting in a display of metaphysical wit, elsewhere in emblematic stasis.

> Tarr's unwieldy playfulness might, in the chequered northern shade, in conjunction with nut-brown ale, gazed at by some Rowlandson (he on the ultimate borders of the epoch) have pleased by its à propos.[23]

> Meanwhile, [Insel's] reserved distinction, as of an aristocrat who should in a lasting revolution have experienced yet unimaginably survived the guillotine, was so consistent it claimed one's respect for his nonsensical manner of being alive. (*I* 30)

The stylistic parallel testifies to related motivations. Both Loy and Lewis seek to differentiate themselves in the name of art not only from the mass of non-artists but from crowd of circumambient identities which batten on the integrity of an imaginary pure selfhood. Tarr rejects those artists who wear the 'uniform of art'[24], the 'Apes of God', while Loy's narrator praises the individualism of the German Insel for his lack of integration with the Surrealist group: 'he's too surrealistic for the surrealists' (*I* 125). Lewis makes repeated use of the metaphor of parasitism in his work to characterize the encroachment of social selfhood on the *psyche*; Loy uses the term 'plagiarism' — identity theft (*I* 47).

While *Tarr* depicts art as the product of the struggle against sexual appetite,[25] *Insel* makes inspiration — if not art itself — the product of hunger. The whole narrative trajectory of *Insel* follows its protagonist's near starvation. As his body decays, Insel achieves more of a magnetic pull on the narrator, in whose construction of events he is approaching a state characterized as surreal, timeless and Edenic, although the narrator registers too the claim of others that Insel's physical (as well as financial and psychological) state is produced by morphine addiction:

> Subconsciously I waived this information. As if my mind were a jury refusing to be influenced by extraneous evidence. [. . .] I was free to pursue my investigation of Insel in my own reactive way.
> Moreover, was not Insel's morphinism a thing of the past? (*I* 126)

In this suppressed aspect, *Insel* may be a lost classic of drug literature to set alongside the work of W.S. Burroughs, whose work Loy's at times uncannily predicts, perhaps because of shared reference to Aleister Crowley, a major presence in Burroughs and an occasional ghost in Loy. Be that as it may, Loy's emphasis is not on the destructive effect of the drug but on the liberation of Insel's state.

While *Tarr* revolves around the contrast between two artists, Tarr and Kreisler, who have no real exchange, *Insel* sets up oppositions between the narrator and the artist which are complicated by the massive psychic transaction which takes place between them. The opposition is distinct, however, between the immateriality of Insel and the indissoluble material definiteness of the narrator: 'under his conjurative power of projecting images, I felt myself grow to the ruby proportions of a colossal beef steak' (*I* 53). The eye and the mouth are repeatedly opposed: the first the narrator sees of Insel are 'the tiny fireworks he let off in his eyes when offered a ham sandwich' (*I* 19). Though Loy could have emphasised herself as an artist, she chooses to present her narrator as an art dealer and writer. As a dealer, trying to help Insel, she is aware of economic encroachment on his authentic state, thus echoing the Surrealist denunciation of organised labour. Orality, economics and sex are all linked in the opening anecdote of *Insel*, where it is explained that Insel needs money to buy teeth to visit a prostitute, so that his ugliness will not frighten her. Insel's authenticity depends on his lack of economic integration which in turn deprives him of the appetitive. Even love cannot draw him into the present, since love for him was lost when his female lover was seduced and taken from him by another woman. Meanwhile the narrator is denied her autonomy as an artist not only by her fascination with Insel, but by the apparent impossibility of writing the biography of a man who has modelled his identity on Kafka — a dependence so complete that he is free to exist timelessly without living out a narrative of his own.

Insel's independence from appetite and event allows him to approach the suspenseful state into which the narrator is drawn:

> In my veritable séances with Insel, the clock alone retrieved me from nonentity — thrusting its real face into mine as a reminder of the temporal.
> Thus I saw how three whole hours went by while Insel asked me what I was thinking of. They passed off in a puff as though, for a change, he had contracted time into an intensity. (*I* 95)

Clock time has a similar function in *Tarr*. In *Insel*, it figures the opposition between the practical, regulated time of work and money and the sublime inner state which is governed by the trope of death. Tarr tropes endlessly in time:

'*Death* is the thing that differentiates art and life. Art is identical with the idea of permanence. Art is a continuity and not an individual spasm: but life is the idea of the person. [. . .]'

'Art is merely *the dead* then?'

'No, but deadness is the first condition of art. The armoured hide of the hippopotamus, the shell of the tortoise, feathers and machinery, you may put in one camp; naked pulsing and moving of the soft inside of life — along with elasticity of movement and consciousness — that goes in the opposite camp. Deadness is the first condition of art: the second is absence of soul, in the human and sentimental sense. With the statue its lines and masses are its soul, no restless inflammable ego is imagined for its interior; it has *no inside*: good art must have no inside: that is capital.'[26]

While Lewis's account focuses on the deadness of art in implied opposition to the liveness of mind, in Loy it is the artist Insel who is continually on the point of death. His existence is 'increate'; he is an 'animate cadaver'; 'I could have sworn I beheld the dead'; 'he moved within an outer circle of partial decease [. . .] he chilled the air, flattened the hour, faded colour' (*I* 88, 69, 103, 51). Lewis certainly wishes to retain a notion of independent mind as a worldly thing; the deadness of art is an acknowledgement that matter and extension do not belong to mind. In Loy, spirit is opposed to flesh according to a model which is both religious and magical, and the emphasis shifts from created objects to the state of creativity itself. In the light of this, *Insel* must be compared to Surrealist notions of the art object and the state of mind accompanying its creation, claims which the text claims to be bettered by the example of Insel.

4. *Insel*, Surrealism and time

Loy's text shows an awareness of the general tenets of Surrealism, and consciously places itself in relation to the work of André Breton, and in particular to *Nadja* which it in part emulates and in part resists in order to generate its own meaning. Loy's negotiation of Surrealism in *Insel* presents an ambivalent picture inasmuch as her evident liking for the notion of going beyond surrealism invites comparison between the politics of Surrealism and her own.

Insel is a surrealist novel, principally in terms of its *topic* rather than its *means* — even if its principal theme concerns the vicarious participation of the narrator in a certain version of the Surrealist moment. Loy's text is systematic, in the manner of the Surrealist manifesto or position piece rather than the 'pure' Surrealist text, intended to examine her relationship to the surrealist impulse, which in her work as in Breton's comes to stand for the artistic impulse *tout court* — rather that to *express* that impulse in the manner which Breton would sometimes claim was the sole aim of surrealist writing.

The 'First Manifesto of Surrealism' (1924) laments the loss in adulthood of the kind of experience that is possible in childhood.[27] It is this kind of immediate and personal/private experience which will be urged and affirmed by Breton in much of his subsequent writing. At his stage however the term 'love' does not play a large part in the argument. By the time of *Mad Love* (1937), love has joined madness as the ideal model of surrealist experience.[28] Love is important in *Nadja* too, as it is in *Insel*. In the first Manifesto the principal focus is on the inability of the contemporary adult to genuinely experience an event. Due to the 'imperious practical necessity' of adult life any event is not grasped in itself but only in relation to others — we would say schematically — it is a 'missed event'.[29] Breton blames materialism in life and logic in thought. There is a vague Weberian resonance in his use of the metaphor of the 'cage' to characterize this limitation of experience.[30] There is a similarly vague suggestion of the opposition between particular and general characteristic of Hegelian thought (which becomes slightly more important for Breton after joining the French Communist Party in 1927). However Breton does not explore the conceptual framework that he touches on, nor does he discuss the politics of labour in the 'materialist' world which he claims has given rise to this loss of experience. Loy's *Insel* adopts this opposition between the world of material demands and the ability of the artist to experience authentically. Like Breton in the first Manifesto, Loy is politically inexplicit and does not draw the connections with Marx or Weber which are latent but unexplored in Breton's text.

Though Breton praises childhood and madness, he does not discuss either at any length in this text. Instead the focus is on the means by which a return to the sources of 'poetic inspiration' can be effected. Breton's main focus is on the dream and on forms of automatic writing. Freud has made the dream a legitimate object of contemplation, although Breton is more interested in the imaginative content of the dream than in its logic. Breton had applied what he takes to be the essence of Freud's method during his war service as a qualified medical practitioner at the army psychiatric centre. The method was designed to obtain from the patient unconscious material which could escape the censorship of the conscious, a method which Breton subsequently resolved to apply to himself, although without the analytical intention. This led him to practice forms of automatic or highly spontaneous writing capable of shattering the dependency of literature on rationality and producing images of beauty of which the conscious mind was incapable.[31] Breton's principal point is that the artist should not consciously impose form on the work.

The affirmation of the momentary and spontaneous would seem to mitigate against the composition of longer works, since the length of any work might depend on the accumulation of its moments but could not be planned. The editor of *Insel* calls it a 'novel' and points out that it is 'difficult'[32]; Loy's literary executor, Roger Conover, calls it a generic hybrid.[33] The difficulty of *Insel* lies in part in the density of its prose. However in part the 'difficulty' of *Insel* as a novel lies in its relationship to Surrealism which in turn had difficulty with the concept of the novel and therefore with the creation of the extended work. In the first Manifesto, Breton rejected the novel as a form, identifying it with the materialist thinking which crushed imagination, and decrying its descriptive and informative style.[34] So rigid was the surrealist declaration against the novel that Louis Aragon, on his own account, had difficulty devising a form which would be narrative but not novelistic, and greater difficulty in persuading Breton to accept it.[35] In the second Manifesto, Breton emphasises that Surrealism takes language itself rather than any represented thing as its ground, in terms that mirror the Futurist concern with *parole in libertà*, and refers to Dadaist and Surrealist literary production as 'hordes of words literally unchained'.[36] This unchaining of the word forms could be construed as part of Loy's agenda in two respects. One would be to interpret Aragon's use of the hallucinatory episode as an unchaining of the subconscious if not of words. Loy's use of hallucinatory episodes reflects those found in *Le Paysan de Paris*, especially in the use it makes of the aquarium. The other would be to interpret Loy's refraction of elements of Lewis's prose style in terms of an aesthetics of the everyday which like surrealism, although in a different manner, paid homage to the idea of a heightened sensibility which both strove to reflect its object in a hyper-sensitized manner, and to incorporate the observing state of mind into the thus stylistically enhanced and re-embodied real. This is worth pursuing. What can be said at this point however is that Loy does not reject the narrative form outright in Breton's manner. However the aesthetic of *Insel* owes something to the first manifesto, if much less to the radicalism of the second which speaks of the 'annihilation of being' and the 'absolute revolt' of shooting people at random in the street — like Marxism, but not in step with it, seeking to destroy ideas of 'family, fatherland and religion'. If Breton's aim is to create a new consciousness, Loy's is, at one step removed, to decide what her own fascination with that form of consciousness is.[37] Despite this difference of objective, Loy shares the surrealist dilemma over narrative, as might be expected of a writer whose verse is lapidary and delights in a complex manipulation of perspectives around and within frugal artefacts. Breton's dictionary definition of surrealism is firmly centred on 'psychic automatism', but he also defines the surrealist poet as a type of 'registering apparatus'.[38] This is done with a view to negating the idea of the 'talent' of the author — a classic 'anti-bourgeois' gesture in the midst of an aesthetic which could hardly be more continuous with romantic aesthetics! However, the notion of the artist as a registering apparatus also defines a rational role for the artist in relation to the irrationality of the 'surreal' experience. This implies a separation between the moment of experience and its realisation as 'image' or artefact. It conserves the parallel with Freud by casting the artist as the neutral analyst of his or her own experience, and conceivably allows a role for the artist as the analyst of the experience of others — an analyst who, unlike the Freudian variety, will make no pronouncement about the analysand.

The need for some form of narrative, the interested and disinterested narrator, and the conservation of the experience of another as a form of record — all of these form part of the make-up of *Nadja*, the most obvious model for *Insel*. Like *Insel*, *Nadja* is concerned with the relationship of two sensibilities, that of the narrator challenged by something elusive in that of the narrative object. 'Who am I?', asks Breton, who proceeds to play on the notion that you are who you 'haunt'. *Insel*'s eyes are made a focus as are those of Nadja. Nadja like Insel has money problems. Yet while *Nadja* focuses on love as the unique force which has made possible the relationship between the narrator and his object, Loy commits her text to a more nuanced account of the dynamics of a relationship which cannot be so glossed. While *Nadja* ends with its heroine confined to an institution in a romanticization of madness and incarceration which apparently set the tone for French literature and thought for the remainder of the Century, *Insel* is wary of romantic excess, and portrays its subject as substantially normalised and returned to the practical world.

As an attempt to supersede Surrealism, *Insel* might be compared to Walter Benjamin's subtle recasting of Surrealist theory in his 1929 essay, 'Surrealism'. Discussing Breton's 'profane illumination', Benjamin praises first his 'discovery' of 'the revolutionary energies that appear in the outmoded', thereby opening out on to praise of the 'Surrealist face' of Paris, and for the strategic goal of Surrealism, said to be 'to win the energies of intoxication for the revolution'.[39] Benjamin's own traversal of concepts of dream, memory, redemption, commodification, history and the everyday are all at stake in some form or another in this essay. Certainly there is always at play in Benjamin a notion of conscious access to a form of time denied by commodification. This gives us a clue to the thread in Loy's novel concerning time, but does not give us access to those concepts of time which organise *Insel*.

Lewis Carroll is among the more subdued presences in *Insel*. His Cheshire Cat provides the model for Insel's autonomous mouth, his disembodied smile, his portrayal of mouthless cats. It is also Carroll who provides us with an oblique route to *Insel*'s handling of time, via Gilles Deleuze's ambitious interleaving of Carroll and the Stoics in *Logique du Sens*. In his description and reappropriation of Stoic philosophy, Deleuze describes the two Stoic readings of time, as Aion and Chronos:

> [. . . T] he past present and future [are] not at all three parts of one single temporality, but form two readings of time, each complete and excluding the other: on the one hand the always limited present, which measures the action of bodies as causes, and the state of their mixing in depth (Chronos): on the other hand the essentially limitless past and the future, which gather incorporeal events at the surface as effects (Aion). The greatness of Stoic philosophy is that it demonstrates at the same time the necessity of the two readings and their mutual exclusivity.
>
> In one case the present is everything, and the past and the future only indicate the relative difference between two presents [. . .]. In the other case the present is nothing, a pure mathematical instant, an entity of reason which expresses the past and future into which it divides itself. In short, *two times, of which one is only composed of boxed presents, and the other only decomposes into an extended past and future*. Of which one is always defined, active or passive, and the other, eternally

Infinitive, eternally neutral. Of which the one is cyclic, measures the movement of bodies, and depends on the matter which limits and fills it; the other is pure straight line on the surface, bodiless, limitless, empty form of time, independent of all matter.[40]

Stoicism proposes a duality between things and their states on the one hand, and effects or bodiless events on the other hand, which, as Deleuze argues, entails a 'throwing into disorder' of philosophy.[41] The sundering of events from things requires it seems this 'double reading' of time, since the event itself has a double structure: on the one hand the moment of the effectuation and embodiment of the event, on the other the future and past of the event which elude the present, are impersonal, pre-individual, neuter and so on. In this analysis, death is the privileged event, existing both in definitive relation to the body and to me, but also impersonal infinitive and bodiless, not related to me at all.[42]

If there is a politics, of time and of art in *Insel*, it is given in the frequent references to money and to watches and clocks. Insel does not eat and lacks teeth even because he has chosen art as an alternative to money — abandoning, he claims, a lucrative career as a forger. Death, art and time are alike tied up in this nexus which concerns both work and experience:

A man who finds himself economically nude, should logically, in the thickset iron forest of our industrial structure, be banged to death from running into its fearfully rigid supports. He is again the primordial soft-machine without the protective overall of the daily job in which his fellows wend their way [. . .]. For them, the atrocious jaws of the gigantic organism will open at fixed intervals and spit at them rations sufficient to sustain their coalescence with the screeching, booming, crashing dynamism of the universal 'works'. (*I* 23–4)

Such reference is rare in *Insel*. We may wish to find that the materiality of the industrial culture is meant to contrast in a simple fashion with the immateriality of Insel, the living bodily person with the near-dead, ghostly Insel. Such a reading would weaken the text, confirming it in a naive ideological impasse — life is material, art is immaterial, except for the artist who is a forger or commercially compromised. The novel does just enough with the metaphorics of time, art and death to produce a more engaging schema.

The narrator meditates on time:

I once heard somebody express surprise that instead of following it onward one should not take a cut across Time to secure a moment which, stretching out in line with oneself, would last indefinitely.

Time that evening lightly came to rest — an unburdened nomad let its three faces linger: the future and the past were with me at present: the whole of time — there was no more pursuing it, losing it, regretting it — while I sat almost shoulder to shoulder with this virtual stranger living the longest period of my life.

It is almost impossible to recover the sequence or the veritable simultaneity of the states of consciousness one experienced in the company of this uncommon derelict. It was so very much as if consciousness were performing stunts. [. . .]

Projected effigies of Insel and myself insorcellated flotsam — never having left any land — never to arrive at any shore — static in an unsuspected magnitude of being alive 'in the light of the eye' dilated to an all enclosing halo of unanalysable insight, where wonder is its own revelation. (*I* 61, 62)

These linked passages make available to us aspects both of the theory and the practice of art in *Insel*. The narrator's attraction to Insel is based principally on a desire to experience time in his way, as opposed to clock time. It would be easy to read this passage in terms simply of the timelessness of the moment of enchantment of love, and *Insel* follows *Nadja* in being, however obliquely, a book about love. But it should be clear that this passage does not deal in a straightforward manner with the moods of love, but with the modalities of time and of art. The division of time into Aion and Chronos described by Deleuze is clearly a logical distinction, not one concerning differing psychological possibilities. However, by analogy with Wyndham Lewis's opposition of the extended temporality of art to temporal incarnate existence, I would like to suggest that the time of art here should be regarded as identifiable with Aion. One of the main attributes of Aion is its infinitive mode — it is tenseless rather than timeless. It is the rare quality of the individual Insel, as Loy's narrator sees him, to be identified in his mind and in his life with this infinitive moment.

The quality of the moment which absorbs the boxed moments of Chronos into an infinitive identity, is to be emblematic. This in turn points us to the conclusion that art in Loy's novel is fundamentally emblematic. In this respect we are as far removed from the Futurism of Loy's earlier years as is Wyndham Lewis in the prose style of *Tarr* and *The Apes of God*. That is to say, the identification of art with Aion, of art as emblem, gives us a style in Loy as in Lewis which is not, as in Futurism, about expressing dynamism, but about grasping the infinitive in the moment, its emblematic stasis. It is true that Loy does here use the term simultaneity to express her mental state, evoking the ideal espoused by Apollinaire when in Futurist company. However, the point is not really the mapping of succession on to a spatial form which this word suggests, but the experience of the emblematic and infinitive stasis which is proper to art and to the artist.

There is no single narrative mode in *Insel*, but a key mode is that of the infinitive emblem. Wyndham Lewis makes a similar use of the emblem. That Lewis refers so often in his discussion of aesthetics to the dominance of the eye, and in his polemics to the priority of the visual and stable, sometimes obscures the frequently conceptual mode of his freeze frame method. In Loy's novel, for all the author's background in the visual arts, and for all that *Insel* continues to locate painting as the art *par excellence*, the frequent refusal of the visual, and especially of the literal, at key descriptive junctures seems remarkable. Yet the emblem, which aspires to Aion, and seeks the event not its incarnation, must take its distance from mere sense. Here the simile of consciousness performing stunts, the extended metaphor of the aquarium of Insel's creative vapour, verge on the emblematic, but more purely emblematic are the 'Projected effigies of Insel and myself insorcellated flotsam — never having left any land — never to arrive at any shore' (*I* 62), a conceptual not a visual image, whatever physicality it has dissolving into the abstractions of 'magnitude', 'insight' and 'wonder'.

While the narrative refers frequently to Insel's intermittency in the physical world, it increasingly transforms him into emblematic existence, leaving open the question of how far the narrator projects the person she believes him to be. The model is Breton's *Nadja*, where the possibility that one is who one haunts has consequences for the haunted quite as much as for the ghost — more so. Indeed we are allowed to believe that it is the narrator who causes Insel's hallucinative phase, and that when she unexpectedly discovers him physically recovered that it is she from the outset who has misunderstood his nature — as if he should have always remained close to death. The emblematic Insel, intermittently incarnate, is given in this passage which realises both the narrator's view of the painter, and the author's ideal of literary art:

No rock, no root, no accident of Nature varied a virgin plain that had conceived no landscape, and I saw Insel reduced to the proportion he would have in the eye of a God — setting out — unaccompanied, unoriented, for here where nothing existed, no sound, no sun, reigned an unimaginable atmosphere he longed to breathe. I could see this, because he was seeing this, as still hanging back, he writhed to its lure. Although I had promised I would send him to a nursing home, we knew I could not come to his aid —. He had never told me *where he was.* His torment tantalized pity. (*I* 94)

At one point, the narrator imputes to Insel an infinitive perspective on time which he does not acknowledge:

'Now', laughed Insel, 'Man Ray should pass again.'
'To conclude, we have no use for time'
'That is not what I mean —'
'You mean that eternity spins round and round?' (*I* 70)

This question goes unanswered. Insel then asks the narrator to take his watch for repair:

Signing for me to hold out my hand, he placed his over it as a cupola showering so discreet a sensitiveness my hand responded as a plot of invisible grasses grazed by an imperceptible breath.
'The girl,' he whispered, and the grasses parted under a couple of atomies cupped in my palm; Insel and his girl embracing – or were they Adam and Eve? 'The girl gave me this,' he said, puckering his face in helpless incomprehension. 'And it won't go.'
I looked at what he had dropped in my hand – a sordid silver watch on a worn leather strap. (*I* 72)

'The girl gave me this'; in infinitive mode, Insel is emblematically assimilated to Adam, his fall into time blamed on the girl. The narrator's allusion at other points to his beatitude, her connecting him with Saint Sebastian, indicate the Christian dimension of the novel's division of time between Aion and Chronos.

Light participates in this division. The light of any seen thing would merely embody its quality, would belong to things, to Chronos. Although Insel is an artist, his ability to actually see anything, physical apperception, is absolutely not at issue. What the narrator finds remarkable is his ability to seize things in their infinitive mode without in effect looking at them at all:

'You have never known ennui,' I laughed [. . .].
'Never,' he assented, beatified. 'I am eternally content. My happiness
is infinite. All the desires of the earth are consummated within myself.'
'Aside from that – what are the people in the next room *doing*?'
'Just being – I ask no more of anyone. *Being* in itself is sufficient for us
all,' he answered, enraptured. (*I* 140)

At this point the novel is sufficiently assured of its main principles
to present them with carefully measured irony. The beatified Insel is
said (elsewhere) to look inward, not outward; his eyes emanate lines
like spears; and in the passage where he begins to pull off his face to
be revealed as a 'man of light' he is shown to consist of a pure light
that reveals no quality, does not participate in visuality – an infinitive
but empty light.

   Finally, this is linked to the narrator's own creative state, the
promise that Insel offers her of an Edenic creative state which is pure
because unconditioned:

> I felt, if I were to go back, begin a universe all over again, forget all
> form I am familiar with, evoking a chaos from which I could draw
> forth incipient form, that at last the female brain might achieve an
> act of creation.
>   I did not know this as yet, but the man seated before me holding a
> photo in his somewhat invalid hand had done this very thing – visu-
> alised the mists of chaos curdling onto shape. But with a male differ-
> ence. (*I* 37)

That photograph of course anticipates Insel/Oelze's commitment to
meticulous rendition, an orientation to which the narrator is indifferent. Insel's creativity, or his access to the surreal timeless state, is
based on his immunity to appetite. Insel's independence from sex is
realised in a kind of androgyny embodied in his painting 'Die Irma',
which as the narrator notes retains his own hands and lip. There is
indeed an androgyny in Oelze's portraits of this period, most notably
in 'Dante allein' (Z 28, 1935). Insel is an organic creator, like a mother,
physically continuous with his offspring: 'His pictures grew, out of
him, seeding through the inter-atomic spaces in his digital substance
to urge tenacious roots into a plane surface' (*I* 103). The image of the
aquarium in *Insel*, while it superficially recalls *Le Paysan de Paris*, is
used to imply that creativity is a kind of maternal state:

Always in his vicinity one had the impression of being surrounded by an arid aquarium – filled with, not water, but a dim transparency; the procreational chaotic vapor in which all things may begin to grow. (*I* 61)

However, there is ambiguity as to the identity of the creator: does Insel form the creative womb from which he comes forth, or is the narrator the mother or essential midwife? The parallel with *Frankenstein* makes a strong link to that work's topic of gender and creativity, with Insel both as the creature and as the warped creator, who resembles an 'incubus' and spawns 'cerebral abortions', 'imbecilic, vampiric [. . .] monsters'(*I* 103). Insel's own state is identified as a regression to pre-human form in the numerous references to primitive, quasi-embryonic, and especially aquatic life forms throughout the text: 'crustacean', 'larva', 'prehistoric fish' (*I* 110), and, completing the link of creation and monstrosity, a 'foetal monster', his head 'swollen in meaningless hydrocephalus' (*I* 101).

As the idealization of the infinitive is mapped on to a somewhat generalized notion of the creative state, Loy's text seems to evoke something about the difference between realised male and unrealised female creative potential, and it seems possible that what may have started life in religious terms as a commitment to the priority of mind, combined with a desire to escape and go beyond existing doctrines, leaves Loy's text in the position of making an important assertion about the nature of female creativity.

However, in *Insel* we do not have a text that is dogmatically worked through. As we have noted, the idea of healing in the text, though central, is eclectically and not dogmatically expressed, according to a range of available vocabularies; the parallels with the artistic egoism of Wyndham Lewis do not, in Loy's case, lead to any pattern of propagandistic argument; comparison with Oelze's work does not reveal that Loy has properly acknowledged, let alone superseded the dialectic of that work, nor does comparison with Breton allow us to claim that Loy's text achieves an appropriation and overcoming of Surrealism in the way that Benjamin's commentary does; it would be hollow, too, to assert that the identification of different modalities of time has much more than a psychologically descriptive, if imagistically impressive function, which cannot rightly be compared to the anti-systematic substance of the work of Gilles Deleuze; *Insel*'s exploration of creativity results in a merely abstract assertion, in which the nature of pure mind is hazily identified with its potential for creation, and some kind of perpetual but comparatively empty present, very different in nature from the politically concrete surrealist encounter with the everyday, is urged as an ideal; finally, the attempt to model gender difference in the very realm of selfhood – the postulation of a kind of 'creation envy' – frustratingly lacks specificity and remains as nebulous as the images of 'vapor' with which it is evoked. Yet *Insel* is a fine work and worth attention. While it proposes a loose system of ideas and images, it was never intended to be as systematic as this study has been. Rather, the various elements are put in place to tell a story, and to evoke the mass of partially formed thinking and above all of varied emotions set in play in this complex relationship between the older writer and the younger artist. Notwithstanding its patina of irony – indeed, because of it – this is text which in its exacting attention to its own immanence projects a remarkable commitment to a fugitive kind of truth.

Notes

1 *A Century of Christian Science Healing* (Boston: Christian Science Publishing Society, 1966), 72–3.

2 Quoted, without reference, in Martin Gardner, *The Healing Revelations of Mary Baker Eddy: The Rise and Fall of Christian Science* (Buffalo: Prometheus Books, 1993), 32.

3 Stephen Gottschalk, *The Emergence of Christian Science in American Religious Life* (Berkeley: University of California Press, 1973), 104–7.

4 Mary Baker Eddy, *Science and Health: with Key to the Scriptures* (Boston: Trustees under the Will of Mary Baker Eddy, 1934), 74, 76, 475, 477, 480, 481, 493.

5 H. A. L. Fisher, *Our New Religion* (London: Ernest Benn, 1929), 102.

6 Gottschalk, 100–129.

7 See the presentation of 'Early American Energy Medicine' at http://www. meridianinstitute. com/eaem/emcont.htm [accessed 8 August 2008].

8 Albert Abrams, *New Concepts in Diagnosis and Treatment: Physioclinical Medicine, the Practical Application of the Electronic Theory in the Interpretation and Treatment of Disease* (San Francisco: Philopolis Press, 1916).

9 Tyrus Miller, '"Everyman his own fluoroscope": Mina Loy's *Insel* Between Aura and Image Machine', in Shreiber and Tuma, eds., 348–55.

10 Elizabeth Arnold, 'Afterword', I, 181.

11 Miller, 348–355.

[12] Renate Damsch-Wiehager, *Richard Oelze: Ein alter Meister der Moderne* (München und Luzern: Bucher, 1989), 24–5.

[13] Wieland Schmied, 'Richard Oelze oder die Präzision des Vagen' in *Richard Oelze: 1900–1980. Gemäldeund Zeichnungen*, herausgegeben von Wieland Schmied (Berlin: Akademie der Künste und Autoren, 1987), 13–23.

[14] Schmied, 18.

[15] Renate Wiehager [sic], 'Paris 1933–1936', in *Richard Oelze: Einzelgänger des Surrealismus*, herausgegeben von Christine Hopfengart (Ostfildern-Ruit: Hatje Cantz, 2000), 107.

[16] Renate Damsch-Wiehager, 47.

[17] Miller, 347–8.

[18] References to art works utilise Schmied. Schmied, G 12, 1935/6).

[19] Claims summarised by Renate Damsch-Wiehager, 90.

[20] Schmied, G 7, 1934.

[21] Ibid., Z 26, 1935 and Z 27, 1935.

[22] Ibid., G 1, 1928.

[23] Wyndham Lewis, *Tarr* (Harmondsworth: Penguin, 1982), 15.

[24] Ibid., 26.

[25] Ibid., 206.

[26] Ibid., 312.

[27] 'Manifeste du surréalisme' in André Breton, *Manifestes du surréalisme* (Paris: Gallimard, 1985).

[28] André Breton, *L'amour fou* (Paris: Gallimard, 1976).

[29] Breton, 'Manifeste du surréalisme', 14.

[30] Ibid., 20.

[31] Ibid., 29, 33, 29–30, 33–35.

[32] Elizabeth Arnold, 'Afterword', *Insel*, 179.

[33] Roger Conover, 'Foreword', *Insel*, 9.

[34] Breton, 'Manifeste du surréalisme', 16–17.

[35] The relevant discussion is quoted in the Introduction to Louis Aragon, *Paris Peasant*, ed. Simon Watson Taylor (London: Cape, 1971), 13–16.

[36] Breton, 'Manifeste du surréalisme', 101.

[37] Ibid., 73–4, 77, 110.

[38] Ibid., 36, 39.

[39] Walter Benjamin, *Selected Writings. Volume 2:* 1927–1934, trans. Rodney Livingstone and others, ed. Michael W. Jennings, Howard Eiland, and Gary Smith (Cambridge MA and London: Belknap Press, 1999), 210, 215.

[40] Gilles Deleuze, *Logique du Sens* (Paris: Editions de Minuit, 1969), 77, 78–9.

[41] Ibid., 16.

[42] Ibid., 179.

Mina Loy's 'Conversion' and the Profane Religion of her Poetry

Suzanne Hobson

Among the unpublished texts in the Mina Loy archive at the Beinecke Rare Book and Manuscript Library is an undated article titled 'Conversion'. Its name suggests that the subject of this piece will be a religious awakening or recognition of spiritual truth. This is indeed the case, but the 'religion' to which the convert turns is not one which is usually known by that name. 'Conversion' explores or rather, exposes, what Loy takes to be the dangerous faith of psychoanalysis. This new religion, she argues, shares rather too many of its concerns with the old. In fact, the discoveries of psychoanalysis are nothing more than reworked versions of Catholic doctrine: '[t]he obsessions prescribed by the "Holy Church" of Rome, are re-edited by the Psychoanalyst.'[1] Whereas man once worshipped at the feet of Our Virgin Mary he now bends to the all-powerful figure of the 'incest complex' or, as if to emphasise the lack of innovation in this respect, the 'Mother complex'. One Eternal Mother, suggests Loy, has simply been substituted for another. In place of God, the psychoanalyst offers the unconscious, which as both first and last principle of the new science nonetheless performs the functions once attributed to God. For Loy, these features reveal psychoanalysis for what it really is: a type of 'mechanized mysticism' in which the convert is granted immediate and automatic access to the Absolute. In this form, and this is the crux of the argument in 'Conversion', psychoanalysis proves a dangerous temptation for the artist. It is not his purpose to provide a short-cut to the Absolute; rather, to strive and then to miss this goal:

The aim of the artist is to miss the Absolute ---- the only possible
creative gesture------whereas the mystic impulse is to embrace a
'ready-made' in the way of absolutes.
    And the absolute of this new mechanized mysticism of the Psycho
Analyst is the Unconscious.[2]

Loy's belief that psychoanalysis had become a twentieth-century,
perhaps *the* twentieth-century religion, is not unfounded. The period
in which this article was written, probably between the mid-1920s
and 1930s, witnessed a number of quasi-religious 'conversions' to the
new science, particularly among artists and writers. The American
poet, H.D., having studied under Freud in 1933 and 1934, remembers
him in *Tribute to Freud* as if he were the founder of a new faith. Freud
is by turn compared to Greek gods, Recording Angels[3] and, as Rachel
Blau DuPlessis remarks, a composite version of Christ himself.[4] H.D.
was not alone in her psychoanalytic faith. In *Psychoanalysis and the
Unconscious*, D.H. Lawrence insists that Freud had created the basis
for a new religion – if only, Lawrence laments, he could have established strong enough foundations on which to 'build his church'.[5]
Ingrid Hotz-Davies and Anton Kirchofer argue that the attitude that
Lawrence adopts towards the study of the Unconscious entirely disre-
gards Freud's own hostility towards religion, maintaining instead that
'the new "science" has all the makings of a candidate for the "religion
of the twentieth century."'[6] Loy's lack of conviction concerning
Freudian theory thus stands in marked contrast to that of H.D., and
even to the qualified interest demonstrated by Lawrence. In her biography of Loy, Carolyn Burke implies that, like several others in her
circle, Loy regretted the fact that Freud did not leave enough room
in his version of the unconscious for 'creative inspiration'. For that
reason, explains Burke, writers such as Loy and Mabel Dodge much
preferred the work of psychical researchers such as Frederic Myers
whose theories suggested the existence of a super-sensible, and therefore potentially artistic or spiritual, dimension to the mind (*BM* 144).
'Conversion', which warns expressly of the dangers of Freudian
thought for the artist, evidently proceeds from a similar concern.
    The aesthetic lesson contained in this article is gleaned from one
writer in particular. Unsurprisingly, considering Lawrence's status
as proselytiser for the new religion, the text is also labelled a 'Critique
of D.H. Lawrence Psycho-Analysis and The Unconscious'. For Loy,
proof of Lawrence's fidelity to the religion of psychoanalysis is
revealed paradoxically in the argument that his study picks with
Freud: 'Inevitably Lawrence like other converts whose reputation

makes it imperative that they preserve their independence, compiles some ingenious terminology of his own and indulges in the well known "truc" of the distinguished desciple [sic], in seeing a quarral [sic] with his master'.[7] In support of her assertion, Loy quotes the passage in *Psychoanalysis and the Unconscious* in which Lawrence ridicules Freud for delving into the cave of the Psyche and returning with a repulsive prize:

> Thus: "But sweet heaven what merchandise.
> What dreams dear heart! What was there in the cave?
> Alas that we ever looked!
> Nothing but a huge slimy serpent of sex————"
> Which transposed to the economic style of 'modernism' would
>   run something like this—'Sweet heart   Alas   Cave serpent
>   ———em' !⁸

The poetic arrangement of these lines, it should be noted, is the work of Loy rather than Lawrence and her quotation stops short of revealing the full horror of Freud's discovery as it appears in *Psychoanalysis and the Unconscious*. Lawrence's text continues: 'Nothing but a huge slimy serpent of sex and excrement and a myriad little horrors spawned between sex and excrement.'[9] Nonetheless, Loy's edited version conveys the essence of what she believes to be the problem with Lawrence's position: by attacking Freud's famous obsession with bodily functions, he reveals himself to be a champion of conservative values and old-church morality. Translated into the 'economic style of modernism', the voice behind *Psychoanalysis and the Unconscious* becomes strangely reminiscent of a heroine in a sentimental novel. Confronted with a threat to her modesty, she descends first into hysteria and then into a dead faint: '"Sweet heart Alas Cave serpent———em"!' Loy's satire delivers an idiosyncratic portrait of Lawrence as a staunch opponent of the kind of talk that threatens common decency. 'Conversion' goes on to explain that it is indeed Freud's perceived attack on morality to which Lawrence takes exception in this text. Loy cites *Psychoanalysis and the Unconscious* again: '"Psycho-Analysis is out under the therapeutic disguise to do away with the moral faculty in man".' Lawrence's mistake is to suggest that too close an examination of sex and excrement poses a threat to man's finer qualities, the mere existence of which, Loy herself is reluctant to countenance: 'My observation of every strata of society leads me to conclude that man has never exhibited the least inclination towards a moral faculty.'[10]

And yet Loy's argument with Lawrence does not end here. Her contention is not that Lawrence has acted against the dictates of Freud in trying to exorcise the less delicate functions of the body from his version of psychoanalysis; rather, that in doing so, he has merely furthered his master's clandestine project, 'the purification of the race'. Although Freud is usually accused of stimulating interest in the grotesque reality of sex and excrement, Loy's Freud (a version that once again departs from the norm) is confronted with an altogether different charge. Like the Fathers of the church, the psychoanalyst has disembodied sex, transforming it from an instinct to a duty:

> If Freud is not in the pay of the Jesuits, the omission should be immediately remedied. For he, contrary to Mr. Lawrence's assertion is in a fair way to accomplish – what the Fathers of the church so signally failed to accomplish – the purification of the race.
> Already the élite, in protest at the epidemic of psycho-exhibitionism among the merely cultured, are dropping 'sex' entirely from their programme.
> Psycho-Analysis has raised sex to the venerable status of a duty; and WHO ——————wants to do his duty?[11]

Admittedly, this is a complicated, perhaps even self-contradictory argument. It is difficult to decide whether Loy accuses Freud of always having been on the side of the church, as she did earlier in her suggestion that the mother complex is a modern version of the Virgin Mary; or, in contrast, whether she asserts that Freud has only latterly become an ally of the church and that he has done so via the circuitous route of turning sex and excrement into matter for common 'merely cultured' conversation and thereby making it unsuitable for the salons of the élite. According to this second interpretation, Freud's ability to succeed where the Church fathers failed would be an unintended consequence of his popularity rather than the 'clandestine project' that 'Conversion' earlier suggested that it was. Lawrence's position in this debate is similarly undecided. Is he a close disciple of Freud focused, like his master, on the erasure of sex and excrement from his moral programme? Or, is he better seen as one of the new élite dropping sex and excrement from his programme for no other reason than that, thanks to Freud, they have become popular topics of conversation for the 'merely cultured'? Neither of these interpretations, needless to say, is a particularly accurate representation of Lawrence's position in *Psychoanalysis and the Unconscious*. Curiously, this is much nearer to Loy's own: thanks to Freud, argues Lawrence, men and women (especially the 'merely cultured' men and women of novels such as *Women in Love*) have got sex on the brain. By over-intellectualizing and over-exposing the act of procreation, Freud had turned a mysterious life-force into a dogmatic duty.

Although 'Conversion' does not offer a very faithful reading of Lawrence, it does, therefore, articulate a concern that Loy shared with Lawrence: namely, that psychoanalysis contains a strand of piety and religiosity that recoils from the human body understood in terms of its sexual, gendered, or even excremental specificity. Regardless of whether the establishment of a church was an unintended conse-quence of Freud's science or not, Loy's point remains that the goal of this new faith repeats that of the old, the banishment of sex or, in Loy's own words, 'what the Fathers of the church so signally failed to accomplish – the purification of the race.'[12] The threat is not simply of eugenics; as Paul Peppis and others have pointed out Loy's poetry and prose sometimes draws openly on the 'eugenicist celebration of biological creativity'.[13] Nor is 'Conversion' purely a feminist protest against the erasure of the gendered body. Although Loy's unpublished works often argue that the chief casualty of the psychoanalytical campaign against the body has been our understanding of female sexuality, the nature of her complaint in 'Conversion' relates to men and women alike.[14] Rather, the problem of the suppression of sex is first and foremost a problem for art. Loy repeatedly states that the new therapeutic religion poses a threat to sources of creativity. The 'mechanical mysticism' of psychoanalysis is impossible for the artist because, explains Loy, he or she must aim for the Absolute and miss; this fore-doomed attempt is 'the only possible creative gesture'. For Loy, Lawrence has compromised himself through psychoanalysis because, by trying to apply Freud's insights to his work, he has 'dangerously damned his own creative flux with a theory.'[15] What is at stake here is a particular type of art; an art that stems from a myste-rious, quasi-Romantic, source of creativity, yet one that is somehow rooted in the physical specificity of the human body. This essay explores the attractions and pitfalls of such an art by focusing on a figure often remarked in Loy's late poetry – the angel-bum – and then exploring how this figure develops some of the themes contained in another, earlier 'star' of Loy's poetry: the artist-angel-bum, provisionally named here for its contradictory bundle of angelic gifts and bum-like incapacities which together add up to something approaching Loy's model for the artist.

1. The angel-bum in 'Hot Cross Bum'

The label 'angel-bum' is often applied to the homeless men and women who feature in poems written by Loy in the late 1930s and 1940s.[16] At this point in her life, the British-born writer was living permanently in New York and spending a significant proportion of her time in the company of the tramps who frequented her chosen neighbourhood, the Bowery in Lower Manhattan. Loy describes these figures as 'bums'; a word perhaps meant to signify the purposeless-ness and immobility that characterizes the condition of being long-term unemployed. As Rachel Potter points out in an article on Loy's late poetry, the men and women living on the Manhattan streets in the post-depression era were far more likely to be long-term unem-ployed than to be economic migrants or itinerant labourers.[17] Loy's work from this period focuses on a cast of bums who were perma-nently denied the social and economic benefits enjoyed by the major-ity of New York's citizens. Trapped at the margins of society, they are ignored by and indifferent to the conventional standards observed by the shoppers and commuters with whom they share the pave-ment.

How, then, do Loy's bums, the representatives of a marginalised and destitute minority, become angel-bums? For critics such as Maeera Shreiber and Carolyn Burke, the answer lies in the spiritual or aesthetic beauty that these figures assume within the context of Loy's work. Shreiber finds an example of this transformation in the 1944 poem, 'Chiffon Velours'. The subject of this poem is an elderly woman whose destitute and decaying body finds aesthetic redemption in the brilliance and radiance of the flowery trim on her skirt – 'a yard of chiffon velours' (*LLB II* 119). For Shreiber, this poem is a celebration of the 'beauty of the thing that is broken' and its homeless subject rather 'more angel than bum'.[18] Burke observes a similar transforma-tion in the Bowery collages that Loy constructed from materials found on the street. One of these compositions, *No Parking*, depicts a pair of 'beatific' bums accompanied, unexpectedly, by a butterfly fashioned out of a paper cup. Burke's description of this butterfly might easily be taken for a wider statement of Loy's artistic aims at this time; bums and paper cups alike manifest the possibility that 'discards' might be 'resurrected as a celestial messenger'.[19] Loy's image of the angel-bum does not, however, encode a moral lesson. It cannot be assumed that sympathizing with what it is to be a bum, Loy sets out to show that there is something inwardly redeeming, in other words angelic, about this condition. Her point is not simply to demonstrate that bums, although outwardly grotesque, actually possess the spiritual qualities of angels; certainly not if these qualities include goodness, radiance and beatitude. Potter cautions against this type of reading in her article 'At the Margins of the Law: Homelessness in the City in Mina Loy's Late Poems'. Loy's texts, she argues, 'problematise' the equation of homelessness and spirituality; they do not simply 'elevate human dereliction to saintly suffering'.[20] No-where in the late poems does bumhood become a condition to be admired or held up as an edifying example. On the contrary, Loy's bums remain, on the whole, degenerate and amoral figures whose mystery, angelic though it may be, cannot be accounted for in terms of inner goodness or the possession of a beautiful soul. The question seems to be, therefore, not how these bums might resemble the angels but how on earth the angels might come to resemble these bums.

'Hot Cross Bum' confirms that it is not only assumptions concerning bums that are at stake in Loy's poetry but also those regarding angels. Published in 1950 in *New Directions* and probably written the year previously, 'Hot Cross Bum' describes the scene before St Mark's in the Bowery. There the church, along with its attendant charities and welfare organisations, is engaged in open competition, even 'warfare' with the bar across the street (*LLB II* 140). The prize is the attention, or more correctly, the souls of the bums who make their homes in the shadow of St Mark's. 'Hot Cross Bum' observes the futility of this struggle, juxtaposing images of the lifeless church with an experience that might be termed the immanent mystery of intoxication. As a funeral procession arrives at the church seeking the 'drudgery / of exoteric / redemption', the 'impious mystics of the other extreme' prostrate themselves at the altar of Bacchus and the gin mill (*LLB II* 141, 139). The 'living' mysteries of religion have quite literally taken up residence on the wrong side of the street and, so too, have the angels. The gutters are populated by a host of 'blowsy angels' who along with 'raffish saints' maintain a kind of vigil to the bottle: 'Blowsy angels / lief to leer / upon crystal horizons' (*LLB II* 134). The epithet 'blowsy', as glossed by Potter with reference to Webster's dictionary, signifies that someone is 'fat, ruddy, dishevelled and rowdy'.[21] The *American Thesaurus of Slang* adds to this definition by simply listing 'blowsy' among countless synonyms for drunk.[22] Needless to say, blowsy is not an epithet easily applied to an angel. While the angel is popularly understood to be an ethereal 'spirit' and theologically associated with concepts such as consciousness and free will, the 'blowsy' angel is identified predominantly by its physical constitution, a constitution that has been upset by the excessive consumption of alcohol. Breaking with tradition, this angel has acquired a body – only to lose control of its bodily functions.

The drunken angel is not, however, unusual in Loy's work. Other poems feature angels who are similarly defined by the unruly and involuntary actions and secretions of their bodies. In 'Property of Pigeons', for example, the blowsy angel gives way to a nauseas angel; it is 'as if an angel had been sick' notes Loy with reference to the 'avalanches' of pigeon excrement covering the walls of her neighbourhood (*LLB II* 120). Resisting the temptation to speculate that the angel in 'Property of Pigeons' is also drunk, this figure is certainly subject to the same physiological mechanics as the one in 'Hot Cross Bum'. An earlier poem, 'The Widow's Jazz', provides another example of an angel whose all-too-present body refuses to be contained within normal boundaries. The jazz musicians featured in this poem are compared to 'black brute-angels' who 'bellow through a monstrous growth of metal trunks' (*LLB II* 96). The cancerous growth of trumpets seems to have transformed these musicians into angel-elephant hybrids. Further instances of embodied angels can be found in 'Jules Pascin', with its prostitute or 'demi-rep' angels dangling in 'tinsel bordels' (*LLB II* 104) and in 'Negro Dancer', in which an animated dancer is compared at once to an ape and an angel (*LLB II* 216). The motif is also explored in Loy's visual art, notably, in the painting re-produced on the front cover of Roger L. Conover's 1997 (Carcanet) edition of *The Lost Lunar Baedeker*. Entitled 'Fallen Angel' (1922), it shows a snail with a human face and an outstretched neck; part-angel, part-creature, this figure seems stuck mid-way-through an awkward phase of metempsychosis.

If the angel approximates bumhood by submitting to the involuntary reactions and mechanics of its body, then, it follows that the bum imitates angelhood not by controlling, but by giving free reign to the same excessive physical traits. In other words, it is when the bum gives himself over to the unruly desires and expressions of his body that he approaches closest to a sacred mode of being. 'Hot Cross Bum' ends with just such a transformation. Observed from a distance by the satirical gaze of the poet, a bum drops to the floor with the Delirium Tremens, memorably portrayed here as the act of making love to the pavement:

> O rare behaviour
>
> a folly-wise scab of Metropolis
> pounding with caressive jollity
> a breastless slab
>
> his cerebral fumes
> assuming
> arms' enlacement
>
> decorously garbed
> he's lovin'up the pavement
>
> —interminable paramour
> of horizontal stature
> Venus-sans-vulva—
>
> A vagabond in delirium
> aping the rise and fall
>
> of ocean
> of inhalation
> of coition. (*LLB II* 144)

Characteristically, Loy's language seems to get in the way of signification in this passage. 'Delirium' in particular points in two directions at once: first, joining with the poetic idiom of 'O rare behaviour', 'interminable paramour' and 'rise and fall / of ocean' to signify self-abandonment in a love-scene on the pavement; and second, joining with 'coition' and 'vulva' to suggest a clinical description of both sex and intoxication. The irony with which these phrases are employed serves to heighten the distance between the poet and the reality which she purports to describe. Loy's poem circles around its subject, but cannot make contact with the unapologetic and resolutely material presence of the bum 'lovin up' the pavement.

The seizure/love-scene in this poem thus strips away the symbolic significance that the sex-act acquires in poetry while simultaneously refusing it the cloak of dignity this stripped back 'reality' often assumes in the languages of the clinic. Left over is an irreducible subject that is closely allied to the angelic experiences of blowsiness, vomiting and defecation in its capacity to suggest both revulsion and mystery. In *Late Modernism*, Tyrus Miller offers a terminology and a framework through which this peculiar mystery might be understood. In a list of features that he identifies as typical of late modernist texts, he includes the phenomenon of 'pure corporeal automatism'; a category comprised of 'images of tics, fits, convulsions, involuntary eruptions and the more arcane phenomena like the bizarre ailments plaguing Beckett's characters'. According to Miller, these experiences define the limits of the human subject: 'They stand as figures of an unthinkable and unrepresentable threshold: a pure laughter in which all subjectivity has been extinguished.'[23] Initially, it seems that a similar meaning could be attached to the figure of the bum making love to the pavement. In his drunken pounding of the stone, he represents a comical, yet nonetheless frightening, challenge to notions of subjectivity bound up with the idea of self-consciousness and social awareness. It is as if the bum is answering to an embodied unconscious (as opposed to the disembodied Unconscious worshipped by the psychoanalytical convert); or, alternatively, as if he is responding to the involuntary memory of an act that he no longer has the opportunity to perform in the socially sanctioned manner.

Yet Miller's definition of 'corporeal automatism' invites another reading of the bum making love to the pavement. While Miller's 'unrepresentable threshold' marks perhaps the lower limit of what it means to be human (to have only the merest hint of a consciousness animating a body that rather seems to be propelled mechanically), religion has often imagined an upper limit: a threshold between human and divine spheres frequently occupied by angels. In the Bible angels stand both as guardians of the threshold – Cherubim guard the gates of Eden (Genesis 3:24) – and as the highest exemplar of what the human might become (Matthew 22:30). Visionaries and mystics, especially those of a Swedenborgian inclination, offer further examples of a limit space in which traffic between humans and angels becomes possible. Loy's poetry, however, frequently collapses these two, upper and lower, limits into a single boundary between the human and the inhuman. In the guise of the blowsy angel 'lovin'up' the pavement, and the nauseous angel of 'Property of Pigeons', the 'limit-experience' of Miller's late modernism is conjoined with the limit-experience of the visionary or mystic: corporeal automatism shades into an angelic encounter, and the angelic encounter is registered by a body mechanically animated by involuntary actions and excretions. Loy's frequent passages between bumhood and angelhood are thus predicated, not on the spiritualization of human destitution and suffering, but on moments of corporeal automatism which offer a glimpse into both sub- and super-natural realms.

2. The artist-angel-bum in 'Apology of Genius' and 'Crab-Angel'

If psychoanalysis erases the body from polite conversation, then perhaps it is the task of Loy's poetic art to put the body back in. 'Conversion' implies that this is necessary, not merely to rescue sex from becoming little more than a duty, but also, indeed especially, to save art itself. The mechanized mysticism of psychoanalysis threatens the artist's most important task: that of aiming for the Absolute and missing. It is not immediately evident, however, that Loy's notion of the angel-bum subject to the involuntary mechanics of his body is any more conducive to the production of great art than psychoanalysis. As both rely on the idea of automatism in order to suggest a relationship between the profane and the sacred, it is not clear that either provides the indirect and ultimately failed route to the Absolute that 'Conversion' demands. Art would seem to fare no better whether it is predicated on the mechanized mysticism of Psychoanalysis or on the automated mystery of the angel-bum; neither of these approaches to the divine appears to leave much room for the agency (aim and failure) of the artist. In the first instance, the artist merely adopts the 'ready-made' Absolute of the Unconscious and in the second, he/she is reduced to a passive observer of the physical ritual that unfolds before him/her in the streets of the Bowery. The poet's detachment from the bum pounding the pavement at the end of 'Hot Cross Bum' permits this figure to retain an air of mystery; at the same time, it gestures towards a poet who is more or less powerless to influence his subject and, more problematically, towards a bum who is little more than an exhibit in a gallery on the pavement.

At an earlier point in her career, Loy imagined a much closer relationship between the artist and the bum. In 1920s poems such as
'Apology of Genius' and 'Crab-Angel', artists appear to be at once holy
and destitute while bums are possessed of the genius of the artist. It
is in this sense that 'Apology of Genius' and 'Crab-Angel' reveal the
existence of another hybrid figure in the poetry of Mina Loy; a figure
that I propose to call the 'artist-angel-bum'. Part-human and part-
divine, this precursor of the 1940s angel-bum more nearly satisfies
the conditions for the creation of good art as laid down in
'Conversion' than does the observing artist constructed by the late
poems. Blessed with an ambition that is god-like yet, simultaneously
restricted by the limitations of his all-too-human body, the artist-
angel-bum reaches for the Absolute and, invariably, misses.

In *Mina Loy: American Modernist Poet*, Virginia M. Kouidis draws a
sharp distinction between the artist figures which appear frequently
in Loy's 1920s poetry and the bums that dominate her later work. The
artist, she explains, is a divine being able to create beauty from the
raw material of the universe: 'He alone among humanity possesses
the vision for intuiting the essence of life's chaos and the skill to
shape his intuitions into form – the divine principle.' The bum, on the
other hand, is a failed artist, an 'emblem of timid or failed vision who
seeks transcendence of worldly care in false Elysiums and Nirvanas'.[24]
Rachel Potter and Mary E. Galvin have rightly questioned the validity of this distinction, given that, in this period, the artist, and the
female artist in particular, was less likely to be God-like than she was
to be subject to the same kind (if not extremes) of exclusionary politics as the bum.[25] If value was to be measured in terms of capital or
the ability to play a productive role in civil society, then bums,
women and artists were all to differing degrees open to the same
charge of worthlessness.

Loy does not, however, deny the divinity of the artist so much as
she demands a recalibration of Godhood in its relationship to the
'failed vision' of artists and bums alike. At times, she seems to follow
peers and predecessors who read Nietzsche as an invitation to endow
the artist with superhuman if not God-like powers. Wyndham Lewis,
for example, explains in the 1918 prologue to *Tarr* that the artist is
blessed with the power of creation, first and foremost with the capacity to create himself.[26] Similarly, T.E. Hulme imagines a 'big artist'
who approaches his art in a vital and pioneering manner.[27] Loy's
version of the artist, with her god-like ability to create 'beauty from

the raw material of the universe', appears at first to have been created in the same mould as these Nietzschean predecessors. All of these figures impose form on unruly matter, understood simply as chaos or, after Bergson, as the uninterrupted flux of inner life.

Loy differs markedly from Lewis and Hulme, however, in her representation of the body of the artist. Lewis, for instance, imagines his artist to be possessed of a strong, vital body and, not infrequently, a body blessed with virile masculinity. The prologue to *Tarr* explains that the artist appears when the sexual energy usually absorbed by a woman is diverted into the production of his art.[28] Loy's artist, by contrast, owns a broken and troublesome body; the kind of body that is subject to the unruly and involuntary actions and secretions that Loy also associates with bums, lepers and circus freaks. In this single but important respect, the artists in Loy's 1920s poems resemble more closely the angel-bums of her 1940s work rather more closely than they do the artist-gods of her predecessors.

'Apology of Genius', first published in 1922, is the poem in which Loy comes nearest to the notion of the artist as a god-like creator. She does so, most notably, in the suggestion that, as geniuses, 'we forge the dusk of Chaos / to that imperious jewellery of the Universe /— the Beautiful—' (*LLB II* 78). Yet the opening lines of this poem suggest that the god to which Loy's artists are compared is anything but the all-powerful Dionysian figure that dominates the Nietzschean imagination:

> Ostracised as we are with God—
>   The watchers of the civilized wastes
>   reverse their signals on our track (*LLB II* 77)

Reading this extract in the light of another of Loy's poems, 'O Hell', Thom Gunn suggests tentatively that the ambiguous preposition 'with' in the first line might be glossed as 'by'; the artists, he implies, have been ostracised, banished or excommunicated *by* God.[29] Gunn's logic is predicated on his reading of 'O Hell' as a celebration of a 'Blakean' underworld in which the artist might find the energy to clear the overworld of the accumulated 'excrement' of tradition.[30] In this context, 'Apology of Genius' provides the confirmation that the Godless artist is the proper figure to access this infernal force; ostracised by God, he or she might plausibly side with the devil. Without dismissing Gunn's reading (Loy's syntax frequently invites more than one interpretation), reference to other versions of 'Apology of Genius' suggest that the preposition 'with' in the first line might more simply be read as 'with'. Loy's drafts and notes contain several alternative openings to this poem; one which reads 'Our eventuality / it is / even to survive with God', and a second, beginning, 'So lonely as God / and laden like his son'.[31] Just as the artist and God are both lonely and merely surviving in these unpublished extracts, it seems reasonable to assume that they are both ostracised in the published version.

Like God, then, the geniuses are not *unlike* the socially excommunicated angel-bums of Loy's 1940s poetry. Gods, angels and bums are all the same in this one respect – civilized man has exiled them to the margins of his domain. The reason for their exclusion again suggests a resemblance to the destitute subjects of Loy's late poems; 'we' (the artists), like the angel-bums, are perceived to possess grotesque bodies that are quickly on their way to becoming corpses:

> Lepers of the moon
> all magically diseased
> we come among you
> innocent
> of our luminious sores (*LLB II* 77)

'Apology of Genius' raises a question that haunts Loy's treatment of the artist in this period; it is simply not clear to what extent their art is understood to be the divine production of the 'Beautiful' and, conversely, to what extent it is associated with the profane display of their 'magically diseased' bodies. To use the terminology supplied by 'Conversion', it is difficult to decide whether good art lies in the leap towards the Absolute or in the failure of the artist to transcend his altogether human body.

'Crab-Angel', a second poem published in the early 1920s, features one of Loy's most unlikely artists. Its subject is a dwarf who, deformed, possibly diseased and almost certainly outcast, again prefigures the bums who feature in her later work. Like them, the eponymous 'Crab-Angel' is firmly situated in a mechanized body: he is hung from a wire manipulated by the circus-master off-stage. Further, like the bum making love to the pavement, the dwarf has an excessively human body; one that is grossly over-determined as a sexual and gendered entity. Markers of virile masculinity alternate with signs of femininity so that 'manly legs' share the page with 'chrysanthemum curls' and a Herculean torso is dressed in 'powder puff' drag. Excessively gendered, it is also difficult to avoid the implication that the dwarf is grossly over-sexed; the 'crab' in the title of this poem refers overtly to the waving of his 'useless pearly claws'; covertly, it cannot help but suggest a sexually transmitted disease (*LLB II* 85–86). On this occasion, however, the bum or 'Crab-Angel' is also an artist, performing as a bareback rider and acrobat in Ringling's circus. In fact, to apply the term artist to this figure does not quite do him justice; at his best, he is the creator of what can only be described as sublime art:

> the horse
> racing the orchestra
> in rushing show
> throw
> his whimsy wire-hung dominator
>
> to dart
> through circus skies of arc-lit dust
> Crab-Angel   like a swimming star
>
> clutching the tail-end of the Chimera
> An aerial acrobat
> floats on the coiling lightning
> of the whirligig
> lifts
> to the elated symmetry of Flight ——— (*LLB II* 86–7)

The image of an angel rushing through sky in pursuit of the impossible 'Chimera' resembles a Romantic tribute to the superiority of imagination over the circumscribed world of the senses. The diminutive, all too human source of this spectacle is temporarily forgotten as centre-stage is taken by an 'aerial acrobat' absorbed in the ecstasy of flight. When the real crab-angel makes his return at the end of this passage, the sense of anti-climax is palpable:

> The dwarf—
> subsides like an ironic sigh
> to the soft earth
> and ploughs
> his bow-legged way
> laboriously   towards the exit
> waving a yellow farewell with his perruque (*LLB II* 87)

There is a sharp disjunction between the unfettered aerial acrobat pursuing the Chimera and the dwarf, who is not only firmly situated in a sexualised and mechanized body, but whose movement is restricted by that body as he 'ploughs / his bow-legged way / laboriously towards the exit'. The question immediately arises as to how these two figures might co-exist in the same subject; the answer lies, not in the dwarf himself, rather, in the type of art he practises.

'Crab-Angel' contains a figurative illustration of the lesson contained in 'Conversion': that the artist should aim for the Absolute and miss. The acrobat is on the brink of conquering the sublime – he dominates the air and catches hold of the 'tail-end' of the impossible – when, in a single moment, he is cast down to the level of a dwarf imprisoned in the unruly machine of his own body. Lawrence's fastidious psychoanalytic faith will never produce such art because it refuses to 'look deep' into the unsightly corners of human life – a world of insistent physicality where sexual acts are performed on the pavement and diseased or deformed bodies take centre stage. Loy's poetry speaks of a different kind of faith; not that the artist has the God-like ability to transfigure this matter (this would be another version of old-church morality) but that once animated such matter is itself a site of divinity: the bum's angelic constitution is no different in this respect to the artist's 'magic disease' which marks her as repulsively God-like in the eyes of the civilized (*LLB II* 77). In this final equation, the divine returns to the abject matter with which Loy's critique of Lawrence began. From bum to angel to artist and back once more to bum, the circular rationale of Loy's poetry turns around a conviction that it shares with 'Conversion': that divinity and poetry are to be found in the places where the 'merely cultured' would rather not look.

Notes

[1] Mina Loy, 'Conversion', Mina Loy Papers, YCAL MSS 6, fol. 153.

[2] Ibid.

[3] H.D., *Tribute to Freud: Writing on the Wall, Advent* (Manchester: Carcanet, 1985), 12, 30.

[4] Rachel Blau DuPlessis, *H.D. The Career of that Struggle* (Brighton: Harvester, 1986), 76.

[5] D.H. Lawrence, *Psychoanalysis and the Unconscious* (New York: Thomas Seltzer, 1921), 11.

[6] Anton Kirchofer and Ingrid Hotz-Davies, 'Introduction: Psychoanalysis as Cultural Material', in Kirchofer and Hotz-Davies, eds., *Psychoanalytic•ism: Uses of Psychoanalysis in Novels, Poems, Plays and Films* (Trier: Wissenshaftlicher Verlag Trier, 2000), 13.

[7] 'Conversion'.

[8] Ibid.

[9] Lawrence, 15.

[10] 'Conversion'.

[11] Ibid.

[12] Ibid.

[13] Paul Peppis, 'Rewriting Sex: Mina Loy, Marie Stopes, and Sexology', *Modernism/modernity* 9 (2002), 570.

[14] See for example, Mina Loy, 'The Child and the Parent', YCAL MSS 6, fols 10–20, especially, 'The Outraged Womb', fol. 19; and Loy, 'Library of the Sphinx', Mina Loy Papers, Beinecke, YCAL MSS 6, fol. 188.

[15] 'Conversion'.

[16] See for example Roger Conover, 'Time-Table', in *LLB II*, lxxvi; and Maeera Shreiber, 'Divine Women, Fallen Angels: The Late Devotional Poetry of Mina Loy', in Shreiber and Tuma, eds., 468.

[17] Rachel Potter, 'At the Margins of the Law: Homelessness in the City in Mina Loy's Late Poems', *Women a Cultural Review* 10 (1999), 256.

[18] Shreiber and Tuma, eds., 480–81.

[19] Burke, 421.

[20] Potter, 256.

[21] Ibid., 261.

[22] *American Thesaurus of Slang*, ed. Lester V. Berrey and Melvin Van den Bark, 2nd edn (New York: Thomas Y. Crowell, 1953).

[23] Tyrus Miller, *Late Modernism* (Berkeley: University of California Press, 1999), 64.

[24] Virginia M. Kouidis, *Mina Loy: American Modernist Poet* (Baton Rouge: Louisiana State University Press, 1980), 109.

[25] Mary E. Galvin, *Queer Poetics: Five Modernist Women Writers* (Westport: Praeger, 1999), 79; and Potter, 263.

[26] Wyndham Lewis, *Tarr* (London: Egoist, 1918), 11.

[27] T.E. Hulme, *Speculations: Essays on Humanism and the Philosophy of Art*, ed. Herbert Read (London: Kegan Paul, Trench, Trubner, 1936), 149.

[28] Wyndham Lewis, 11.

[29] Thom Gunn, 'Three Hard Women: HD, Marianne Moore, Mina Loy', in *On Modern Poetry: Essays Presented to Donald Davie,* ed. Vereen Bell and Laurence Lerner (Nashville: Vanderbilt University Press, 1988), 37–52, n47.

[30] Gunn, 45–6.

[31] Mina Loy, 'Apology of Genius', YCAL MSS 6, fol. 76; 'Lady Asterisk', YCAL MSS 6, fol. 163.

Selected Bibliography

Published Poetry Collections and Prose by Mina Loy

Lunar Baedecker [sic]. Dijon: Contact, 1923.

Lunar Baedeker and Time-Tables. Edited by Jonathan Williams. Highlands NC: Jonathan Williams, 1958.

The Last Lunar Baedeker. Edited by Roger L. Conover. Manchester: Carcanet, 1982.

The Lost Lunar Baedeker. Edited by Roger L. Conover. Manchester: Carcanet, 1996.

Insel. Edited by Elizabeth Arnold. Santa Rosa: Black Sparrow Press, 1991.

Biography

Burke, Carolyn. *Becoming Modern: The Life of Mina Loy.* New York: Farrar, Strauss and Giroux, 1996.

Criticism on Loy

Armstrong, Tim. *Modernism, Technology and the Body: A Cultural Study.* Cambridge: Cambridge University Press, 1999.

Arnold, Elizabeth. 'Mina Loy and the Futurists'. *Sagetrieb* 8 (1989), 83–117.

Benstock, Shari. *Women of the Left Bank: Paris, 1900–1940*. London: Virago Press, 1987.

Borshuk, Michael. '"A Synthesis of Racial Caress": Hybrid Modernism in the Jazz Poems of William Carlos Williams and Mina Loy'. In *William Carlos Williams: A Commemoration*, edited by Ian A. Copestake, 255–71. Bern, Switzerland: Peter Lang AG, 2003.

Burke, Carolyn. 'Getting Spliced: Modernism and Sexual Difference'. *American Quarterly* 39 (1987), 98–121.

Churchill, Suzanne. *The Little Magazine Others and the Renovation of American Poetry*. Burlington, VT: Ashgate, 2006.

Dunn, Susan. 'Fashion Victims: Mina Loy's Travesties', *Stanford Humanities Review* 7 no. 1 (1999). www.stanford.edu/group/SHR/7–1/html /body_dunn.html [accessed September 2006].

Eliot, T.S. [T.S. Apteryx]. 'Observations'. *Egoist* 5 (1918), 64–71.

Feinstein, Amy. 'Goy Interrupted: Mina Loy's Unfinished Novel and Mongrel Jewish Fiction'. *MFS: Modern Fiction Studies* 51 (2005), 335–53.

Galvin, Mary E. *Queer Poetics: Five Modernist Women Writers*. Westport: Praeger, 1999.

Goody, Alex. *Modernist Articulations: A Cultural Study of Djuna Barnes, Mina Loy and Gertrude Stein*. Palgrave Macmillan, 2007.

Gunn, Thom. 'Three Hard Women: HD, Marianne Moore, Mina Loy'. In *On Modern Poetry: Essays Presented to Donald Davie*, edited by Vereen Bell and Laurence Lerner, 37–52. Nashville: Vanderbilt University Press, 1988.

Hancock, Tim. '"You couldn't make it up"': The Love of "bare facts" in Mina Loy's Italian Poems'. *English: The Journal of the English Association* 54 (2005), 175–94.

Januzzi, Marisa. 'Dada Through the Looking Glass, or: Mina Loy's Objective'. In *Women in Dada: Essays on Sex, Gender, and Identity*, edited by Naomi Sawelson-Gorse, 578–612. Cambridge MA: MIT Press, 1998.

Kinnahan, Linda. *Poetics of the Feminine: Authority and Literary Tradition in William Carlos Williams, Mina Loy, Denise Levertov, and Kathleen Fraser*. Cambridge: Cambridge University Press, 1994.

Kouidis, Virginia. *Mina Loy: American Modernist Poet*. Baton Rouge: Louisiana State University Press, 1980.

Miller, Cristanne. *Cultures of Modernism: Gender and Literary Community in New York and Berlin*. Ann Arbor: Michigan, 2005.

Miller, Tyrus. *Late Modernism*. Berkeley: University of California Press, 1999.

Paul Peppis. 'Rewriting Sex: Mina Loy, Marie Stopes and Sexology'. *Modernism / Modernity* 9 (2002), 561–570.

Potter, Rachel. ' "At the Margins of the Law": Homelessness in the City in Mina Loy's Late Poems'. *Women: A Cultural Review* 10 (1999), 253–65.

— *Modernism and Democracy: Literary Culture 1900–1930*. Oxford: Oxford University Press, 2006.

Pound, Ezra. 'Others'. *The Little Review* 5, no. 11 (4 March 1918), 56–8.

Roberts, Andrew Michael. ' "How to Be Happy in Paris": Mina Loy and the Transvaluation of the Body'. *Cambridge Quarterly* 27, no. 2 (1998), 129–47.

Scott, Bonnie Kime, ed. *The Gender of Modernism: A Critical Anthology*. Bloomington: University of Indiana Press, 1990.

Shreiber, Maeera and Keith Tuma, eds. *Mina Loy: Woman and Poet*. *Orono*: The National Poetry Foundation, 1998.

Stauder. Ellen Keck. 'Beyond the Synopsis of Vision: the Conception of Art in Ezra Pound and Mina Loy'. *Paideuma* 24, no. 2/3 (Fall and Winter 1995), 195–227.

Vetter, Lara. 'Theories of Spiritual Evolution, Christian Science, and the "Cosmopolitan Jew": Mina Loy and American Identity'. *Journal of Modern Literature* 31 (2007), 47–63.

Winters, Yvor. 'Mina Loy'. *The Dial* 80 (1926), 496–99.

Contexts

Literary Modernism

Altieri, Charles. *The Art of Twentieth-Century Poetry: Modernism and After.* Oxford: Blackwell, 2006.

Kolocotroni, Vassiliki, Jane Goldman and Olga Taxidou, eds. *Modernism: An Anthology of Sources and Documents.* Edinburgh: Edinburgh University Press, 1998.

Nicholls, Peter. *Modernisms: a Literary Guide.* London: Macmillan, 1995.

North, Michael. *Reading 1922: A Return to the Scene of the Modern.* Oxford: Oxford University Press, 1999.

The Avant-garde

Apollonio, Umbro. *Futurist Manifestos.* New York: Viking Press, 1970.

Blum, Cinzia Sartini. *The Other Modernism: F.T. Marinetti's Fiction of Power.* Berkeley: University of California Press, 1996.

Breton, André. *Manifestes du surréalisme.* Paris: Gallimard, 1985.

Marinetti, F.T. *Marinetti: Selected Writings.* Edited by R.W. Flint and translated by R.W. Flint and Arthur A. Coppotelli. London: Secker and Warburg, 1971.

Perloff, Marjorie. *The Futurist Moment: Avant-garde, Avant Guerre and the Language of Rupture*. Chicago: University of Chicago Press, 1986.

Saint-Point, Valentine. 'Manifesto of Futurist Woman' (1912), in *Manifesto: A Century of isms*. Edited by Mary Ann Caws. Lincoln and London: University of Nebraska Press, 2001.

Watson, Steven. *Strange Bedfellows: The First American Avant-garde*. New York, London and Paris: Abbeville Press, 1991.

Jazz

Appel, Alfred Jnr. *Jazz Modernism: From Ellington and Armstrong to Matisse and Joyce*. New York: Alfred A. Knopf, 2002.

Archer-Straw, Petrine. *Negrophilia: Avant-Garde Paris and Black Culture in the 1920s* London: Thames and Hudson, 2000.

Berliner, Brett A. *Ambivalent Desire; The Exotic Black Other in Jazz-Age France*. Amherst and Boston: University of Massachusetts Press, 2002.

Blake, Jody. *Le Tumulte Noir: Modernist Art and Popular Entertainment in Jazz-Age Paris, 1900–1930*. University Park, PA: Pennsylvania University Press, 1999.

Goddard, Chris. *Jazz Away from Home*. New York: Paddington Press Ltd, 1979.

Haney, Lynn. *Naked at the Feast: the Biography of Josephine Baker*. London: Robson, 2002.

Shack, William A. *Harlem in Montmartre: A Paris Jazz Story Between the Great Wars*. Berkeley and London: University of California Press, 2001.

Autobiography

Burke, Carolyn. 'Supposed Persons: Modernist Poetry and the Female Subject'. *Feminist Studies* 11, no.1 (1985), 131–48.

Gilmore, Leigh. *Autobiographics: A Feminist Theory of Women's Self-Representation*. Ithaca, NY; London: Cornell University Press, 1994.

Marcus, Laura. *Auto/biographical Discourses: Theory, Criticism, Practice*. Manchester: Manchester University Press, 1994.

Sexology

Bland, Lucy. *Banishing the Beast: English Feminism and Sexual Morality 1885–1914*. London: Penguin, 1995.

Greenway, Judy. 'It's What You Do With It That Counts: Interpretations of Otto Weininger'. In *Sexology in Culture: Labelling Bodies and Desires*, edited by Lucy Bland and Laura Doan. Chicago: University of Chicago Press, 1998.

Sengoopta, Chandak. *Otto Weininger: Sex, Science, and Self in Imperial Vienna*. Chicago: University of Chicago Press, 2000.

Stevens, Hugh and Caroline Howlett. *Modernist Sexualities*. Manchester: Manchester University Press, 2000.

Weininger, Otto. *Sex and Character: An Investigation of Fundamental Principles*. Edited by Daniel Steuer and Laura Marcus and translated by Ladislaus Löb. Bloomington, IN: Indiana University Press, 2005.

Christian Science and Joseph Cornell

Cornell, Joseph. 'Some Dreams, 1947–1969'. In *Surrealist Painters and Poets: An Anthology*, edited by Mary Ann Caws. Cambridge, MA: MIT Press, 2001.

—*Shadowplay Eterniday*. New York: Thames & Hudson, 2003.

Eddy, Mary Baker. *Science and Health, with Key to the Scriptures*. Boston: First Church of Christ, Scientist, 1994.

Gardner, Martin. *The Healing Revelations of Mary Baker Eddy: The Rise and Fall of Christian Science*. Buffalo: Prometheus Books, 1993.

Gill, Gillian, *Mary Baker Eddy*. Cambridge, MA: Perseus Books, 1998.

Gottschalk, Stephen. *The Emergence of Christian Science in American Religious Life*. Berkeley: University of California Press, 1973.

Morgan, David and Sally Promey. *The Visual Culture of American Religions*. Berkeley: University of California Press, 2001.

Peel, Robert. *Christian Science: Its Encounter with American Culture*. Harrington Park, NJ: Robert H. Soames, 1958.

Podmore, Frank. *Mesmerism and Christian Science: A Short History of Mental Healing*. London: Methuen, 1909.

Ross, Peter V. *Lectures on Christian Science*. New York: Hobson Press, 1945.

Solomon, Deborah. *Utopia Parkway: The Life and Work of Joseph Cornell*. New York: Farrar, Strauss and Giroux, 1997.

Lightning Source UK Ltd.
Milton Keynes UK

175997UK00002B/2/P

9 781876 857721